THE ECONOMICS OF NATURAL DISASTERS

THE FREE PRESS, NEW YORK

COLLIER-MACMILLAN LIMITED, LONDON

The Economics of Natural Disasters

Implications for Federal Policy

By

DOUGLAS C. DACY

and

HOWARD KUNREUTHER

In memory of RICHARD M. HALFYARD
Colleague, friend, fighter of tragedy

$\mathcal{F}$ oreword

MODERN MAN, for all his technological sophistication, is still at the mercy of his environment, particularly the weather. Raging storms, flood waters cascading over low-lying areas, and other freaks of nature can spell catastrophe for millions of Americans, urban or rural. Indeed, one of the most vivid and dramatic yardsticks for American history is the continuing saga of great floods, tornadoes, and hurricanes.

The cost of these frequent eruptions is enormous. Besides the tragic and immeasurable loss of human life, natural disasters cause many millions of dollars of economic loss each year. In spite of certain limited forms of disaster assistance already available, the private citizen and the commercial interest stand vulnerable to crippling loss from nature's fury.

To bring relief after disasters strike, the Federal government has provided various kinds of rehabilitation assistance. Unfortunately, the Federal role in disaster assistance has been crisis-oriented—*ad hoc*, fragmented, and occasionally inequitable. Congress, and the Administration, respond to floods or hurricanes by approving enormous temporary loans, grants, and other relief measures. The result is often less satisfactory than anyone could have imagined: high-risk areas become heavily populated with "speculators" in disaster relief; financial aid is often meted out in amounts disproportionate to the need; and the responsible economics of disaster relief are hidden behind the headlines.

We need to stop relying on this sporadic approach to disaster assistance, and develop a workable system of national insurance to provide consistent, predictable, efficient aid.

One way to accomplish this would be to create a Federal reinsurance system for a private network of disaster insurance coverage. This is the formula behind the National Flood Insurance Act of 1968. I introduced flood insurance legislation to the Congress early in 1963—and it took five years of legislative maneuvering to win acceptance for this form of disaster protection. Nevertheless, the struggle was worth the outcome: millions of businessmen and householders will now be able to call on an insurance network to protect them from economic collapse should a disaster strike.

I am delighted that the authors of this book share my enthusiasm for a nationwide program of disaster insurance. I would hope that the pattern of *ad hoc* responses to disaster would give way to a comprehensive, coordinated program of disaster insurance which would put an end to the reliance on crisis-oriented procedures after a flood or hurricane. National disaster insurance would mean that businessmen and homeowners could depend on rehabilitation assistance, and could budget the costs involved over a period of time. It would also mean that the risk of living in a disaster-prone area would be distributed more evenly, between private and public bodies.

Reliable, comprehensive disaster insurance—perhaps built on the model of the National Flood Insurance Act of 1968—is a realistic goal. It ought to be given a thorough hearing, and a careful analysis. This book should do much to enhance our understanding of the economics of natural disaster, and to clear the way for an efficient system of fiscal protection for those who suffer from the storm.

Harrison A. Williams, Jr.
U.S. Senator

Preface

THE MAIN objective of this book is to formulate a clear-cut case for the development of a comprehensive system of disaster insurance as an alternative to the current paternalistic Federal policy. This was not our aim when we were asked to undertake a detailed analysis of the economic problems facing Alaska in the wake of the severe Good Friday earthquake there in 1964. In fact, our impressions of disasters were not any more profound than those of the average person for whom the word *disaster* conjures up a series of different images, generally centering around the words *suffering*, *destruction*, and *helplessness*.

The first part of the project, undertaken at the Institute for Defense Analyses, was devoted to searching through the existing literature. These studies and reports were primarily concerned with organizational problems during the emergency postdisaster period and only occasionally referred to economic phenomena. We gained a perspective on the general subject but not a great deal of specific knowledge for our purposes. However, our reading did reinforce a point of view we shared before we began our work—that fruitful economic analysis must be pursued within the context of actual environmental conditions. Thus, as we shall indicate throughout the book, we feel that sociological and psychological factors play an important role in influencing economic behavior and must be explicitly considered in order to develop meaningful and workable policy formulations.

If the Alaska earthquake had been the only major disaster to affect the country during 1964 and 1965, our case study might have remained just that. The forty-ninth state is so highly dependent on Federal aid that one would have been justified in regarding the government's role there as rather special. However, during the next eighteen months, the United States experienced an unparalleled series of hurricanes, tornadoes, and floods that caused damage to all parts of the nation. We were surprised to find that the unusual treatment given the Alaskans was actually used as the vehicle for passing new congressional legislation that liberalized Federal aid available to these other areas. Thus, what was special in 1964 is now part of the normal Federal response to disaster.

A principal reason for the increasing role of the government in disaster relief is the absence of adequate insurance coverage to homeowners and businesses in hazard-prone areas. Protection against floods is not available today; earthquake insurance, although on the market, is not purchased by property owners living in high-risk areas; and water damage from hurricanes is not covered by the extended-coverage endorsement that normally accompanies fire insurance. Only loss from tornadoes is protected by the standard policies, and here many individuals are underinsured. As a result, people have been forced to cry for help and the government has responded.

Our studies, however, soon led us to the firm conviction that only by understanding the peculiar economics of disaster and recovery could some really constructive policy recommendations be made. We have, therefore, presented here a large amount of empirical economic data on short- and long-term recovery not only from Alaska but from studies of other disasters. Our presentation of statistical data related to the economic effects of disasters runs through hurricane Betsy (September 1965), the last in the series of natural catastrophes that affected the country during the unusual eighteen-month period following the Alaska earthquake. On the basis of these findings we have formulated certain theoretical hypotheses that we hope will provide some impetus for future economic analyses of disasters. We are fully aware that some of these ideas are nebulous and controversial, but our hope is that, with the help of our theoretical framework, interesting empirical studies will be undertaken that will inject more substance into this form.

In this connection we might also suggest that our analysis of economic behavior following natural disasters may have some relevance in understanding reactions of individuals following man-made disasters, such as riots. Behavior *during* the disaster will, of course, be considerably different: natural disasters produce very little looting or panic on the part of residents in the community whereas riots are noted for these phenomena. Once the activity has died down, however, short-run economic behavior appears to follow similar patterns. For example, after the Chicago riots following Dr. Martin Luther King's assassination, residents who were spared destruction or who lived outside the damaged area offered free food and housing to the victims. As we shall see in the empirical section on short-term recuperation problems, this is precisely the same phenomenon that occurs following natural disasters. On the other hand, the long-term recovery characteristics following natural disasters may not shed much light on patterns in riot-torn areas. Businesses that were burned out and /or looted frequently decide to locate elsewhere or to discontinue operations. In contrast, communities hit by a natural disaster are often rebuilt so that they emerge bigger and better than they were before the event.

Our treatment of the economics of disaster can be conveniently divided into three parts. Part I provides the framework for analysis. In Chapter 1, we offer detailed statistical evidence on the increasing cost of natural disasters over the years, using data from 1925 to 1965. Since the early 1950s, the number of organizations providing some form of disaster relief has pyramided. Chapter 2 not only catalogs the sources of this aid but statistically analyzes Federal trends by using figures from specific disasters. In Chapter 3 we present a theoretical analysis of the recuperation and long-term recovery periods using basic statistical and economic concepts.

Part II presents empirical evidence on short-term recuperation behavior. Problems of information and communication immediately following the catastrophe are illustrated in Chapter 4 with data from several different types of disaster (i.e., hurricanes, tornadoes, and earthquakes). Chapter 5 examines short-run supply and demand problems with particular emphasis on emergency food and shelter requirements. Once these demands are satisfied, reconstruction problems become prominent.

Part III focuses on the capital and labor needs facing disaster areas. The problem of damage assessment is studied in Chapter 6 by using specific figures from the Alaska earthquake to illustrate changes over time in these estimates and in proposed expenditures. Chapter 7 concentrates on the labor side of the coin by analyzing migration patterns following disasters. Chapter 8 presents empirical evidence illustrating differences in the recovery pattern of a disaster region in a relatively underdeveloped country (Skopje, Yugoslavia) and an area that is part of an industrialized nation (southcentral Alaska). We also demonstrate that the crisis situation generated by a disaster may be a blessing in disguise by permitting modernization of facilities and encouraging technological innovations.

Part IV of the book critically examines the Federal government role in providing disaster relief to the private sector. The Small Business Administration (SBA) is the principal agency offering low-interest loans for replacing or repairing damaged homes and businesses. The features of its disaster loan operation are described in Chapter 9, and a statistical analysis of the distribution and size of agency loans is presented. Chapter 10 explores the inequities of the present SBA program and suggests alternative policies for eliminating these perverse effects. Chapter 11 then estimates the costs to the Federal government of its disaster relief program. These figures offer further statistical evidence for developing a comprehensive system of disaster insurance. After detailing several criteria that an insurance system must meet, we outline in Chapter 12 the elements of a program to be operated by private companies but that will initially rely on Federal subsidies and some form of government reinsurance. Comprehensive disaster protection under this system should not only lead to a more efficient and equitable recovery than we have today but it will also curtail the growth of hazard-prone areas that has resulted from our present relief program.

Recently Congress and the Small Business Administration have taken significant steps to remedy some of the disaster relief abuses we have described in this book. We have not attempted to evaluate these actions in the text because the book was already in press when the measures were taken. However, we feel that the reader ought to be aware of their existence.

Specifically, during the past year the Budget Bureau investigated certain disaster relief practices of the Small Business Administration. We submitted certain parts of the draft of our book for the Bureau's consideration and are pleased that their conclusions are similar to those we present in Chapter 10. Following the Bureau's study the Small Business Administration placed a limit on the size of disaster loans and prohibited the use of funds for the purpose of debt retirement. We applaud these actions but are not confident that they will be effective safeguards, insofar as they have been promulgated only as internal directives. We have found in the course of our study that internal directives are frequently ignored once disaster has struck and sympathies have been aroused.

Late in the second session the 90th Congress passed the National Flood Insurance Act of 1968. The provisions of this program are still vague with respect to coverage, premiums, and mode of operation; however, passage of the act is a step in the right direction. We would prefer a more comprehensive disaster insurance system (one that includes all types of disasters) but the fact that Congress has recognized the need for flood insurance marks a major advance toward this objective. We hope that this program will not suffer the same fate as its predecessor, the Federal Flood Insurance Act of 1956, which was passed by Congress but was never implemented.

Acknowledgements

NUMEROUS INDIVIDUALS have contributed diverse skills to the completion of this book and we would like to acknowledge their contributions here. Our first debt of gratitude is to John Hause of the University of Minnesota, who carefully read a good part of the manuscript and served as general critic and advisor. We received helpful suggestions and comments from a number of our colleagues and former colleagues at the Institute for Defense Analyses, especially Steven Brams, Louis de Alessi, Richard Halfyard, William Niskanen, Elissandra Fiore Roy, and Wade Sewell. Also Charles Fritz from the Institute provided us with insight into the sociological aspects of the problem. We benefited from our discussions with James Brown of the George Washington Law School on legal matters relating to disaster insurance.

Jack Hirshleifer of UCLA and Harry Roberts of the University of Chicago provided useful comments on the manuscript and offered encouragement in our efforts. Through discussions with George Rogers of the University of Alaska and his comments on portions of the manuscript, we obtained a greater understanding of the economic problems that faced Alaska after the earth-quake.

Several individuals gave a great deal of their time in providing data and critical comments on parts of the manuscript. Roy Popkin of the American National Red Cross made his files available to us and corrected any misimpressions we may have had as to the specific role his group plays in disaster relief. Padraic Frucht, formerly of the Small Business Administration, gave us access to statistical information on the agency's disaster loan program and allowed us to sample SBA loan files related to the Alaska earthquake. Fred Lupro of the Alaska Department of Labor furnished us with detailed employment data·on the communities affected by the earthquake. In Anchorage Elmer Gagnon, director of the Federal Housing Administration, provided us with statistical material on the pre- and post-earthquake housing situation in the city.

We wish to thank the following official and quasi-official Federal agencies for providing us with data and information on their natural disaster activites: the Small Business Administration; the Office of Emergency Planning; the Department of Housing and Urban Development; the Corps of Engineers; the Environmental Data Service of the Environmental Science Services Administration; the National Academy of Sciences—National Research Council Committee on the Alaska Earthquake; the Rural Electrification Administration; the Farmers Home Administration; the Alaska Railroad; the Bureau of Commercial Fisheries; and the Geological Survey.

Both the American Insurance Association and the Fire Insurance Research and Actuarial Association were extremely patient and helpful in answering our questions relating to current insurance practices. They cleared up any misunderstanding we had on the types of coverage available to homes and businesses today. The views expressed by Karl Steinbrugge of the Pacific Fire Rating Bureau also proved helpful to our study. Thanks are also due to Mrs. Evelyn Cole for her typing and proofreading assistance.

Finally, we acknowledge the generous financial support we received through the central research program at the Institute for Defense Analyses, which allowed us to pursue our study without interruption. While this book does not necessarily represent the views of that organization, it does provide an example of the Institute's continuing concern with a broad range of national problems.

Contents

Part I

FRAMEWORK OF ANALYSIS

| Chapter One | The Cost

of Natural Disaster

in the United States

THE COST of natural disasters is on the rise. Yet, fierce winds, torrential rains or complete lack of them, unusual tidal waves, and great earthquakes probably are no more frequent today than in the past. However, only when these natural phenomena cause damage to man and his artifacts can they properly be called *disasters*. In modern times man has built up his physical environment at a rapid rate, thus increasing the likelihood that a violent storm or convulsion of the earth will cause great damage. The potential for destruction is growing each day and so are the problems associated with any violent natural disturbance. As a nation we are becoming concerned if not alarmed.

DAMAGE ESTIMATION AS A MEASURE OF COST

▷ LOSS OF LIFE AND PROPERTY OVER TIME

Violent acts of nature have always posed a formidable threat to mankind. Yet in highly developed parts of the world the character of the threat has changed within the past century from one in which an expectation of significant loss of

4

life has given way to an expectation of significant loss of property. A great hurricane struck Galveston Island in 1900 leaving in its wake six thousand deaths and destroying an estimated $30 million in property. Sixty-one years later another storm described as "one of the largest, most intense, and destructive hurricanes ever to strike the Gulf Coast"[1] took its toll in human life, but the number killed, forty-six, was small in comparison with the earlier storm. However, property loss was estimated at something over $400 million.[2]

The reversal of the life-property loss relationship is a consequence of the advance of civilization. On the one hand, the movement toward urbanization and agglomeration of building has provided a bigger target for violent natural occurrences, and so the likelihood of property destruction for any given occurrence has increased. This would be true even without a trend to urbanization so long as real property were built up faster than the increase in population. On the other hand, advances in meteorology and communications have made it possible to give ample warning to the population of an area of an approaching storm or building flood. In the case of hurricane Carla (1961) mentioned above, preparations to meet the emergency began even before the storm had received its name and while it was still 1150 miles away.[3] Within a week an estimated 350,000 persons had fled the coastal region of Louisiana and Texas. In those areas where danger was greatest, evacuation was virtually complete; in larger towns it was 75 to 90 per cent complete; in the cities of Corpus Christi and Galveston about one fourth of the population left.[4] Evacuation undoubtedly was a major factor in limiting the loss of life. In the twenty-five years before 1950, hurricanes, floods, and tornadoes claimed an average of 445 lives per

1. Gordon E. Dunn and Banner I. Miller, *Atlantic Hurricanes*, rev. ed., Louisiana State University Press, 1964, p. 344.

2. The most deadly Atlantic hurricane on record struck the Windward and Leeward Islands on October 11–12, 1780. Known as the "Great Hurricane," that storm caused a British fleet "to disappear" off Barbadoes and completely ravished the island where 6000 persons were "crushed under the ruins." It then "enveloped" a convoy of French ships sinking forty of them with 4000 troops aboard. Nine thousand persons perished on Martinique, and the governor of the island released the English war prisoners stating that "in such a disaster all men should feel as brothers." Ivan Ray Tannehill, *Hurricanes: Their Nature and History*, Princeton University Press, 1956, pp. 131, 146.

3. Harry E. Moore et al., ... *And the Winds Blew*, The Hogg Foundation for Mental Health, University of Texas, Austin, 1964, p. 2. See Chapter 4 for a detailed account of the role played by the press and radio in dispensing information.

4. Weather Bureau, U.S. Department of Commerce, *Climatological Data*, National Summary, 1961, vol. 12, no. 13, p. 63.

year; since 1950 the average has fallen to 247. Tornadoes continue to be the most destructive of human life, accounting for 44 per cent of all deaths in the last fifteen years. Floods and hurricanes have accounted for equal shares of the remainder.

Recently, average damage to the United States from hurricanes, floods, tornadoes, and earthquakes has exceeded $600 million annually.[5] This figure excludes destruction due to other cyclonic[6] and noncyclonic storms, tidal waves, fires, droughts, freezes, and rainstorms. Between 1950 and 1964 floods alone have caused property loss of almost $300 million annually, hurricanes approximately $200 million, and tornadoes about $50 million. The losses would be about 17 per cent higher if taken in 1964 dollars. Concealed in those averages is a yearly pattern of extreme variation. In the three years 1950 to 1953 hurricane damage was estimated at $11 million, but for the next year it rose to $755 million. In 1963 hurricane damage was small, about $13 million, but in 1965 it was at least 100 times that large. The variation in destruction brought by floods is also large, ranging from over $1 billion in 1951 to $65 million in 1956. Tornado damage has ranged from $14 million in 1950 to about $500 million in

---

5. The presentation of damage estimates is undertaken with considerable trepidation. In a study on *Federal disaster insurance*, the reader is warned that flood damage figures "unfortunately cannot be accepted as an exact mathematical calculation of the evil effects." (*Federal Disaster Insurance, Report of the Committee on Banking and Currency, U.S. Senate*, Staff Study, January 1956, p. 36.) That is an understatement, and the reader should consider all the estimates that follow only as rough approximations of actual damage. These figures, usually taken from Weather Bureau reports, are not always comparable. In most cases they pertain only to real property damage, but sometimes they include damage to crops and indirect effects such as economic loss and damage attributable to other classes of disasters (e.g., floods) caused by the primary type (e.g., hurricanes). Thus, there may be some double counting, although we have attempted to eliminate this source of error where possible. These technical problems, coupled with the sheer difficulty in esti-

mating damage for a wide area, must be taken into account in any appraisal of conclusions to be made.

6. Cyclonic is a term used to designate all classes of storms that have low atmospheric pressure at the center. Tropical cyclones are usually the most destructive. They originate near the equator and form over all the oceans with the exception of the South Atlantic. In various parts of the world they are referred to by different names: In the North Pacific they are called *typhoons*; in the Bay of Bengal and the northern Indian Ocean they are called *cyclones*; in the South Pacific, eastern North Pacific, southern Indian and North Atlantic Oceans (including the Gulf of Mexico and Carribean Sea) they are known as *hurricanes*. (See Ivan Ray Tannehill, *op. cit.*, pp. 1–3). The term *tropical storm* is frequently used to refer to a tropical cyclone when the speed of the storm wind is less than 75 miles per hour; *hurricane* is used when the wind speed exceeds 75 miles per hour. *Federal Disaster Insurance*, p. 123.

Table I-I   LOSS OF LIFE AND PROPERTY DAMAGE IN THE UNITED STATES DUE TO HURRICANES, FLOODS, TORNADOES, AND EARTHQUAKES—1925–1965

| Years | PROPERTY LOSS IN MILLION $ DUE TO | | | | | | LOSS OF LIFE DUE TO | | | | |
	Hurricanes	Floods	Tornadoes	Earthquakes	Total	Total in 1964 Prices[a]	Hurricanes	Floods	Tornadoes	Earthquakes	Total
1925–29	133	495	95	8	731	1550	2114	579	1944	13	4650
1930–34	51	76	44	40	211	563	80	146	1018	117	1361
1935–39	314	966	39	4	1333	3327	1026	783	921	4	2734
1940–44	222	481	60	7	770	1537	149	315	835	9	1308
1945–49	298	133	126	34	1291	1953	67	304	953	8	1332
1950–54	802	1680	331	65	2778	3619	217	293	885	15	1410
1955–59	539	1695	209	16	2459	2842	660	498	523	34	1715
1960–64	1576	1151	207	405	3339	3409	175	242	230	115	762
1965	1420	788	500	13	2721	2667	75	119	299	3	496

Data Source: Weather Bureau data for hurricanes, floods, and tornadoes; for earthquakes, Coast and Geodetic Survey, U.S. Dept. of Commerce "Earthquake Investigation in the United States," special publication no. 282, 1964.
[a] GNP implicit price deflator used to obtain these estimates; from 1928 to 1929 a linked wholesale price index was used.

1965, when a series of tornadoes struck with unusual violence throughout the Midwest on Palm Sunday.[7]

Table 1-1 is presented as a quick historical summary of the costs of natural disasters in the United States since 1925. It shows that although the cost in lives is generally declining, property loss is on the rise. The grouping by five-year periods is arbitrary but any other interval would tell much the same story. The life-property loss relationship for floods, hurricanes, tornadoes and earthquakes is depicted in Figure 1-1. Between 1930 and 1935 nearly three lives were lost for every million dollars of property loss. Thirty years later approximately one fourth of a life was associated with a million dollars property loss. This amazing reduction can be attributed to advanced warning and preventive actions taken in local communities.

The detailed statistical work in this book covers the forty-year period 1925–64, yet it would be a serious mistake to exclude 1965 in any general discussion of natural disasters, for it was the worst year in U.S. history. Hurricane damage was almost twice as large as losses from this kind of storm in any previous year. Virtually all the destruction in 1965 from hurricanes can be attributed to hurricane Betsy, which struck the southeastern states in September. The year was also the worst on record for tornadoes; these storms destroyed

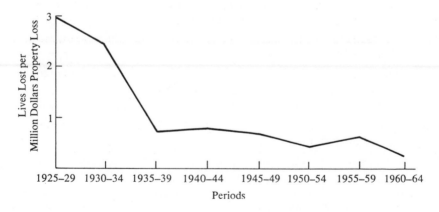

FIGURE 1-1. *Lives lost per million dollars of property loss (in 1964 prices) from floods, hurricanes, tornadoes, and earthquakes.*

7. See Table 1-8 at the end of this chapter.

close to $500 million in property,[8] or about twice the amount for any previous year. Flood damage broke no record although it was about $2\frac{1}{2}$ times higher than the previous ten-year average. In all $2.7 billion of property was destroyed, a figure larger than the financial economic assistance we currently give to foreign nations.

In athletic events, records are broken every year. Apparently this applies to natural-disaster damage as well. Certainly the costs of such damage have escalated in recent decades, and there is no reason to expect a reversal of this long-term trend. That disasters are becoming a major problem in the United States is evident from the recent concern of many legislators and the increasing involvement of the Federal government in the reconstruction of devastated areas.[9] A detailed analysis of damage over time follows; but before we turn to that subject, it is necessary to comment upon the reliability of estimates made immediately following a disaster.

▷ IMMEDIATE POSTDISASTER ESTIMATES

In the immediate aftermath of severe disasters, there is a general feeling within the stricken community that destruction is greater than it actually is. Radio, television, and newspapers focusing on human-interest reporting convey a similar impression to the outside world. At the same time, state and local officials view the situation in its darkest light, and their sight is usually faulty. Destruction is hardly ever total, and sometimes it turns out to be small in comparison with early guesses. Corps of Engineers officials responsible for damage estimates have observed that actual losses usually run about one third of the figures given in the earliest statements. Following are a few examples of this variation in damage estimates.

---

8. This very rough estimate was made by the authors from data obtained from Weather Bureau publications, "Storm Data" (monthly issues) and *Climatological Data*, National Summary, Annual 1965. In the latter publication total damage is estimated at $1 billion (p. 50), but there appears to be a discrepancy in the reporting. *Climatological Data* states that damage due to the Palm Sunday tornadoes was in excess of $200 million; yet an entry in "Storm Data" (April 1965, vol. 7, no. 4, p. 35) indicates the damage to Branch, Hillsdale, Lenawee, and Monroe counties, Illinois, was in excess of $500 million. We have used the $200 million estimate for the Palm Sunday tornadoes.

9. Some documentation of this growing concern is given in Chap. 2.

Hurricane Diane, August 1955: *The New York Times* first reported damages "in the billions of dollars."[10] Four days later the figure was pinned down to approximately three billion, with Connecticut and Massachusetts suffering one billion each and lesser damage in Pennsylvania, Rhode Island, New Jersey, and New York.[11] Six days after the storm struck, a Corps of Engineers estimate was given at approximately $1.7 billion.[12] The final Weather Bureau estimate of damage to the six-state area was $832 million.[13]

It is instructive to look at one of the components of that total. Damage in Pennsylvania was estimated by Governor Leader as between $500 million and $1 billion.[14] The Weather Bureau later set Pennsylvania damage at $77 million.[15]

Iowa Floods, March 1961: The flooding of Cedar River in March 1961 caused an estimated $70 million damage in Waterloo, Iowa,[16] yet the final Weather Bureau report placed all damage along Cedar River for that year, including Waterloo, at $5.4 million.[17]

Alaska Earthquake, March 1964: More than two weeks after the Alaska earthquake, the Office of Emergency Planning (OEP) thought that damage exceeded $600 million.[18] In its progress report nine months later the same agency placed the damage at $311 million.[19]

This list of examples easily could be extended to dozens, but the conclusions would remain the same: Damage estimates made on the spot and before the shock has worn off grossly exaggerate the extent of losses caused by natural disasters. Yet these early guesses frequently make headlines and are the ones remembered longest by the public. Overstatements of damage have at least two effects: (1) They make it appear that recovery was much faster than it actually

10. *The New York Times*, August 20, 1955, p. 1.

11. Peter Khiss, "Many Units Study Easing of Floods," *The New York Times*, August 24, 1955, p. 1.

12. *The New York Times*, August 26, 1955, p. 1.

13. See Table 1-6.

14. *The New York Times*, August 24, 1955, p. 1.

15. Weather Bureau, U.S. Department of Commerce, *Climatological Data*, National Summary, Annual 1955, vol. 6, no. 13, p. 82.

16. *The New York Times*, April 2, 1961, p. 87.

17. Weather Bureau, U.S. Department of Commerce, *Climatological Data*, National Summary, Annual 1962, vol. 13, no. 13, p. 20.

18. *Anchorage Daily News*, April 18, 1964.

19. Office of Emergency Planning, *The Alaska Earthquake: A Progress Report*, December 29, 1964, pp. 18–19. See Chap. 6 for a detailed discussion of damage estimates and expenditures following the Alaskan earthquake.

was, and (2) they make it easier politically for the Federal government to dispense aid more generously than it otherwise might. But overestimates are hardly necessary to convince one that natural disasters are costly and are becoming even more so. None of the damage figures presented throughout the rest of this chapter is a first guess; rather they are the last figure reported in most cases from the Weather Bureau.

▷ FACTORS CAUSING INCREASE IN DAMAGE
General Hypotheses

As the value of real property increases over time, it is to be expected that losses from natural disasters will rise. If we assume that the occurrence of potentially destructive natural phenomena is a random variable, then, *ceteris paribus*, the expected losses will be proportional to the value of damageable property accumulated. Many factors, however, work against having a proportional increase in damage. Some of the major ones are the following:

1. Technological advancement in building materials and building design. With the present state of the building art, it is possible to construct buildings capable of withstanding extreme stress due to earthquakes and wind gusts.
2. Building-code regulations. In certain disaster-prone areas, regulation of design and materials is written into building codes. A severe earthquake shook Long Beach on March 10, 1933, causing about $40 million in damage and taking 115 lives.[20] Noticeable among the buildings that collapsed were schools, and loss of life would have been considerably larger had the quake occurred when classes were in session. The Field Act, passed after this earthquake, restricted the use of state funds to the construction of schools capable of withstanding collapse.
3. Damage-prevention projects. Since 1936 $6.3 billion has been spent by the Corps of Engineers on flood-control projects. All other things being equal, the amount of damage should be reduced in any area where these projects have been constructed.
4. Better information on hazard areas. The knowledge that an area is disaster prone should tend to discourage movement into the area. Certainly it would make an investment in building more risky and ought to make mortgage capital more expensive, thus indirectly limiting growth.

---

20. *Earthquake History of the United States*, Part II, Coast and Geodetic Survey, U.S. Department of Commerce, 1961, pp. 38–39.

This listing above is not, by any means, exhaustive. It is intended only as a background for our discussion on losses due to natural disasters over the past forty years. Also it is suggestive of the hypothesis that disaster losses over time tend to increase at a slower pace than the rate at which real property is accumulated.

A recent study on flood insurance by the Department of Housing and Urban Development commented that flood damages have "trended irregularly upward."[21] It is evident from Figure 1-2 that this is a more accurate description of damage when applied to total destruction than when used in the special case of floods. Figure 1-2 is plotted on the basis of a ten-year moving average; thus the damage indicated for any year is really an average of the ten-year period ending with the year under consideration. The moving average exhibits a most definite trend upward. Since 1925, damage due to the four types of disasters combined has increased at an annual compounded rate of 1.7 per cent,[22] or 2.5 per cent if we use average annual rate.[23]

To compare the rise in natural-disaster loss with other important indicators, we divided the forty-year period into two equal twenty-year intervals separating them at 1945. This is an arbitrary division, but at least one may feel more comfortable with long-period averages than with annual data. Relevant data for the comparisons are given in Table 1-2.

Between the first and second periods, average annual losses increased 67 per cent. It was somewhat higher than population increase, as one would expect, and lower than the growth in GNP.[24] We are particularly interested in

---

21. "Insurance and Other Programs for Financial Assistance to Flood Victims," U.S. Department of Housing and Urban Development, August 8, 1966, p. 35. Hereafter this report will be called the HUD study.

22. More precisely, a linear regression fit to natural logarithms has a coefficient of .017. The raw data consisted of forty annual observations (1925–1964) in 1964 prices.

23. We define *average annual rate* as the average annual (absolute) increase as determined by a least-squares regression line divided by the mean value of damage over time. This is a satisfactory definition for purposes of comparison, and it probably is closer to the method used in the HUD study. Although it yields a higher

value than the compounding rate, we have eschewed use of the latter measure because of inherent difficulties in computing such a rate if any of the annual observations are zero, which is the case for hurricanes and earthquakes. In general, it is more meaningful to use the logarithmic trend where we attempt to measure the rate of growth of a stock in which case the above problem usually does not exist.

24. Although damage has increased more slowly than GNP, it has increased at about the same pace as per capita GNP. It can be argued, therefore, that relative to our ability to pay, natural disasters are no more of a problem today than they have been in the past even though their absolute costs have risen.

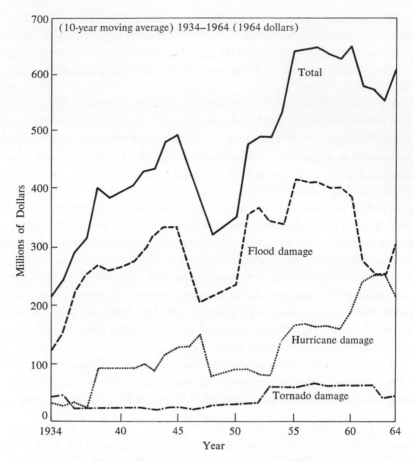

FIGURE 1-2. *Natural disaster damage in the United States.*

Table 1-2	COMPARISON OF DISASTER LOSSES WITH CHANGES IN POPULA-TION, GNP, AND NATIONAL WEALTH FROM 1925–1944 TO 1945–1964

	(1) Average 1925–1944	(2) Average 1945–1964	Average Percentage Increase Over Time (2)/(1)
Damage ($million, 1964 prices)	348	580	1.67
Population (millions)	127	165	1.30
GNP ($million, 1964 prices)	228	460	2.02
Reproducible tangible assets[a] ($million, 1964 prices)	867	1451[b]	1.67

[a] Basic data was taken from U.S. Dept. of Commerce, *Statistical Abstract*, 1964.
[b] This figure is based partly on an extrapolation to 1965 made by the authors.

comparing damage with growth in national reproducible assets, the capital goods that are destroyed in natural disasters. A remarkable feature of Table 1-2 is the identical percentage rise in both damage and tangible assets between the two periods. How can we account for the fact that natural-disaster losses have kept pace with the build-up in national wealth despite the factors tending to mitigate disaster losses listed earlier? The data, of course, are crude; but we do not consider shortcomings in the data a sufficient reason to ignore the statistical result indicated in Table 1-2. Of course, it is possible that improved reporting of natural disasters may have led to a systematic understatement of damage in the earlier period relative to the post war years. Or it may be that twenty-year periods are not long enough to smooth out the variations in damage. For example, it is quite possible that the second period was extraordinary in terms of the violence of the natural disruptions that occurred, although concrete evidence on this point is lacking. On the other hand, it is possible that the factors we listed as tending to reduce disaster losses have not actually operated in any strong way.

For the present we offer the tentative conclusion that losses due to natural disasters have risen proportionately with the increase in national wealth. Since there is some underlying logic why that relationship should hold in the long-run, we predict that the pattern will continue in the future.

Specific Examples

[FLOOD-CONTROL PROJECTS]

To investigate this question further, we shall take a closer look at the effects that flood-control projects have had on limiting flood damage.[25] Flood losses have increased more slowly than total damage, rising only 1.3 per cent per

---

25. For a full discussion on flood damage estimation see William G. Hoyt and Walter B. Langbein, *Floods*, Princeton University Press, 1955, Chap. 4, and Gilbert White et al., *Changes in Urban Occupancy in Flood Plains in the United States*, Department of Geography, University of Chicago, Research Paper No. 57, 1958, p. 4. The U.S. Department of Agriculture, Corps of Engineers, and Weather Bureau make separate estimates. They differ in that the Corps' figures give some consideration to indirect damage, the Department of Agriculture to damage along small tributary streams, while the Weather Bureau concentrates mainly on direct losses in larger floods. As a consequence, USDA estimates usually are much larger and Weather Bureau figures smaller than those given by the Corps of Engineers. However, since the Weather Bureau is the only agency that has reported consistently over a long period of time, we have used their estimates.

year.[26] The fact that they have grown at all, in the face of considerable Federal effort to contain floods, raises an interesting and controversial question. Between the enactment of the Flood Control Acts of 1936 and 1966, Congress appropriated $6.3 billion for new flood control and related projects;[27] but apparently that large expenditure was not sufficient even to hold flood losses to the level of the year 1936.

At the time of the 1936 act, annual damage was estimated at $95 million, or $200 million in 1964 prices. In 1957 a staff report of the Committee on Public Works of the House of Representatives conjectured that *potential* average annual flood loss was $911 million, of which $712 million had been or would be prevented by flood-control projects completed or authorized.[28] The remainder, or $199 million, is approximately equal to the direct loss that was estimated in 1936. Gilbert White et al. have raised the question of "why the losses believed to have been prevented by engineering works during that period exceeded the total estimated losses at the outset."[29] Flood-control projects should have decreased the average annual loss. When the White study was published in 1958, it appeared that flood losses had increased significantly since 1936, and the HUD study extended that conclusion to the present.[30] To rationalize this reported increase despite considerable efforts at controlling damage, three factors are listed:

1. Better reporting and more extensive coverage of flood losses.
2. Increases in frequency and magnitude of floods.
3. Increased occupancy of flood plains.[31]

---

26. Compare this estimate with the 5.5-per cent figure given on page 35 of the HUD study. This large discrepancy probably is a result of the length of the series. We go back only to 1925 whereas the HUD study traces the series from 1903 when flood damages were relatively small. However, it is not clear how the HUD figures were computed.

27. Figures from Corps of Engineers.

28. "Costs and Benefits of the Flood Control Program," U.S. House Committee on Public Works, House Committee Print no. 1, 85th Congress, 1st Session, 1957, p. 2.

29. White et al., *op cit.*, p. 2. Of course,

poor estimation in 1936 might be the answer.

30. "Insurance and Other Programs for Financial Assistance to Flood Victims," p. 24. See especially the footnote on that page referring to the White study: "Although the White study was able to examine the record only to the mid-1950s, available evidence suggests that average annual flood losses have become greater, not less, since that date, and additional sums have been spent for flood protection."

31. White et al., *op. cit.*, pp. 8–9. For other evidence see Hoyt and Langbein, *op. cit.*, who show an increase of 35 per cent in their "flood index" for the first

The HUD study places major reliance on the third reason.

In spite of the flood protection programs of the past 30 years, the average annual flood hazard is now greater than before such programs began because people have moved themselves and their property into flood prone areas faster than flood protection works have been built. Many factors have been responsible for the development of flood prone areas—the general growth of population, income, and wealth among others; but it is also clear that the substantial separation of costs from benefits—whereby the general public bears most of the costs of flood protection works while individual members primarily receive the gains—has been a major factor encouraging such development.[32]

Paradoxically, Federal policies on flood control are partially responsible for the lack of success in reducing flood damage. Because they engender optimistic expectations of future improvements and play down the flood danger, they encourage the occupancy of flood plains. Other programs such as highway construction to and within hazardous areas and Federal financial assistance to persons who, presumably, have accepted the risks of living in those areas have also contributed to increased losses.[33] Gilbert White has estimated that "every $6 of potential flood damage reduced each year by new flood protection measures is offset by at least $5 of additional flood damage resulting from growth in the number and value of new residential, commercial, transportational, and industrial structures placed on flood plains."[34] Weather Bureau figures on flood damage do not refute this statement. Expenditures on flood-control measures following the Flood Control Act of 1936 certainly did slow down the very rapid increase in flood damage that had taken place prior to the completion of the first projects coming after the act;[35] but they did not reverse the trend.

---

half of this century (p. 88), and Roland C. Holmes, "Composition and Size of Flood Losses" in *Papers on Flood Problems*, Gilbert White, ed. Department of Geography, University of Chicago, Research Paper No. 70, 1961.

32. "Insurance and Other Programs for Financial Assistance to Flood Victims," p. 51.

33. White et. al., *op. cit.*, pp. 227–228.

34. *Ibid.*, pp. 226–227.

35. This is not necessarily a point of conflict between our own analysis and that of HUD and White. Absolute damage has risen slightly since the act was passed even if the rate of increase has been reduced considerably.

[Hurricane Losses]

Hurricane damage has not been the subject of any controversy, nor has it been reviewed or scrutinized in any significant detail.[36] However, the overall trend is evident. Since 1934 hurricane damage has increased at a rate of 4.5 per cent per year, and since 1950 the rate of increase has been 10 per cent per year. Average annual damage for the period 1925–1949 was $83 million; since 1950 the average has increased to $217 million. Although we have no "hurricane index" that combines frequency and intensity into one measure of hurricane occurrence, there are data on the number of hurricanes reaching the U.S. coast. From 1950 to 1964, twenty-six hurricanes reached the United States, or 1.8 per year, causing an average of $120 million damage each. In the previous twenty-five years, forty-nine hurricanes reached the U.S. shoreline, a rate of 1.96 per year, causing an average damage in 1964 prices of $43 million. Evidently, the very large rise in hurricane damage in recent years cannot be attributed to stepped-up storm occurrence. We speculate that the increased losses are due ultimately to a rising standard of living with more leisure time that has turned coastal lands into attractive recreation places and living sites.[37] As coastal areas have been built up, no damage-limiting programs comparable to flood projects have been undertaken, and that probably is the reason why hurricane damage in the last decade has approached the amount caused by floods. And in the last five-year period shown in Table 1-1, hurricane damage

---

36. In some cases it is almost impossible to separate flood damage from that caused by hurricanes since much of the latter comes as a result of flooding. Gale-force winds and tidal inundation are major causes of hurricane destruction, although the heavy rains that accompany hurricanes can cause severe flooding due to river and stream overflow. Hurricane Diane, although not a violent cyclone, brought as much as 12 inches of rain in a twenty-four hour period to parts of New England in August 1955, causing record flooding and extensive damage in that area. The hurricane section of the Weather Bureau usually will attribute all the damage to the hurricane, but the flood section will report it as flood damage.

For every year for which a major hurricane has been reported, we have taken a very close look at the flood damage likely to have been induced in the affected river basins. Only in the case of hurricane Diane did we observe considerable double counting and after consultation with knowledgeable persons in the Corps of Engineers, we separated the flood damage due to river overflows from damage due to winds and tidal inundation. As a result our estimate of hurricane damage for 1955 is only about one third that reported by the Weather Bureau.

37. The same speculation is voiced in "Insurance and Other Programs for Financial Assistance to Flood Victims," p. 52.

exceeded flood damage for the first time over any extended period. It seems likely that the trend will continue.

[EARTHQUAKE AND TORNADO OCCURRENCES]

Neither earthquakes nor tornadoes constitute so dangerous a threat as floods or hurricanes. Tornadoes occur frequently in the United States, and the destruction they bring is more predictable than for any of the other types of disaster we have considered. Earthquakes occur much more infrequently with a large variability in damage.

Testing Hypotheses

By regressing the value of damage (in 1964 prices) on time for each of the four kinds of disasters, relevant information on trends can be obtained; they are summarized in Table 1-3.

These time trends in disaster losses have been computed on the basis of groupings into five-year periods. Because no kind of disaster occurs at regular intervals and with equal destructiveness, it is to be expected that these five-year period losses will, in some sense, be a more reliable measure of growth in damage than those fit to annual losses.[38] As can be seen in column 4, damage due to each type of disaster has a definite upward trend.

Table 1-3	AVERAGE, VARIABILITY AND ANNUAL INCREASE IN DAMAGE BY TYPE OF DISASTER—1925–1964[a]

Type	*(1)* Mean of 5-year Periods *($million)*	*(2)* Coefficient of Variation	*(3)* Regression Coefficient *($million)*	*(4)*[b] Per cent Annual Increase
Hurricanes	665.1	.71	149.3	.045
Floods	1395.5	.52	107.2	.013
Tornadoes	201.1	.49	19.6	.019
Earthquake	77.0	1.34	22.4	.058
All	2338.8	.46	293.8	.025

[a] Data in table from linear regressions fit to 5-year groupings. Damage (1964 prices) = f (time).
[b] (4) = (3)/[(1) × 5].

38. Data presented in Table 1-10 show that the R^2s and t-values associated with the five-year period losses are greater than those applicable to annual losses.

From the evidence presented in Table 1-10, on which Table 1-3 is based, it is clear that none of the least-squares trend lines is a good fit in the statistical sense. The R^2s and t-values are low. For that reason the regressions cannot properly be used to predict losses that will be caused in any future year by any particular type of disaster or all of them combined. This is just another way of saying that a natural catastrophe can occur at any time. Thus, predicting disaster losses is a dangerous game, and prediction for any one year in the future is particularly hazardous. Predicting averages over a long period for total damage probably makes some sense. Accordingly, we venture to estimate that total disaster losses over the next decade will average about $750 million annually in 1970 prices and easily could be 10 to 20 per cent higher than that in 1964 prices.

In summary, although disaster losses show a strong upward trend, the year-to-year variation is too large for us to make any meaningful annual point prediction. Yet the aggregate over a longer period is more predictable than any of the components. In any given year it is not likely that nature will feel consistently benevolent. Some disaster will strike somewhere, and we believe it will happen more and more frequently in the future, and with greater damage because of the rapid accumulation of buildings in disaster-prone areas. Our analysis indicates that in the long run disaster losses increase proportionately with the build-up in damageable property; therefore, we take seriously the strong upward trend in disaster losses as a realistic guide to the future.

COSTS OF DISASTERS BY REGION

▷ FORMING GEOGRAPHICAL BOUNDARIES

Natural disasters do not recognize geographical divisions. The historical record is replete with examples of catastrophes striking areas where, today, we are not accustomed to expect them. New Madrid, Missouri—not California or Alaska—was the center of the greatest earthquake ever to rock the United States. Three quakes occurring between December 1811 and February 1812 shook an area of two million square miles and left a permanent "sunken country" of thirty to fifty thousand square miles in southeastern Missouri and northeastern Arkansas. Other severe quakes have shattered eastern Massachusetts

(1755) and Charleston, South Carolina (1886), as well as San Francisco (1906) and Alaska (1964).[39] Two of the most destructive tornadoes of this century struck Waco, Texas, a town reported by an ancient Indian legend and the local Chamber of Commerce to be immune from such unfriendly acts of nature,[40] and Worcester, Massachusetts, in the same year.

These isolated cases are not intended to suggest that earthquakes are as likely to occur in the central part of the United States as in the West or that the Midwest is no more prone to tornadoes than the East Coast. Earthquakes do occur primarily in the West, but they are not so rare in the eastern half of the United States as is commonly thought. Between 1638 and 1956, one fourth of all earthquakes with an intensity of VII or greater on the Modified Mercalli scale occurred in the nonwestern, nonmountain states.[41] However, almost all the damage caused by earthquakes has been in the West. A similar case can also be made for tornadoes. Although they are not infrequent in the East and Southeast, over the years they have been most destructive in the central part of the United States. They have caused negligible damage in the West.

If regions are defined broadly, every part of the country has its problems with natural disasters. Although hurricanes strike only the East and the Gulf Coast, sometimes their rains are felt inland as far as the Midwest.[42] Earthquakes, as noted above, are a phenomenon mainly in the West, particularly in California and Alaska. Of approximately nine thousand tornadoes counted in the United States between 1916 and 1958, 74 per cent occurred in the central

---

39. Although the great earthquake in San Francisco caused much more damage than any other, its intensity on the Modified Mercalli scale was less than that for the New Madrid earthquake. The ratings are X, XI, and XII respectively, for Charleston, San Francisco, and New Madrid. *Earthquake History of the United States*, Parts I and II. The Good Friday earthquake in Alaska was rated between VIII and X with the lower rating in Anchorage. Damage in the San Francisco earthquake is stated at $500 million, or, in today's prices, about $1.6 billion.

40. Harry E. Moore, *Tornadoes Over Texas*, The University of Texas Press, Austin, 1958, p. 3.

41. P. G. Buffington, "Earthquake Insu-

rance in the United States—A Reappraisal," *Bulletin of the Seismological Society of America*, vol. 51, no. 2, April 1961, p. 321. A rating of VII means that damage to poorly built or badly designed structures is considerable but is negligible to buildings of good design and construction. In the case of severe earthquakes, X and over, four of a total of seventeen in the continental United States have occurred east of the Rockies.

42. Heavy rainfall was caused during the extra tropical stage of hurricane Carla (1961) in Missouri, Kansas, Iowa, Illinois, and Michigan a couple of days after it hit the Texas coast with full hurricane force. Weather Bureau, U.S. Department of Commerce, *Climatological Data*, National Summary, Annual 1961, vol. 12, no. 13, p. 16.

part of the country,[43] only 3 per cent in the West, and the remainder in the Northeast and Southeast. Floods occur in every part of the country, but their occurrence is more predictable since they are confined to river basins.

To determine the geographical distribution of loss due to natural disasters, we have divided the United States into six fairly large regions. Our selection of regional boundaries was dictated by the areas designated as major flood districts by the Weather Bureau. Flood districts are established in accordance with drainage systems, and therefore do not necessarily correspond to political or state boundaries. But whereas flood damage is tabulated by drainage systems, tornado damage is reported by state. Hurricane damage, on the other hand, is reported by storm, although it is possible to obtain estimates by state. Even though flood districts are not drawn up to match state lines, it is evident from a map delineating the districts that one does not have to stretch their boundaries too far to obtain a reasonable correspondence with state borders. A transformation of drainage areas into states and a grouping of states into regions suggests the six areas shown in Figure 1-3.

The regions and their corresponding flood districts are

1. Northeast: North Atlantic Flood District (Connecticut, Delaware, Dist. of Columbia, Maine, Maryland, Massachusetts, New Hampshire, New Jersey, New York, Pennsylvania, Rhode Island, Vermont, Virginia).
2. Southeast: South Atlantic, East Gulf, and Lower Mississippi Flood Districts (Alabama, Florida, Georgia, Louisiana, Mississippi, North Carolina, South Carolina).
3. Ohio Valley: Ohio Valley and Great Lakes Flood District (Indiana, Kentucky, Michigan, Ohio, Tennessee, West Virginia).
4. North Central: Missouri, Red River, and Upper Mississippi Flood Districts (Illinois, Iowa, Kansas, Minnesota, Missouri, Montana, Nebraska, North Dakota, South Dakota, Wisconsin, Wyoming).
5. South Central: Arkansas, Red River (south), and West Gulf Flood Districts (Arkansas, New Mexico, Oklahoma, Texas).
6. Western: Pacific, Great Basin, and Colorado Flood Districts (Alaska, Arizona, California, Colorado, Hawaii, Idaho, Nevada, Oregon, Utah, Washington).

---

43. In the central USA we include the North Central, Ohio Valley and South Central regions shown in Fig. 1-3. These data were taken from "Tornado Occurrences in the United States," U.S. Department of Commerce, Technical Paper no. 20, 1960, Table 2. The exact number counted is 9167 corrected for boundary-crossing tornadoes.

FIGURE 1-3

ANALYSIS: THE COST OF NATURAL DISASTER IN THE UNITED STATES

▷ EVALUATING DAMAGE ESTIMATES

The reader again must be cautioned about the proper use of our damage estimates. We do not present them as exact measures, but we do think they are sufficient for the purpose of broad generalizations about area damage. Table 1-4 displays this data by five-year periods.

Taken in isolation, the figures give a striking impression that natural disasters do affect all parts of the country on a significant scale. However, they are somewhat misleading because of the considerable variation in the sizes and populations of the regions. And it certainly is true that the broader one draws the regional boundaries, the more uniform damage will appear. To gain a better perspective on relative disaster costs, we have deflated the regional damage figures by average population. The adjusted figures, given in Table 1-5, more accurately depict the direct dollar cost of disasters over the past forty years for

| Table 1-4 | DAMAGE ESTIMATES FOR SIX REGIONS BY FIVE-YEAR PERIODS— 1925–1964 ($MILLIONS) |

Region

DAMAGE IN CURRENT PRICES

Years	North- east	South- east	Ohio Valley	North Central	South Central	Western	Total
1925–29	36	321	76	113	170	12	728
1930–34	29	36	26	22	37	58	208
1935–39	505	69	570	64	69	55	1,332
1940–44	134	98	84	237	180	36	769
1945–49	43	320	136	416	211	167	1,293
1950–54	678	331	172	1,349	198	158	2,775
1955–59	850	433	376	222	276	303	2,460
1960–64	306	1,040	342	247	489	911	3,335
Total	2,581	2,648	1,782	2,670	1,630	1,700	13,001

DAMAGE IN 1964 PRICES

Years	North- east	South- east	Ohio Valley	North Central	South Central	Western	Total
1925–29	76	681	161	239	367	26	1,550
1930–34	82	98	66	55	99	163	563
1935–39	1,266	175	1,414	161	174	137	3,327
1940–44	253	198	170	467	370	79	1,537
1945–49	67	482	214	617	328	245	1,953
1950–54	828	413	220	1,710	247	201	3,619
1955–59	1,040	489	418	245	308	342	2,842
1960–64	319	1,065	348	254	508	913	3,407
Total	3,931	3,601	3,011	3,748	2,401	2,106	18,798

Data Source: Table 1-9; implicit GNP price deflator was used to convert damage into 1964 prices.

each of the six regions. Although the per capita variation is greater than the variation in regional totals, it is still evident that natural disaster is more of a national problem than we commonly assume.

If loss per capita can be considered a rough measure of the hazard of living in a particular area, the South Central appears to be the most disaster-prone region in the country. However, about one third of the relatively high per capita figure of $196 is due to severe flooding of the Red River in 1927 and to hurricane Carla in 1961. Second is the Southeast, which is the major hurricane area in the United States. If damage for 1965 were included, the Southeast probably would replace the South Central as first in damage per capita, and the figure for the North Central would also be considerably higher. Also, the Southeast probably is the most *consistently* disaster-prone region, that is, some significant disaster usually occurs there each year. Because of its considerable concentration of population, the Northeast shows the least damage per capita, even though it is first in total damage.[44]

More information relating to regional disaster loss is contained in Tables 1-6 and 1-10. These tables differ in that the former is based on damage figures grouped in five-year periods whereas the latter is based on annual observations. The grouped data reduce the variation to a significant degree and, therefore, are subject to a more meaningful interpretation. Even so, the five-year variation

Table 1-5	ACCUMULATED DISASTER DAMAGE PER CAPITA BY REGION[a]

Region	1925–1944	1945–1964	1925–1964
USA	$57.02	$70.74	$129.76
Northeast	42.21	46.23	88.85
Southeast	67.93	108.61	182.19
Ohio Valley	80.59	42.03	118.01
North Central	36.88	93.25	134.08
South Central	92.87	102.43	196.35
Western	34.47	74.05	120.46

[a] Period 1925–1944 uses average of 1930 and 1940 population; period 1945–1964 uses average of 1950 and 1960 population.

44. If property damage due to the recent riots in large cities were also included in the same category with natural disasters, the variation in regional totals undoubtedly would be smaller than that shown in Table 1-5. These riots generally have caused damage in those regions which have a relatively low per capita damage due to natural disasters. For example, riot damage has occurred in the Western region (Los Angeles), the Ohio region (Detroit), the Northeast region (Newark, Washington, and Baltimore), and the North Central region (Chicago).

is large as can be seen by the ratios in column 2 of Table 1-6. The larger the coefficient of variation, the more precarious any prediction on five-year loss becomes. Note that the coefficient of variations for the United States (.46) is considerably less than that for all except the South Central region. Of course, this is not surprising since the likelihood of the occurrence of a major catastrophe increases as the size of the area increases. For example, the likelihood of a flood in California or a hurricane in Florida is greater than the likelihood of either event in one of those states.

In the previous section we compared growth in tangible reproducible assets with the growth in disaster losses and observed that the two have increased proportionately. It would be of interest to make this same comparison at the regional level, but the requisite data do not exist. On the basis of the information already presented on regional and national damage, we would not expect to observe so close a correspondence between regional damage trends and growth in regional wealth as had been observed at the national level, since the variability in regional losses over time is greater than the variability in national losses. However, if we had data over a period of, say, one hundred years, we would expect to find that disaster losses within each region would vary more or less proportionately with the build-up of regional wealth.

If we use population growth as a proxy for rate of increase in tangible reproducible assets, we observe some interesting relationships. Referring to Table 1-6, one notices that population has grown most rapidly in the Western and Southeast regions and that those areas rank first and second respectively in the rate at which damage has increased. But beyond these areas there appears to be no consistent relationship. The cases of the Ohio Valley and North

Table 1-6	VARIABILITY AND RATE OF GROWTH OF DISASTER LOSSES BY FIVE-YEAR PERIODS—1925–1964[a]

	(1) Average of 5-year periods ($million)	(2) Coefficient of Variation	(3) Annual Rate of Change[b]	(4) Population Growth
USA	2338.8	.46	.025	.013
Northeast	491.8	.97	.024	.010
Southeast	449.5	.70	.030	.015
Ohio Valley	376.5	1.15	−.003	.011
North Central	468.4	1.08	.029	.006
South Central	300.3	.42	.018	.012
Western	252.3	1.00	.065	.018

[a] Based on information in Table 1-10.
[b] Rate of change is computed as the 5-year damage increase as determined by the regressions given in Table 1-10 divided by the mean of the series divided by 5.

Central regions are anomalies. For the Ohio Valley region the trend in damage is negative, whereas the rate of population change is significant. That relationship is not likely to hold in the long run, for the negative trend in damage is due to extreme flooding that occurred in the Ohio Valley in 1936 and 1937 compared with relatively minor flooding in recent years. Likewise the strong upward trend in damage in the North Central region is due primarily to the rampage of the Missouri River in 1951 that caused over $1 billion in damage. The relatively high coefficients of variation for those two regions provide one way of confirming these erratic occurrences. We believe that a longer period of observation is necessary to demonstrate a close relationship between the trends in damage and property accumulation in the various regions. For the present we must be satisfied with a statement that disaster losses are increasing faster than population by a good margin, perhaps two to two-and-a-half times as fast. That estimate can serve as a rough guide as to what the future portends in the way of losses due to natural disasters.

▷ CATALOGUING RECENT DISASTERS

We conclude this chapter with some estimates of damage in particular disasters. Because of the limitation on data pertaining to disaster relief—the subject of the following chapter—we have singled out no disaster before 1954. Also, only those disasters with damage of approximately $100 million or over were selected. No attempt has been made to give a detailed account of these disasters; the major purpose is to put them in the perspective of what has preceded and what follows.

Every disaster is unique, and almost every year brings a new one in the East or West. Over a decade ago a Weather Bureau annual report claimed, "From the standpoint of property damage the hurricane season of 1954 was the most destructive on record . . . 'Carol' alone did more damage than any single storm or natural catastrophe . . . and more than that resulting from any previous entire hurricane season."[45] In the following year hurricane Diane struck the East Coast causing record flooding in New England and also record

---

45. C. E. Rhodes in Weather Bureau, U.S. Department of Commerce, *Climatological Data*, National Summary, Annual 1954, vol. 5, no. 14, p. 72. Statement refers to damage in current prices.

losses. Thus, one reads in the annual Weather Bureau report for 1955, "For the second consecutive year all records were broken for hurricane destruction."[46]

Hurricane Audrey in 1957 claimed more lives than any other natural disaster during the period under consideration. Hurricane Donna in 1960 was "the most destructive tropical cyclone ever to strike Florida and one of the most damaging ever to affect the United States."[47] Hurricane Carla in 1961 has previously received mention. Then in September 1965 hurricane Betsy became "the most destructive hurricane in history,"[48] devastating the coast of Louisiana and especially New Orleans.

Table 1-7	MAJOR DISASTERS—1954–1965

Disaster	Month/Year	Region[a]	Damage ($million)	Deaths
Hurricane Carol	9/54	Northeast	456	60
Hurricane Hazel	10/54	Southeast	232	94
Hurricane (and Floods) Diane	8/55	Northeast	832	180
Northwest Flood	12/55	Western	193[b]	74
Hurricane Audrey	6/57	Southeast	150	390
Hurricane Donna	9/60	Southeast	360	60
Hurricane Carla	9/61	South Central	431	46
Great Atlantic Storm	3/62	Northeast	245[c]	33
Ohio Basin Floods	3/63	Ohio Valley	98	26
Alaska Earthquake	3/64	Western	311[d]	115
Pacific Northwest Flood	12/64	Western	462[e]	45
Upper Mississippi Floods	4/65	North Central	140[f]	16
Palm Sunday Tornados	4/65	North Central	200	247
Colorado and Kansas Floods	6/65	Western	405[g]	16
Hurricane Betsy	9/65	Southeast	1420	89

Data Sources: Weather Bureau, *Climatological Data*, various issues except where noted.
a Region where major losses occurred.
b Estimated by authors from river-basin flood data in *Climatological Data*, December 1955, and National Summary, Annual 1956, vol. 7, no. 13.
c Corps of Engineers, "Report on Operation Five High," Civil Works Branch, Construction Operation Division, North Atlantic Division, August 1963, p. 2-2.
d Office of Emergency Planning, *The Alaska Earthquake: A Progress Report*, December 29, 1964, pp. 18–19.
e "The Northwest Floods of December, 1964 and January, 1965," *Report of the Special Subcommittee to Inspect Flooded Areas in the Northwestern United States*, Committee on Public Works, U.S. House of Representatives, Print no. 8, April 1, 1965.
f "Upper Mississippi River Basin Floods of April–May 1965," *Report of the Special Subcommittee to Inspect Flooded Areas of the Upper Mississippi River Basin*, Committee on Public Works, U.S. House of Representatives, Print no. 13, June 1965.
g "The Colorado and Kansas Floods of June 1965," *Report of the Special Subcommittee to Inspect Flooded Areas in Colorado and Kansas*, Committee on Public Works, U.S. House of Representatives, Print no. 15, June 1965, p. 9.

46. C. E. Rhodes in Weather Bureau, U.S. Department of Commerce, *Climatological Data*, National Summary, Annual 1955, vol. 6, no. 12, p. 80.
47. Dunn and Miller, *op. cit.*, p. 337.

48. George W. Cry and Richard M. DeAngelis in Weather Bureau, U.S. Department of Commerce, *Climatological Data*, National Summary, Annual 1965, vol. 16, no. 13, p. 59.

The years 1964 and 1965 brought a spate of other disasters in addition to Betsy. A great earthquake on Good Friday 1964 in Alaska and nine months later a devastating flood in the Pacific Northwest brought on a wave of legislative discussion. The central portion of the country suffered most in early 1965 from flooding on the Mississippi and the worst tornadoes in history, which touched down on Palm Sunday and left ruin and rubble scattered throughout the Midwest. Figures on loss of life and damage from these and other less well-known disasters are given in Table 1-7.

Every disaster seems worse in some way than the previous one. Superlatives highlight their description. Perhaps because disasters have been well publicized in recent years, there is a growing public awareness of their potential danger, and they have created interesting problems in relief assistance. Gone are the days when the victims sought no aid or when they received little outside financial support. A new generosity on the part of the Federal government is a major feature of the new era. To that subject we turn in the next chapter.

APPENDIX

| Table 1-8 | ESTIMATES OF DISASTER LOSSES IN THE UNITED STATES BY TYPE OF DISASTER—1925–1965 ($MILLION IN CURRENT PRICES) |

Year	Hurricanes	Floods	Tornadoes	Earthquakes	Total	Year	Hurricanes	Floods	Tornadoes	Earthquakes	Total
1925	—	10	24	8	42	1945	80	166	22	—	268
1926	107	24	4	—	135	1946	5	71	12	—	88
1927	—	348	44	—	392	1947	136	272	24	—	432
1928	25	45	13	—	83	1948	18	230	41	—	289
1929	1	68	10	—	79	1949	59	94	27	34	214
1930	—	16	12	—	28	1950	36	176	14	—	226
1931	—	3	3	—	6	1951	2	1029	30	3	1064
1932	—	10	9	—	19	1952	3	254	35	60	352
1933	46	37	16	40	139	1953	6	122	224	—	352
1934	5	10	4	—	19	1954	755	99	28	2	884
1935	12	127	5	4	148	1955	326[a]	911[a]	34	4	1275
1936	2	283	26	—	311	1956	27	65	49	—	141
1937	—	441	3	—	444	1957	152	360	73	1	586
1938	300	101	9	—	410	1958	11	218	28	—	257
1939	—	14	6	—	20	1959	23	141	25	11	200
1940	5	41	6	6	58	1960	370	93	27	5	490
1941	8	40	5	1	54	1961	431	154	46	—	636
1942	27	99	15	—	141	1962	247[b]	75	18	—	340
1943	17	200	12	—	229	1963	13	176	34	—	223
1944	165	101	22	—	288	1964	515	653	82	400	1650
						1965	1420	788	500	13	2721

Data Sources: *Hurricane damage* for 1925–1952: U.S. Weather Bureau, *Climatological Data*, National Summary, Annual 1952, vol. 3, no. 13, p. 68; for 1953–1965, annual issues of *Climatological Data*.
Flood damage: U.S. Weather Bureau, *Climatological Data*, National Summary, Annual 1964, vol. 15, no. 13, p. 87 and Annual 1965, vol. 16, no. 13.
Tornado damage for 1925–1958: Laura Wolford, "Tornado Occurrences in the United States," *Technical Paper No. 20*, U.S. Weather Bureau, 1960; for 1959–1965, estimates made by authors from range data and storm descriptions in monthly and annual issues of *Climatological Data and Storm Data*, U.S. Weather Bureau. *Earthquakes* for 1925–1964, Coast and Geodetic Survey, "Earthquake Investigation in the United States", Special Publication No. 282, 1964; for 1965, Coast and Geodetic Survey.

[a] Authors have separated flood and hurricane damage from hurricane Diane on basis of information obtained from Corps of Engineers.
[b] This figure includes the great Atlantic coastal storm in March 1962.

Table I-9 — ESTIMATES OF DISASTER LOSSES IN SIX REGIONS OF THE UNITED STATES—1925-1964 ($MILLION IN CURRENT PRICES)

Year	North-east	South-east	Ohio Valley	North Central	South Central	Western
1925	.8	4.5	4.9	21.2	1.8	8.7
1926	.6	107.6	5.8	8.3	10.6	.6
1927	30.4	159.5	34.9	58.0	132.6	.9
1928	2.7	19.0	12.0	15.4	7.0	1.4
1929	1.2	30.6	18.0	10.0	18.2	.2
1930	—	1.2	9.0	6.5	8.2	.5
1931	1.0	5.8	.2	2.1	1.5	.6
1932	.1	3.4	1.3	2.4	6.8	.1
1933	28.2	22.0	13.7	5.1	18.9	51.6
1934	.1	3.5	1.3	5.4	1.5	5.0
1935	16.6	20.3	21.9	42.5	41.7	4.6
1936	147.2	26.5	122.5	2.3	11.0	.9
1937	3.2	8.3	414.9	3.8	4.1	9.5
1938	337.4	4.8	5.0	12.4	10.1	40.3
1939	.2	9.4	5.8	2.6	1.6	—
1940	2.5	19.6	8.4	3.2	9.1	14.4
1941	.7	2.2	1.2	17.4	27.7	3.7
1942	22.3	3.5	19.3	31.9	54.9	9.0
1943	—	3.2	47.1	107.0	63.7	7.8
1944	108.8	69.1	7.7	77.1	24.3	.7
1945	10.9	67.6	54.3	50.8	74.1	11.2
1946	8.6	13.3	13.9	20.8	23.7	7.5
1947	1.7	140.8	14.5	255.2	19.0	.9
1948	12.7	31.3	43.8	44.9	46.7	111.8
1949	9.4	66.6	9.3	44.1	47.8	37.0
1950	9.6	49.3	61.3	50.0	13.7	41.7
1951	1.6	13.8	7.9	981.7	49.2	8.9
1952	3.0	8.8	18.6	212.9	18.1	90.9
1953	64.6	82.3	48.4	62.1	86.3	8.9
1954	599.3	177.1	36.2	42.2	30.3	6.9
1955	835.1	178.3	23.1	11.3	28.2	199.2
1956	3.9	38.3	45.4	16.3	7.9	28.3
1957	.7	164.5	140.8	77.4	177.9	25.1
1958	.7	34.6	69.6	83.9	34.7	33.7
1959	9.8	17.2	97.0	32.6	26.8	5.7
1960	35.7	372.7	11.1	50.4	17.7	1.1
1961	5.2	72.2	43.7	75.1	429.2	8.8
1962	237.7	24.5	32.8	24.8	7.7	15.8
1963	11.4	23.1	142.9	21.0	5.5	18.8
1964	16.3	547.6	111.2	75.8	28.1	866.8

Data Sources: See references for Table 1-8. Hurricane damage was separated by state on basis of information contained in descriptive write-ups in annual issues of *Climatological Data* and in Gordon E. Dunn and Banner I. Miller, *Atlantic Hurricanes*, rev. ed., Louisiana State University Press, 1964. Flood damage was arranged by regions from flood data by flood districts.

ANALYSIS: THE COST OF NATURAL DISASTER IN THE UNITED STATES

| $Table$ I-IO | REGRESSION COEFFICIENTS, STANDARD ERRORS, AND OTHER DATA PERTAINING TO DAMAGE TRENDS[a] |

VALUES DERIVED FROM ANNUAL OBSERVATIONS

	(1) Mean	(2) Standard Deviation	(3) Constant Term	(4) Standard Error of (3)	(5) Regression Coefficient	(6) Standard Error of (5)	(7) Standard Error of Estimate	(8) R^2
Hurricanes	132.8	216.0	4.9	66.3	6.26	2.82	205.9	.11
Floods	279.3	312.9	201.5	101.1	3.78	4.30	313.8	.02
Tornadoes	40.2	43.7	23.1	13.9	.83	.59	43.1	.05
Earthquakes	15.4	52.8	−5.6	16.8	1.03	.71	52.1	.05
USA	467.8	403.0	225.4	123.8	11.66	5.26	384.2	.11
Northeast	98.4	289.9	50.3	74.2	2.26	3.16	230.4	.01
Southeast	89.9	119.2	34.3	37.5	2.71	1.59	116.4	.07
Ohio Valley	75.2	163.2	79.3	53.3	−.20	2.26	165.3	.00
North Central	93.9	182.8	40.7	58.9	2.43	2.51	182.9	.02
South Central	59.9	84.9	40.1	27.5	.97	1.17	85.3	.02
Western	50.5	128.4	−20.8	39.8	3.47	1.69	123.5	.10

VALUES DERIVED FROM 5-YEAR GROUPS

	(1) Mean	(2) Standard Deviation	(3) Constant Term	(4) Standard Error of (3)	(5) Regression Coefficient	(6) Standard Error of (5)	(7) Standard Error of Estimate	(8) R^2
Hurricanes	666.1	472.8	−5.9	—	149.3	49.9	323.5	.60
Floods	1396.5	727.0	913.2	570.6	107.2	113.0	732.3	.13
Tornadoes	201.1	97.7	113.1	71.7	19.6	14.2	92.0	.24
Earthquakes	77.0	103.5	23.9	73.9	22.4	14.6	94.8	.28
USA	2338.8	1074.1	1000.0	671.2	293.8	132.9	861.4	.45
Northeast	491.8	481.5	223.9	386.2	59.5	76.5	495.7	.09
Southeast	449.5	316.1	148.4	227.8	66.7	45.1	292.4	.27
Ohio Valley	376.5	433.4	401.5	364.6	−5.5	72.2	467.9	.00
North Central	468.4	490.7	159.4	390.4	65.3	77.3	501.1	.11
South Central	300.3	126.8	181.7	91.8	26.3	18.2	117.8	.26
Western	252.3	251.1	114.5	128.1	81.5	25.4	164.4	.63

[a] Regressions were run with time as the independent variable and damage in 1964 prices as the dependent variable.

Chapter Two | Relief in

Natural Disasters

IN RECENT years the general taxpayer has assumed an ever increasing role in the financing of recovery from natural catastrophe, relieving substantially the distress of the comparatively few caught by such misfortune. The socialization of the burden of disaster has progressed to a remarkable extent and is likely to advance even more in the future with the further institutionalization of relief programs. This chapter has a twofold purpose: to demonstrate quantitatively the extent of the socialization of disaster costs and to indicate qualitatively how the process of Federal aid is becoming institutionalized.

While the cost of natural disasters has climbed rapidly since the early 1950s, the amount of financial assistance given to disaster victims has grown even faster. It is intriguing to speculate that the conspicuous rise in aid is due to the emergence of a new social attitude toward assistance on the part of both recipients and givers. Following the San Angelo tornado in 1953 some local school officials were persuaded by Federal representatives to apply for Federal funds to repair a school damaged by the twister; however, the officials were reluctant to ask for Federal money because most of the repair expenses were covered by insurance. Eventually they did forward a request that was promptly granted. But a year later they returned the money in an act of conscience.[1] Today one rarely reads of such independent conduct. With regard to the principal giver of aid, the Federal government, there can be little doubt of a changed

---

1. Harry E. Moore, *Tornadoes Over Texas*, The University of Texas Press, Austin, 1958, p. 74.

attitude in recent years, as Congressmen and government officials have become more and more concerned with finding ways to help communities that have been struck by sudden disaster.

ORGANIZATIONS PROVIDING ASSISTANCE

Over the past decade and a half, the Federal government has joined the American Red Cross in rendering financial assistance to devastated communities on a very large scale. The figures in Table 2-1 show that Federal involvement has increased from several million dollars in 1953 to several hundred million in 1965, and as we shall indicate in the last section of this chapter, legislative changes, beginning with the Alaska earthquake in 1964, hold a promise for

$Table$ 2-I	ANNUAL FEDERAL DISASTER AID UNDER PL 875 AND SMALL BUSINESS ADMINISTRATION LOANS AND RED CROSS EXPENDITURES—1953–1965[a]

| | | FEDERAL AID | | | |
YEAR	DAMAGE	PL 875 *Allocations*	*SBA Loans*	*Total*	RED CROSS
1953	352	2.7	.5	3.2	4.5
1954	884	11.4	7.5	18.9	3.5
1955	1275	59.6[b]	42.8	102.4	28.5
1956	141	4.4	3.3	7.7	2.7
1957	586	17.3	8.2	25.5	10.3
1958	257	5.0	1.1	6.1	1.3
1959	200	.9	4.4	5.3	3.8
1960	490	9.8	14.3	24.1	2.8
1961	636	17.1	23.4	40.5	7.8
1962	340	41.0	22.6	63.6	1.7
1963	223	12.5	9.3	21.8	3.4
1964	1562	140.8	120.1	260.9	11.0
1965	2721	103.4	170.5[c]	273.9	21.0

Data Sources:
Damage: Table 1-8.
PL 875 Allocations: Office of Emergency Planning, "Major Disaster Declarations," mimeographed.
SBA Loans: Small Business Administration, "Disaster Loans Approved and Applications Pending—By Disaster—By State."
Red Cross: American Red Cross, "Operations Directed by National Headquarters 1946–47 through 1962–63," mimeographed. Figures for 1963–65 were derived from data supplied by the American Red Cross.
[a] Pertains only to aid for floods, hurricanes, tornadoes, and earthquakes occurring within the United States. One exception is the Atlantic coastal storm in March 1962 which is covered by the figure in this table.
[b] This figure includes a supplemental appropriation of $32.9 million made by Congress to the Corps of Engineers and $3.6 million made by the OEP to the Corps for work performed under PL 875.
[c] This figure is based upon worksheets supplied by the Small Business Administration.

still deeper involvement in the future. Today, the number of Federal agencies that participate in disaster assistance is so staggering that it has become necessary to publish a *Federal Disaster Relief Manual*[2] in addition to dozens of pamphlets circulated by the various departments just to inform communities and individuals of the multiple Federal services of which they may avail themselves.

Where misadventure strikes, the Red Cross has been a familiar symbol. It serves as the nation's most effective linkage between thousands of sympathetic private citizens and persons in distress. Because of its historic claim to distinction among relief agencies, the following discussion starts with this well-known government-chartered, privately operated charitable organization.

▷ THE AMERICAN NATIONAL RED CROSS

Until the early fifties the major disaster relief agency in the United States was the American National Red Cross (ARC). Established by Federal statute[3] in 1905 as an official instrument of the Federal government for carrying out duties assumed under an international treaty, the Red Cross has had a long and distinguished history of private charity. Raising all of its funds through private donations, the Red Cross uses them to "carry on a system of national and international relief in time of peace and apply the same in mitigating the sufferings caused by pestilence, famine, fire, floods, and other great calamities."[4]

Since its founding the Red Cross has dispensed more than $300 million to individuals and families suffering from natural disaster in the United States. All its efforts are directed toward relief and restoration of the private sector in contrast with some government programs designed to finance the rebuilding of public facilities. Red Cross aid can be separated into (1) emergency assistance and (2) rehabilitation support.

In the emergency period following a disaster, Red Cross activities are concerned mainly with mass care. It prepares shelter for persons forced to leave their homes, offers food, clothing, and emergency medical treatment to disaster

---

2. *Federal Disaster Relief Manual*, rev. ed., Committee on Government Operations, U.S. Senate, U.S. Government Printing Office, 1963.

3. Public Law 4, 58th Congress, January 5, 1905 (33 Stat. 599).

4. 36 U.S. Code, Sec. 3.

victims, and provides food for many thousands of volunteer workers. While these services hardly ever cost more than 15 per cent of total Red Cross expenditures in any disaster, they frequently involve the handling of hundreds of thousands of people. In hurricane Carla, for example, the Red Cross gave emergency care to over 400 thousand persons.

The emergency operation is widely publicized and always appears dramatic and humane, so that the Red Cross's principal function of rehabilitation assistance is frequently put in the background. Table 2-2 indicates the relative importance of this role very clearly. Specifically, the Red Cross supplies food, clothing, rental payments, financial aid for the repair and rebuilding of owner-occupied homes, replacement of household furnishings, occupational supplies and inventories for small family businesses, tools and equipment, and medical and nursing care extending well beyond the emergency period. Persons who receive Red Cross help are under no obligation to repay since the organization is strictly charitable, granting funds to families in need. It makes no loans.

In order to qualify for a Red Cross grant a family must show clear need caused by the disaster. Need implies that financial resources such as savings, insurance, or a line of credit either are small or do not exist. Thus, if a family has not accumulated any savings but is able to obtain a low-cost loan for repair or rebuilding from the Small Business Administration, it is not likely to qualify for a Red Cross grant for that same purpose unless supplemental funds are deemed necessary. For example, an individual may apply for an SBA loan of $2000, but only $1500 will be approved because of the agency's concern with his ability to repay. If the Red Cross felt that the extra funds were needed for rehabilitation, they would supplement the SBA loan with a grant of $500.

Some information on Red Cross rehabilitation assistance is given in Table 2-3. The figures indicate the flexibility of the ARC's assistance program. Grants for building and repair and household furnishings usually account for most Red Cross expenditures, but in disasters like the Palm Sunday tornadoes, which caused great bodily injury and for which homeowner's comprehensive insurance covered much rebuilding, the major expenditure was on medical and nursing care. One should note also the relatively large variation in average grant per family for different disasters. The number of families assisted in each of the separate categories add up to more than the total number assisted because many families receive aid in more than one category. In summary, the Red Cross does not adhere to any preplanned schedule for providing assistance; its help is tailored to the special situation.

Table 2-2 — RED CROSS AID BY MAJOR CLASS OF EXPENDITURE, NUMBER OF PERSONS GIVEN MASS CARE, AND FAMILIES GIVEN REHABILITATION ASSISTANCE IN MAJOR DISASTERS SINCE 1954

Disaster and Year		Total Expenditures $000	Emergency Mass Care $000	Rehabilitation Assistance $000	Administrative Costs $000	Per cent for Mass Care	Per cent for Rehabilitation	Per cent for Administrative	No. of Families Rehabilitated	No. of Persons Given Mass Care
Hurricanes Carol and Edna[1]	1954	1,116	125	894	97	11.2	80.2	8.6	1,883	42,000
Hurricane Hazel[2]	1954	840	10	738	92	1.1	87.9	10.9	1,922	10,000
Eastern States Floods[3]	1955	18,288	1,321	15,649	1,319	7.2	85.6	7.2	14,750	144,000
West Coast Floods[4]	1955	8,563		7,325			85.5		10,342	86,000
Hurricane Audrey[5]	1957	2,566							3,343	70,000
Hurricane Donna[6]	1960	2,042	169	1,680	193	8.3	82.3	9.3	7,143	156,000
Hurricane Carla[7]	1961	5,605	561	4,769	274	10.0	85.1	4.9	17,574	421,000
Atlantic Coastal Storm[8]	1962	1,000	95	804	101	9.5	80.4	10.1	3,277	26,000
Alaska Earthquake[9]	1964	1,271	248	899	124	19.5	70.7	9.8	930	11,000
Pacific Northwest Floods[10]	1964	4,233	433	3,417	382	10.2	80.7	9.1	5,632	49,000
Palm Sunday Tornadoes[11]	1965	879	62	708	109	7.1	80.5	12.4	1,081	78,000
Upper Mississippi Floods[12]	1965	1,844	275	1,380	188	14.9	74.8	10.2	3,650	152,000
Hurricane Betsy[13]	1965	16,749	810	13,925	2,014	4.8	83.1	12.0	34,600	267,000

Data Sources: *Total expenditures and breakdown:* (1) "Wind and Fury 1954, Disaster Operations in the New England Hurricanes—Carol and Edna," undated; (2) "Hurricane Hazel," February 1955; (3) "In Disaster a Friend—1955 Eastern States Floods," January 1956; (4) "Disaster in the West," undated; (5) "ARC Disaster Relief Operations," mimeographed; (6) "Donna," December 1960; (7) "Hurricane Carla," March 1962; (8) "The Great Mid-Atlantic Coastal Storm, March 5-6-7, 1962," July 1962; (9) "Alaskan Earthquake Disaster, March 1964," undated; (10) "West Coast Floods, Christmas 1964," undated; (11) "Palm Sunday Tornadoes, 1965," August 1965; (12) "North Central Plains Floods and Minnesota Tornadoes, Spring 1965," September 1965; (13) "Betsy," undated. All published by the ARC. *Number of families rehabilitated and persons given mass care:* data supplied by the American Red Cross except for hurricane Donna for which data was taken from source 6 above.

Table 2-3	RED CROSS REHABILITATION ASSISTANCE BY SPECIFIC USAGE, NUMBER OF FAMILIES AIDED, AND AVERAGE GRANT PER FAMILY IN MAJOR DISASTERS SINCE 1954	

VALUE OF ASSISTANCE IN THOUSANDS OF DOLLARS

	Total	Food, Clothing, Maintenance	Building and Repair	Household Furnishing	Medical and Nursing	Occupational Supplies
Hurricanes Carol and Edna	894		507	284	20	84
Hurricane Hazel	738	60	424	129	5	119
Eastern States Floods (Diane)	15,649	1,294	7,043	5,305	132	1,875
West Coast Floods	7,325	794	3,647	2,171	67	646
Hurricane Audrey						
Hurricane Donna	1,680					
Hurricane Carla	4,769	674	1,292	2,608	67	128
Atlantic Coastal Storm	804	131	305	308	12	47
Alaska Earthquake	899	107	607	100	19	65
Pacific Northwest Floods	3,417	565	1,652	1,015	51	134
Upper Mississippi Flood	1,380	219	761	354	31	15
Palm Sunday Tornadoes	708	140	181	178	192	17
Hurricane Betsy	13,925	2,651	3,029	7,766	110	370

NUMBER OF FAMILIES ASSISTED

Hurricanes Carol and Edna	1,883		724	957	144	257
Hurricane Hazel	1,222	844	989	510	48	389
Eastern States Floods (Diane)	14,750	10,800	5,400	8,400	1,350	1,660
West Coast Floods	10,342	7,947	3,045	5,312	716	1,023
Hurricane Audrey	3,343					
Hurricane Donna	7,143					
Hurricane Carla	17,574	12,798	3,816	7,549	628	418
Atlantic Coastal Storm	3,277	2,691	602	1,336	142	155
Alaska Earthquake	930	841	197	195	82	119
Pacific Northwest Floods	5,632	4,879	1,278	2,396	442	347
Upper Mississippi Flood	3,650	2,758	1,267	1,444	97	50
Palm Sunday Tornadoes	1,081	886	119	392	283	44
Hurricane Betsy	34,600	29,880	6,011	22,730	3,395	1,860

AVERAGE GRANT PER FAMILY IN DOLLARS

Hurricanes Carol and Edna	475		700	297	140	326
Hurricane Hazel	383	72	429	252	110	307
Eastern States Floods (Diane)	1,061	120	1,304	632	98	1,130
West Coast Floods	708	100	1,198	409	94	632
Hurricane Audrey						
Hurricane Donna	235					
Hurricane Carla	271	53	339	346	106	306
Atlantic Coastal Storm	245	49	507	231	82	306
Alaska Earthquake	967	128	3,081	515	235	547
Pacific Northwest Floods	607	116	1,293	423	116	386
Upper Mississippi Flood	378	79	601	245	320	307
Palm Sunday Tornadoes	655	158	1,522	454	680	397
Hurricane Betsy	402	89	504	341	32	199

Data Sources: See Table 2-2.

As the disaster-loan programs of Federal agencies continue to grow, it follows that fewer and fewer families will be completely without financial resources so long as the ability to borrow is considered a possible source of support. Yet it would be foolish to assume that the Red Cross will wither and die because some other, richer agency has taken over many of its traditional functions. Rather, one would expect to see this famous relief organization gradually shift away from grants given for the purpose of rebuilding and repair —the primary purpose of SBA loans—and place greater emphasis on grants for household furnishings and other things, depending also, of course, on the extent to which these items are covered by insurance.

There is one other interesting hypothesis that can be made. Federal disaster-loan programs do not guarantee everyone a loan regardless of his financial position. In its loan program the Federal government presumably will turn down a prospective borrower if he cannot be expected to pay back the loan. Such a poor risk is obviously a charity case. Some of the poor-risk borrowers who would have relied on the Red Cross for aid at some time in the past can now obtain financing from the Small Business Administration as a result of more liberal Federal loan policies. Consequently, one would suppose that families aided by the Red Cross today would have a lower relative income on the average than those given assistance ten years ago by the same organization. But we must leave this a verifiable proposition rather than a fact since we have no information on the incomes of families aided by the Red Cross.

▷ ROLE OF THE FEDERAL GOVERNMENT

Within the past fifteen years the Federal government has assumed a leading role in the disaster arena. Presently some fifty Federal agencies, bureaus, and offices are involved in domestic relief including all of the cabinet offices with the lone exception of the State Department. A detailed discussion of the roles of these agencies and the ways in which they become involved in disasters is outside the scope of this book.[5] The following thumbnail sketch covering the major

---

5. For a start, the interested reader should refer to *Federal Disaster Relief Manual*, rev. ed.

Federal relief organizations is intended to serve only as an introduction to a subsequent discussion on governmental aid since 1953.

The Federal government has many avenues for providing assistance to the people of a disaster area. It can aid the community as a whole with Federal grants for the restoration of public property, or it can aid individuals separately with loans and grants. It most frequently intervenes through the Federal Disaster Act (PL 81-875), but it also makes its presence felt through other statutory legislation pertaining to specific departments and agencies. Figure 2-1 schematically represents the ways in which the most important governmental disaster-relief agencies can come to the aid of the public and private sectors. Since the figure is only a schematic representation it cannot be taken as a catalogue of all agencies which can become involved in disaster relief. To become involved in a disaster a governmental organization requires either the explicit authority contained in some Federal statute or the delegated authority of the President under the Federal Disaster Act. Any Federal organization which the President can command may participate in disaster relief under the Federal Disaster Act. That is the meaning of the left-hand side of the flow diagram. On the other hand, some important governmental organizations do not require the specific authority of the President; they can become involved in disaster relief through statutory authority granted them in previous acts of Congress. As examples of the right-hand portion of the diagram, the Small Business Administration has its own statutory authority to give low cost business and home loans to disaster victims, and the Corps of Engineers has specific legal authority to assist in flood fighting and rescue operations, or to restore flood control works. While Figure 2-1 does not give an exhaustive listing of disaster organizations the reader can generalize by assuming that any agency having statutory authority can be called upon to perform under the Federal Disaster Act; but the converse is not true. Also, when agencies become involved under the Federal Disaster Act their activities are usually broader in scope than is possible when they act under their own statutory authority. For example, the Small Business Administration cannot grant economic injury loans under its own statutory authority, but it can grant them under Presidential authority; the Corps of Engineers requires authority under the Federal Disaster Act to engage in activities such as debris clearance and emergency repairs to public facilities; and the Internal Revenue Service can be more generous in allowing disaster victims to deduct losses from the previous year's taxes when the President has declared a major disaster than is possible under the normal interpretation of the Internal Revenue Code.

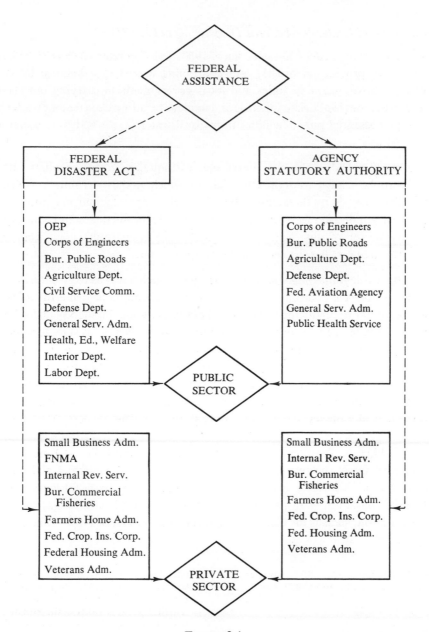

FIGURE 2-1

Intervention Under the Federal Disaster Act (PL 875)

The intent of the Federal Disaster Act of 1950, hereafter referred to as PL 875, is clear: "to provide an orderly and continuing means of assistance by the Federal Government to states and local governments in carrying out their responsibilities to alleviate suffering and damage resulting from major disasters, to repair essential public facilities in major disasters . . ."[6] It defines a major disaster as

> any flood, drought, fire, hurricane, earthquake, storm, or other cata-
> strophe in any part of the United States which, in the determination of the
> President, is or threatens to be of sufficient severity and magnitude to
> warrant disaster assistance by the Federal Government . . . and which the
> Governor of any State . . . in which such catastrophe may occur or
> threaten certifies the need for disaster assistance.[7]

It is evident that *major disaster* is defined in such a way as to give the President *carte blanche*. The only way in which his hands might be tied is the refusal of a governor to certify the need, and, of course, it would be slightly farfetched to imagine that a governor today would not claim a need of his state to receive Federal money. Once the President has decided that some event is a major disaster, he then is authorized to direct any Federal agency "to utilize its available personnel, equipment, supplies, facilities, and other resources"[8] to aid disaster communities. It thus seems evident that any service that may be performed by any agency under appropriate statute may also be performed under PL 875.

In 1953 the President vested in the Director of the Office of Emergency Planning (OEP) the responsibility for coordinating all Federal activities in disaster relief.[9] Recently this responsibility has been given to the OEP in specific Federal legislation.[10] In performing that role, the OEP utilizes operational organizations such as the Corps of Engineers, the Bureau of Public Roads, the

---

6. Public Law 875, 81st Congress, September 30, 1950 (64 Stat. 1109).

7. *Ibid.*, Sec. 2.

8. *Ibid.*, Sec. 5(2).

9. Executive Order No. 10427 (January 16, 1953) and Executive Order No. 10737

(October 29, 1957) as amended by Executive Order No. 11051 (September 27, 1962). The Office of Emergency Planning is in the Executive Office of the President. It is not a separate Federal agency like the others listed in Figure 2-1.

10. Public Law 89-769, 89th Congress, November 6, 1966 (80 Stat. 1316).

Public Health Service, and the Community Facilities Administration to make estimates of damage and to undertake disaster recuperation measures such as debris clearance (Corps of Engineers). Funds are appropriated annually by Congress, and the operating agencies are reimbursed through the OEP. On authority of the President, the OEP may direct any Federal agency to perform a disaster recovery service it is capable of performing. Federal agencies may be called upon to lend equipment, supplies, and food, to provide housing and emergency shelter (frequently through the Red Cross), or to supply feed grains for commingled livestock. Finally, and most importantly, the OEP is responsible for disbursing Federal funds under PL 875 for emergency repairs and reconstruction of public facilities. As will be noted later, allocation of these funds has increased rapidly in recent years.

Intervention Under Own Statutory Authority

Many of the same agencies that are called upon under the Federal Disaster Act may also respond to an emergency under their own statutory authority. For example, the Public Health Service does not have to wait for a call from the OEP since it is authorized under PL 410[11] to enter an area of pending disaster to estimate the health resources it may need to commit and actually to commit them if the need arises. Under PL 99[12] and subsequent amendments in the Flood Control Act of 1962,[13] the Corps of Engineers is charged with the responsibility of fighting floods, rescue work, repair and restoration of flood-control works, and other operations incidental to flood control and hurricane protection.

Aid to the Public Sector

In the immediate aftermath of disaster, much of the Federal effort is directed toward the restoration of community activities. Rubble is cleared, the water supply is restored, protective health measures are undertaken, and public facilities are put back into operation. Most of this kind of assistance to the public sector is supervised by the OEP under the Federal Disaster Act. But much assistance can be given under statutory authority pertaining to various agencies. The Bureau of Public Roads is a major contributor to disaster relief

---

11. Public Law 410, 78th Congress.
12. Public Law 99, 84th Congress.

13. Public Law 874, 87th Congress, October 23, 1962 (76 Stat. 1173).

when serious damage has occurred to highways. As a consequence of the Alaska earthquake in March 1964, this bureau spent $37.7 million on highway repairs, and as a result of the Pacific Northwest floods in December of the same year, it spent another $76.4 million.[14]

Aid to the Private Sector

At the same time, the private sector is not neglected since other parts of the Federal government may offer assistance to individuals with or without a Presidential declaration. Principal among these agencies are the Agriculture Department, the Federal Housing Administration (in the Department of Housing and Urban Development), the Internal Revenue Service, and the Small Business Administration.

The Department of Agriculture is a major contributor to disaster relief. Through the Farmers Home Administration it supplies credit to repair and rebuild farm buildings or to replace livestock and equipment lost in a disaster. The Consumer and Marketing Service can provide food for emergency mass feeding and technical assistance on sanitation, feeding, and rehabilitation. The Agricultural Stabilization and Conservation Service is authorized to supply feed grains owned by the Commodity Credit Corporation at reduced prices in order to maintain livestock herds, and the Federal Crop Insurance Corporation makes indemnity payments to farmers on insured crops. Much aid rendered by various divisions of the Agriculture Department is automatic (e.g., insurance), some depends upon a declaration of disaster by the Secretary, and some is contingent upon Presidential declaration. Unfortunately, the Agriculture Department does not keep a separate account for aid given in the particular disasters we have studied, and, hence, we are forced to exclude their operations in subsequent discussions. It should be kept in mind, however, that this department annually makes loans on the order of $100 million, much of which is for drought relief.

The Federal Housing Administration (FHA) can offer some relief to FHA homeowners by deferring loan payments or otherwise rearranging payment schedules. A sister organization, the Federal National Mortgage Association

---

14. These figures were supplied by the Bureau of Public Roads. They are not representative. For example, the BPR spent about $800,000 because of hurricane Betsy and $4 million in the Upper Mississippi floods in 1965.

(FNMA), has a special assistance program by which it may purchase mortgages on FHA and Veterans' Administration (VA) homes destroyed as a result of a major disaster. In the Alaska earthquake disaster of 1964 the mortgagor was allowed to make a relatively low forgiveness payment in return for FNMA assumption of his obligation. This source of relief to the private sector, used only in the Alaska earthquake, has the potential of becoming one of the Federal government's most expensive disaster relief programs.

The Commerce and Interior Departments are authorized to make loans to the private sector. For example, Commerce's Business and Defense Services Administration can give various kinds of assistance to defense plants damaged in a natural disaster, and Interior's Bureau of Commercial Fisheries can use PL 84-1024 to make loans to replace fishing boats lost to storms and tidal waves. The Bureau of Reclamation of the Interior Department can provide funds for restoring hydroelectric power facilities in a devastated region.

The U.S. tax laws provide another source of relief to private citizens. Under existing arrangements, an uninsured person who has received damage to his property in a disaster can write off the loss against his income. Thus, the government will bear a percentage of this reduction in net worth, which will vary with the tax rate of the injured person. Depending upon the wealth of a community struck by disaster, anywhere from 5 to 15 per cent of the total disaster loss will be borne by the Federal government.[15]

By far the biggest lender in disaster situations is the Small Business Administration. In most instances this agency becomes heavily involved after the President has declared a major disaster, but it need not wait for that declaration. The Administrator of SBA has been empowered by the Small Business Act[16] to offer 3 per cent, thirty-year loans to homeowners and businesses suffering injury from natural disasters. Loans may be made directly by the SBA or in an arrangement with local banks by which the latter furnish some of the capital. However, certain kinds of loans such as economic injury loans, where disaster damage results from loss of future business activity rather than from tangible property, require a prior declaration by the President or the Secretary of Agriculture. Past operations of the Small Business Administration are discussed in some detail in Chapters 9 and 10.

---

15. See Chap. 11, "Federal Losses due to Tax Relief."

16. Public Law 536, 85th Congress,

amended subsequently by Public Law 70, 87th Congress; Public Law 264, 88th Congress; Public Law 560, 88th Congress; and Public Law 59, 89th Congress.

TREND IN FEDERAL AID

▷ ANALYSIS OF ANNUAL FIGURES

This section is concerned with describing the trend in Federal aid since 1953 and then attempting to infer whether the governmental attitude toward disaster relief has changed during this period. The statistical story as read from Table 2-1 is clear enough. Under the two major programs, SBA loans and PL 875 grants, Federal aid was almost one hundred times as large in 1965 as it was in 1953.

Of course, a better indication of Federal intent may be seen in legislation. Legislation is qualitative evidence and will be presented in the next section. For the time being, we center our attention first on the statistical facts and then draw inferences from these data. We shall use the term *Federal aid* to mean Federal assistance from the SBA and PL 875, which are by far the principal sources of disaster relief. The term *Federal participation* refers to the ratio of Federal aid under those two programs to total damage.[17] The terms PL 875 *allocations* and SBA *approvals* properly should be taken as measures of the intent of the Federal government to help distressed communities rather than as precise statements about the actual amount of aid received, since they refer to the maximum financial commitment that the Federal government is willing to make. Public Law 875 allocations almost always exceed the amount actually used for the restoration of public facilities. For the large disasters we have studied, actual expenditures run about 80 per cent of allocations.[18] The same is

---

17. To eliminate a possible source of bias in investigating the trend due to an increase in damage caused by natural catastrophes over the years, we have looked at the ratio of Federal aid to total damage over time rather than at the magnitude of Federal aid.

18. Expenditure data after 1963 are not complete, and the 80 per cent figure is based on allocations and expenditures for the nine major disasters occurring before that time. In all cases, with the exception of hurricane Diane (1964), the percentage of allocations actually expended is between 74 per cent and 86 per cent. In the case of hurricane Diane, it was only 53 per cent. For a dozen smaller flood disasters for which we were able to obtain information, the percentage varied between 27 per cent and 100 per cent and the average was 60 per cent. However, in the past two years the OEP estimates that "costs" will be 90 to 95 per cent of allocations indicating, perhaps, that allocations are now being made after a more careful assessment of damage.

true of the relationship between SBA approvals and disbursements, since some loans initially authorized are canceled at a later date. The ratio of disbursements to approvals varies with disasters, but on the average it is 85 to 90 per cent. Thus, the figures on Federal aid indicate the maximum amount that the Federal government is willing to administer under two of its programs.

The bar chart in Figure 2-2 depicts the per cent of Federal aid to total damage from natural disasters. Federal participation has increased markedly. Up to 1962 the two Federal programs had never supplied more than 8 per cent of the capital required to rehabilitate an area and the average was less than 5 per cent. For the following four years, however, the average was about three times

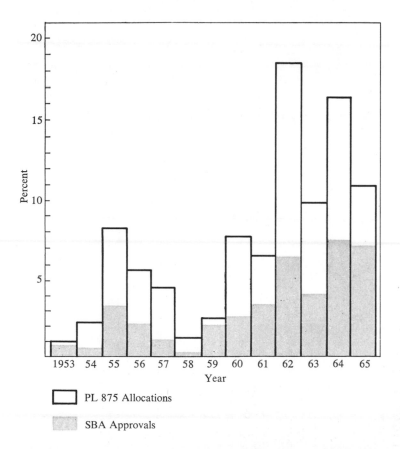

PL 875 Allocations

SBA Approvals

FIGURE 2-2. *Percent of annual disaster losses covered by PL 875 allocations and SBA approvals, 1953–65.*

Table 2-4 PL 875 ALLOCATIONS, SBA LOAN APPROVALS, AND INSURANCE LOSS PAYMENTS IN SELECTED DISASTERS—1954-1965 (MILLION DOLLARS)

	(1)	(2)	(3)	(4)	(5)	(6)	(7)	(8)	(9)
						PER CENT OF DAMAGE			
Disaster	Date	Damage	PL 875 Allocations	SBA Approvals	Insurance Payments	PL 875 Allocations	SBA Approvals	Federal Aid	Insurance
Hurricane Carol	9/54	456	6.8	2.8	129.7	1.5	.6	2.1	28.4
Hurricane Hazel	10/54	232	2.6	4.0	122.1	1.1	1.7	2.8	52.6
Hurricane and Flood Diane	8/55	832	42.1	29.1	5.1	5.1	3.5	8.6	.6
Northwest Flood	12/55	193	11.5	7.0	11.7	6.0	3.6	9.0	6.1
Hurricane Audrey	6/57	150	6.0	3.0	32.2	4.0	2.0	6.0	21.5
Hurricane Diane	9/60	360	5.7	12.3	91.0	1.6	3.4	5.0	25.3
Hurricane Carla	9/61	431	9.0	18.0	100.0	1.9	4.2	6.1	23.2
Great Atlantic Coastal Storm	3/62	245	33.1	18.4	6.2	13.5	7.5	21.0	2.5
Ohio Basin Floods	3/63	98	5.9	6.0	—	6.0	6.1	12.1	—
Alaska Earthquake	3/64	311	59.3	90.8	—	19.1	29.2	48.3	—
Pacific Northwest Floods	12/64	462	54.1	15.8	—	11.7	3.4	15.1	—
Upper Mississippi Floods	4/65 }	340	25.8	7.1	70.0	7.6	2.1	9.7	20.6
Palm Sunday Tornadoes	4/65								
Colorado and Kansas Floods	6/65	405	21.7	27.9	—	5.4	6.9	12.3	—
Hurricane Betsy	9/65	1420	44.1	126.5	715.0	3.1	8.9	12.0	50.4

Data Sources: *Damage*: Table 1-7.

PL 875 Allocations: Office of Emergency Planning, "Major Disaster Declarations."

SBA Approvals: Small Business Administration, "Disaster Loans Approved and Applications Pending—By Disaster—By State."

Insurance Payments: Insurance Information Institute, "Insurance Facts, 1966," pp. 43–47.

larger. As our subsequent review of recent legislature will indicate, Federal participation is not likely to be reduced in the future.

A more interesting question concerns the intent of the Federal government. If the Federal government, in its total operations, has increased its participation in disaster relief, why has it done so? Has the government undergone a change in attitude toward relief? If so, did it occur gradually, or is it possible to isolate a single event or time when the new attitude became apparent? Are the annual data misleading because they ignore other governmental disaster relief programs aside from the PL 875 and SBA activities? Are there any factors that may account for the apparent increased Federal participation that would invalidate an inference regarding intent from the bare statistical facts presented?

The annual data do not contain sufficient detail to answer these questions, and consequently it will serve our purpose better to turn to specific disasters, for which more information is available. Table 2-4 presents some relevant data on those disasters. Before 1962 the Federal government had not offered financial assistance exceeding 9 per cent of total losses in any of the major disasters. Federal aid was especially slight for the first two disasters listed in Table 2-4. Of course the Small Business Administration was just beginning its disaster-loan program, a rather novel experiment by the Federal government, and the grant program under PL 875 had been in operation only four years.

There was a noticeable jump in Federal participation in the great Atlantic coastal storm; the extent of aid surpassed all previous levels by a wide margin, and it has remained high in every major disaster since that time. In fact, in every case since 1962 governmental participation has been higher than it was in any case before. (See column 8 of Table 2-4.) Yet this fact alone is not sufficient to indicate a change in governmental attitude toward disaster relief. To affirm any causal relationship between the figures and a supposed intention, it is necessary to consider the effects of several other variables.

▷ CHANGES IN SPECIFIC FACTORS OVER TIME

Losses Covered by Insurance

In most of the early disasters a substantial part of the loss was covered by insurance. To test the hypothesis that a change in attitude occurred, it is convenient to divide the fourteen disasters into two groups, comparing the first seven in Table 2-4 with the last seven. This division makes 1962 the dividing line and is consistent with the impression gained from Figure 2-2. Whereas insurance financed a considerable part of disaster recovery in five disasters of the first group, it was an important element in only two of the last group. Furthermore, considering only the first group, Federal assistance was highest in the two 1955 disasters, precisely the ones for which insurance payments were the least. In the last group, Federal participation was lowest in the only two catastrophes for which insurance payments were an important element of disaster relief. This suggests that the Federal government responds most favorably to those situations least covered by insurance.

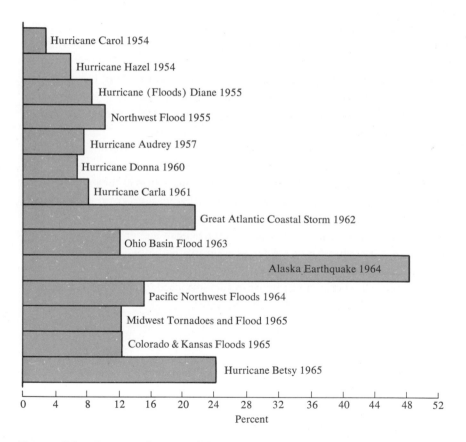

FIGURE 2-3. *Percent of uninsured losses covered by PL 875 allocations and SBA approvals in selected disasters.*

Water damage generally is not insurable, wind damage is included in comprehensive coverage, and earthquake insurance, while possible to obtain, is practically nonexistent. The increasing popularity of homeowners' comprehensive insurance has decreased the need for assistance to tornado victims in particular. Since winds are responsible for much hurricane damage, some of those losses are insurable; in fact, insurance payments did contribute significantly to reconstruction after all the hurricanes we have studied except Diane (1955), where practically all damage was caused by heavy rains and flooding. The most straightforward way of eliminating the influence of insurance availability is to subtract insurance payments from total damage to obtain a measure of non-insured losses in each disaster. The bar chart in Figure 2-3 shows Federal government financial assistance as a percentage of all noninsured losses for the disasters under consideration. Even though the difference between the first seven and last seven disasters is not so spectacular as that indicated in Table 2-4, where insurance is not taken into account, it is nevertheless obvious that the level of Federal help has increased markedly. On the average, the level of Federal aid is about three times as high for the disasters starting with the great Atlantic coastal storm in 1962 as for those occurring before it, even after insurance payments have been taken into account. The variation in Federal aid is also greater in the later disasters.

Agricultural Losses and Relief

In some disasters, notably hurricanes, agricultural losses are fairly high and frequently are included in total damage estimates. However, agricultural aid is not included in our figures on Federal relief. Unfortunately, estimates of agricultural losses for all disasters are not available, precluding a similar treatment accorded insurance payments. For two hurricanes where agricultural damage was relatively large, however, we do have some estimates.

In hurricane Audrey (1957) agricultural damage was one third of the total damage, or $50 million, and in hurricane Carla (1961) it was about 15 per cent of the total, or $60 million.[19] If we subtract insurance payments and agricultural losses from total damage for those two disasters, the percentages of Federal assistance are 13.2 and 9.6 per cent, respectively. The weighted average is 10.3 per cent. For two other hurricanes, Carol and Hazel, agricultural damage

19. Weather Bureau, U.S. Department of Commerce, *Climatological Data*, vol. 8, no. 13 and vol. 12, no. 13. Hurricane Donna (1960) was very destructive to the Florida citrus crop, but those losses are not included in total losses for that hurricane.

was relatively small so that the participation ratios would be only slightly higher than those shown in Figure 2-3; in fact, they would probably differ only slightly from the other five ratios in the first disaster grouping. Betsy was the only hurricane after 1962 on our list, but the Weather Bureau did not report an approximate damage estimate for agriculture, although it is known to have been "extensive"[20] in sugar cane, cotton, rice, and pecans. In any event, knowledge of the exact amount of agricultural damage for this disaster does not affect the conclusion that Federal participation increased significantly after 1962.

Composition of Losses Between Public and Private

If the composition of losses between the public and private sectors systematically changes over time, aggregate statistics on Federal participation could give a misleading impression of Federal intent. Even without a new attitude toward relief, the participation ratio, as we have defined it, could change simply because the distribution between private and public loss might have been altered. As a good example of this, suppose that a disaster caused damage only to public schools and that Federal funds were available for repairs of these educational facilities on a fifty-fifty matching basis. In that case, Federal financing would cover 50 per cent of total damage. But assume that in some earlier disaster only private homes had suffered damage and the SBA had provided a liberal 20 per cent of the financing for reconstruction. In this case the participation ratio would be only 20 per cent. The larger participation ratio in the later disaster would give an entirely false clue as to any change in the attitude of the Federal government toward disaster relief. Thus, without some knowledge of the composition of disaster losses between the private and public sectors, it is not safe to make any inference concerning Federal intentions on the basis of the share of losses covered by its funds.

Unfortunately, Weather Bureau figures do not separate private and public damages. Occasionally, however, reports from various Corps of Engineers districts do make some distinctions, even if somewhat vaguely. Recently a breakdown on damage figures has also been made in several congressional reports. From these sources we have extracted the information on eight disasters given in Table 2-5, but we caution our readers that we have had to make subjective judgments as to whether some of the damage categories in these

---

20. Weather Bureau, U.S. Department of Commerce, *Climatological Data*, vol. 16, no. 13, p. 63.

reports constitute public or private losses. The figures, therefore, should be treated as rough approximations only. The percentage of total damage in the public sector was unusually high in the Alaska earthquake and the Pacific Northwest floods in 1964. For the other disasters the share of public damage was no greater, on the average, for those beginning with the great Atlantic coastal storm than the share in public damage for disasters before it. Excluding, then, the two 1964 disasters, a comparison between the other six catastrophes, for which the composition of private and public losses was similar, reinforces the conclusion that Federal participation ratios have changed with the great Atlantic coastal storm.

Miscellaneous Factors

Several other factors, such as a possible systematic change in measuring disaster losses and the extent to which other Federal agencies have become involved in relief, should be considered. Suppose, for example, that recent disaster-loss estimates have included economic injury (e.g., loss of business) whereas previous ones have not, and suppose also that the Federal policy with regard to economic-injury loans is more stringent than its policy toward home or regular business disaster loans. The effects of such a change would be substantially the same as that indicated in the preceding section, "Composition of

Table 2-5	DAMAGE TO THE PUBLIC SECTOR AS PERCENTAGE OF TOTAL DAMAGE IN SELECTED DISASTERS[a]

Disaster	Per cent
Hurricane Diane (1955)[1]	25
Northwest Flood (1955)[2]	31
Hurricane Carla (1961)[3]	7
Great Atlantic Coastal Storm (1962)[4]	15–25
Alaska Earthquake (1964)[5]	75
Pacific Northwest Floods (1964)[6]	54
Colorado and Kansas Floods (1965)[7]	12
Hurricane Betsy (1965)[8]	15

Data Sources:
(1) Corps of Engineers, North Atlantic Division, "Report on Operation Noah," undated; (2) Corps of Engineers, Sacramento District, "Report on December 1955 Floods Sacramento–San Joaquin River Basins, California and Truckee, Carson, and Wilkes Rivers, California and Nevada," May 1956, p. 8; (3) Corps of Engineers, Galveston District, "Hurricane Carla, September 9–12, 1961," undated, Table 5; (4) Corps of Engineers, North Atlantic Division, "Report on Operation Five High," August 1963, Table, Appendix 4–7; (5) Chapter 6 of this book; (6) "The Northwest Floods of December, 1964 and January, 1965" *Report of the Special Subcommittee to Inspect Flooded Areas in the Northwestern United States,* Committee on Public Works, U.S. House of Representatives, print No. 8, April 1, 1965, p. 7; (7) "The Colorado and Kansas Floods of June 1965," *Report of the Special Subcommittee to Inspect Flooded Areas in Colorado and Kansas,* Committee on Public Works, U.S. House of Representatives, Print no. 15, June 1965, p. 9; (8) Corps of Engineers, New Orleans District, "Report on Hurricane Betsy 8–11 September 1965 in the U.S. Army Engineer District, New Orleans," Tables 15 and 16.

[a] The Corps of Engineers reports cited cover a district, whereas most disasters cover more than one district. Thus, the estimates in this table assume that the damage patterns in other districts were similar.

Losses Between Public and Private." Also suppose that other agencies are involved in disaster relief to a lesser extent today than previously. In that case, the computed ratios would understate the degree to which the Federal government participated in earlier disasters relative to those occurring in the last four years, and the ratios would be an inadequate and misleading proxy regarding Federal intent. The last supposition can easily be dismissed as being factually incorrect—more agencies are involved today—and there are no hints of any systematic change in disaster accounting, and so the likelihood of that source of error is reduced.

Concluding Comments

Taking into account insurable losses and agricultural losses in those cases where they have been estimated, and eliminating the Alaska earthquake and the Northwest floods as catastrophes in which the share of public damage was unusually high, we can now compute some Federal participation ratios reasonably indicative of Federal intent. For the first seven disasters, grants under PL 875 and SBA loan approvals accounted for 7.8 per cent of the relevant losses, whereas the ratio for the last five is 17.9 per cent. Since this comparison probably is biased in favor of the early disasters, the disparity is convincing evidence that there has been a significant change in Federal attitude over the period.

The most interesting questions are "How did such a change in attitude come about? Why is the U.S. government more involved today than before? Is there a greater need? Are individuals less self-sufficient?" It is not our purpose to attempt to answer these questions. We simply have presented facts that, after a moment's reflection, should not be surprising. That the Federal government has become more generous in its attitude toward disaster relief is consistent with its growing concern with problems of welfare.

RECENT FEDERAL LEGISLATION

The great Atlantic coastal storm has been used as a divide for separating the major disasters that have occurred since 1954. The reason for selecting that catastrophe is obvious from a glance at Figure 2-3, which shows that Federal assistance in that disaster was unusually large compared with previous disasters. Yet no special legislation was considered necessary to cope with the relief problems arising from the storm; existing machinery was sufficient.

▷ EFFECT OF ALASKA EARTHQUAKE

From a legislative point of view, the Alaska earthquake in March 1964 must signal a change in Federal relief attitudes, for it triggered a wave of congressional action that has not yet been consummated. Because of its importance as a point of demarcation between the old and new attitudes toward relief, subsequent chapters will treat the various economic aspects of the earthquake in considerable detail. Now it will suffice to outline the permanent changes that have resulted from Federal actions following that catastrophe.

The United States has experienced many natural catastrophes more destructive than the Alaska earthquake. In fact, of the major disasters in the period 1954–1965 it would rank as only average in terms of property damage sustained. On the other hand, it is unique in the amount of Federal aid it received both absolutely and relative to the damage suffered. Almost 50 per cent of its total losses were covered by SBA loans and grants under PL 875. Adding defense expenditures on military installations, expenditures by the Bureau of Public Roads, the Department of Interior (including repair on the Alaska Railroad), and Urban Renewal Projects,[21] the expenditures were almost as large as the total estimated physical losses.

Up to the Alaska earthquake there had been no disaster legislation specific to a single disaster in the United States.[22] As we have seen, PL 875 is the major piece of legislation governing Federal disaster relief. This law, known as the Federal Disaster Act,[23] was first enacted on September 30, 1950, and was subsequently amended in 1953[24] and 1962.[25] Following hurricane Diane in

---

21. For a detailed description of Federal expenditures see Chap. 6 and particularly Tables 6-3 and 6-7.

22. The Territory of Guam with its large military base did merit two special relief bills to provide assistance after typhoon Olive in 1962 and typhoon Karen in 1963. Public Law 502, 87th Congress, June 27, 1962 (76 Stat. 111).

23. Public Law 875, 81st Congress, September 30, 1950 (64 Stat. 1109).

24. Public Law 134, 83rd Congress, June 17, 1953 (67 Stat. 180).

25. Public Law 502, 87th Congress, June 27, 1962 (76 Stat. 111).

1955, Congress passed the Federal Flood Insurance Act of 1956,[26] but later refused to appropriate the funds required to get the insurance program started. In 1958 the Small Business Act was amended to allow that agency to make loans in areas of excessive rainfall as well as drought.[27] Although four hurricanes between 1954 and 1964 had caused more damage than the Alaska earthquake, no action has been taken by Congress to aid these areas.

Following the Good Friday earthquake, special disaster legislation became a familiar topic in Congress. Of the many new provisions regarding relief to Alaska, three deserve special attention since they will be discussed in some detail in later chapters:

1. Alaskans were the first disaster victims to receive thirty-year SBA disaster loans, the previous maturity being limited to twenty years by statute.
2. They were the first to receive the privilege of writing off mortgage debt on HHFA-held loans.
3. They were the only citizens ever to receive additional low-cost loans for the purpose of retiring existing higher-cost loans.[28]

An amendment to the Alaskan Omnibus Act cleared Congress in August 1964,[29] allowing the Small Business Administration to extend loan maturities for Alaskans to thirty years, and also provided for mortgage forgiveness in favor of homeowners whose mortgages were held by the Federal National Mortgage Association. Thirty-year SBA loans were generalized by another amendment to the Small Business Act in 1965[30] that also allowed the Administration to waive payments on principal and interest up to five years.

▷ POST-ALASKA EARTHQUAKE CONGRESSIONAL ACTION

The Pacific Northwest floods in December 1964 brought more special legislation. "We seek no preferential treatment," testified Congressman Al Ullman of Oregon in the Northwest flood hearings, "only assistance parallel to that

---

26. Public Law 1016, 84th Congress, August 7, 1956 (70 Stat. 1078).
27. Public Law 335, 85th Congress, February.22, 1958 (72 Stat. 27).
28. See Chap. 9 for a full discussion.

29. Public Law 451, 88th Congress, August 19, 1964 (78 Stat. 505).

30. Public Law 59, 89th Congress, August 30, 1965 (79 Stat. 206).

given other natural disaster areas of the past year such as the Alaska earthquake."[31] Congressman Wendall Wyatt, also from Oregon, noted that "the State of Alaska was the recipient of prompt relief" and continued, "We need relief likewise."[32] Their colleague from Oregon, Congressman Robert Duncan, admitted to "look[ing] to the Alaska bills" for guidance.[33] A California Congressman, Harold T. "Bizz" Johnson, requested certain measures "similar to proposals contained in the Alaska Earthquake relief bill,"[34] and Governor Brown also turned to the Alaska relief bill for certain of his recommendations.[35]

The hearings led to the Pacific Northwest Relief Act of 1965.[36] Although the act did not go as far as Alaskan relief in the way of mortgage forgiveness, it did provide for thirty-year loans and made available an additional $70 million for repair and reconstruction of highways.

Although special legislation was proposed, no bill actually was passed immediately after the Upper Mississippi floods and the most destructive tornadoes in U.S. history, which struck the Midwest on Palm Sunday 1965. But hurricane Betsy, the most destructive tropical storm ever to hit the United States, did produce congressional action. The most prominent feature of the Southeast Hurricane Disaster Relief Act of 1965[37] is a provision by which the recipient of an SBA loan in excess of $500 is able to write off an amount up to $1800. This write-off privilege of the borrower transforms part of the loan into a grant from the Federal government.

Some of the changes that have been embedded in special legislation are now a part of the Federal Disaster Relief Act of 1966[38] In the Senate's initial version of this bill[39] and the one that eventually passed the Senate,[40] a fundamental alteration in government disaster policy was recommended. Section 4

---

31. "Pacific Northwest Flood," *Hearings Before the Subcommittee on Flood Control*, Committee on Public Works, U.S. House of Representatives, 89th Congress, First Session, March 9–11, 1965, p. 42.

32. *Ibid.*, p. 64.

33. *Ibid.*, p. 55.

34. *Ibid.*, p. 9.

35. *Ibid.*, p. 151.

36. Public Law 41, 89th Congress, June 17, 1965 (79 Stat. 131).

37. Public Law 339, 89th Congress, November 8, 1965 (79 Stat. 1301).

38. Public Law 769, 89th Congress, November 6, 1966 (80 Stat. 1316).

39. "Disaster Relief Act of 1965," *Hearings Before the Subcommittee on Flood Control—Rivers and Harbors*, Committee on Public Works, U.S. Senate, 89th Congress, First Session, June 21–22, 1965.

40. See "Disaster Relief Act of 1965," *Hearings Before the Subcommittee on Flood Control*, Committee on Public Works, U.S. House of Representatives, 89th Congress, First Session, October 14–15, 1965, pp. 1–8.

provided for Federal grants to any state suffering a natural disaster to help homeowners and businesses get back on their feet. The Federal government had previously provided funds for this purpose but always via some special legislation. However, in the form in which the bill finally passed both legislative bodies a year later, the grant provision was not included. Although the changes included in the new act certainly do involve the Federal government still more deeply in disaster relief, they do not represent any fundamental change in policy. Among other features the Federal Disaster Relief Act of 1966 provides for

1. Federal loan adjustment by HUD and the Veterans Administration on damaged homes lengthening the maturity to forty years in some cases and reducing interest payments to 2 per cent.
2. Grants to unincorporated communities for public facilities.[41]
3. Grants to institutions of higher learning for repair and replacement of buildings.
4. SBA loans at 3 per cent to institutions of higher learning regardless of whether other financing is available.

What is the attitude of the American people with regard to disaster relief? We do not pretend to know the answer, but perhaps Congressman William C. Cramer of Florida does.

> Disaster relief is an accepted Federal responsibility and has been for years. I know of no partisan difference relating to a proper Federal responsibility for disaster relief. There never has been . . . there is no partisanship and no territorial delineation. When nature strikes, it hurts everyone . . . That is my attitude about this. I think that is the attitude of all Americans.[42]

---

41. Unincorporated communities were not provided for under PL 875.

42. "Southeast Hurricane Disaster," *Hearings Before the Committee on Public Works*, Committee on Public Works, U.S. House of Representatives, 89th Congress, First Session, October 13, 1965, p. 22. Compare this statement with one made eighty years earlier. After vetoing an appropriation for $25,000 to buy seed corn for Texas farmers ruined by a drought, President Grover Cleveland said, "I can find no warrant for such an appropriation in the Constitution, and I do not believe that the power and duty of the general government ought to be extended to the relief of individual suffering which is in no manner related to the public service or benefit. A prevalent tendency to disregard the limited mission of this power and duty should, I think, be steadfastly resisted, to the end that the lesson should be constantly enforced that though the people support the government, the government should not support the people." G. F. Parker, ed., "Veto of the Texas Feed Bill, February 16, 1887," *The Writings and Speeches of Grover Cleveland*, Cassel Publishing Co., 1892.

Whatever the attitude of the American people, it is very likely that future disasters will continue to break records both in destruction and in Federal participation in recovery from them. In response to this anticipation of further Federal involvement, based on the record of the past, we shall propose at the end of this book an alternative, a Federally subsidized insurance program that would eliminate many of the inequities of the present schemes.

| Chapter Three | Economic Theory

and Natural

Disaster Behavior

A THEORETICAL analysis of behavior following natural disasters will be developed in this chapter using basic concepts of economic and statistical analysis. Most of the ideas were stimulated by empirical observations, so they are only abstract models in the informal sense of the word. Fruitful economic work on both short- and long-term postdisaster problems requires some framework for analysis. The ideas in this section should thus be viewed as exploratory and subject to testing and revision as additional data are obtained.

Our interest in this first section is in the economic choices facing the community immediately after a natural disaster. During this recuperation period there are basic problems of information and communication that impede the decision-making process. Potential shortages may also loom on the horizon during this time; however, prices of these emergency goods appear to be somewhat lower than would be predicted if each individual behaved as a rational "economic man." The long-term recovery phase or the rebuilding process that brings the community back to its predisaster level is analyzed in the second half of the chapter. By describing the effect that disaster has on losses to the capital sector, we can develop rules for recovering in the most efficient way. To conclude Part I, we will analyse the speed of recovery from a disaster.

In practice it is impossible to draw a fine line between the recuperation period and the long-term recovery phase since the two overlap. For example, rebuilding activity begins immediately after a disaster with the clearing of debris and informal damage surveys. At the same time, shortages of certain goods that are characteristic of the recuperation phase may be present during the period when rebuilding is well under way. We have preferred to separate these two periods from each other to illustrate the different types of problems that characterize them.

*S*HORT-TERM RECUPERATION PHASE

▷ PROBLEMS OF INFORMATION AND COMMUNICATION

Accurate data and effective communication are fundamental needs of any organization under normal circumstances. Following a disaster, they become even more important, because quick action is often necessary to cope with emergencies. But the difficulties of acquiring and communicating information are often compounded because of physical destruction and the breakdown of normal mechanisms.

This section discusses, in theoretical terms, information and communication problems existing during an emergency period. In the first part, we describe the effect of uncertainty on decision making by showing how actions taken after a disaster differ from behavior during normal times. We can then determine the *potential* savings if postdisaster uncertainty is reduced by developing systematic procedures for gathering more accurate information.

Effects of Uncertainty on Decision Making

The term *decision making* implies a choice between two or more alternatives. In most circumstances the decision maker is forced to act under conditions of uncertainty, i.e., only incomplete information exists about the future. As an example of decision making in an organization, consider the plight of a manager who must plan production of two items during the coming month. To simplify the exposition, assume that costs of changing production or work force from one period to the next do not enter into the manager's decision. He is solely concerned with inventory-related expenses of each item (i.e., storage and shortage costs). If demand for both items is known with certainty, he will try to schedule production equal to sales, so that inventory at the end of the month will be zero. However, when there is imperfect information regarding sales of each product, he will plan production in a way that minimizes overall inventory-related costs. His decision is based on implicit values regarding the cost of holding each item and the cost of shortage as well as on the assumptions he makes about the probability distribution of future demand for the product. As his ratio of shortage cost to holding cost of item A increases relative to that of item B, the desired product mix will shift in the direction of item A. Of course, capacity restrictions may limit the production of both items, but the proportion of each will still be determined by the shortage/storage cost ratio. Reliable outside cues from the environment, such as market surveys and branch-office reports, may influence behavior because they increase the knowledge about each product and thus reduce the uncertainty of future demand. Naturally, if these external hints fail to materialize, unexpectedly high inventory costs may result.

Community officials making decisions on relevant needs immediately following a disaster have a somewhat different frame of reference than managers in a profit-making organization, although the criteria they use in taking action are identical. The expressed willingness of the Federal government to lend a hand shifts to all taxpayers the cost of sending and storing unnecessary items. For example, if the call went out for emergency hospital supplies that turned out not to be needed, then the government would incur the round-trip transport fees. The only cost that the community might have to bear is the storage expenses for articles that could not be used and would not be shipped back to their source. This form of convergence behavior, discussed in Chapter 4, plays a minor role in influencing decisions during the emergency period. Thus, the prime concern of decision makers in a disaster-torn area is in obtaining as many emergency supplies as possible to minimize potential shortages, There may, however, be some capacity constraint restricting the overall quantities that can be transported to the area during a given period of time. In this sense, the community official must implicitly assign *storage costs* to each item. These charges will normally not be based on dollar value, as in a profit-making organization, but rather on size or weight depending on which factor limits the total shipment. We may prefer another system of allocation following a disaster, but it would not appropriately describe current operations.

If a person were asked to calculate the *shortage cost* of each item without having any specific information regarding the disaster, he would have to make certain value judgments regarding priorities. If saving a human life through medical treatment was ranked much higher than provision of food supplies, then first-aid equipment would assume a relatively greater shortage cost than orange juice. Of course, once specific information from the disaster became available, these values would most likely be modified. For example, if all existing medical buildings were found to be intact whereas severe damage to the sewer system was reported to have contaminated the water supply, then the demand for hospital units might be very low relative to the demand for canned juices. Our definition of shortage cost for any good will be based on both an a priori system of values and reported damage to the area.

Even if the resulting shortage cost figure is high, there may still be no reason to ship large quantities to the area if the probability of using the item is small. Thus, a disaster may damage some medical facilities so that the relative cost of a shortage would be ranked high. If very few people were actually injured, then the immediate value of first-aid equipment would be much less than the actual shortage cost figure would have indicated. In other words, to obtain the relative value of any unit to the community, we must also consider the probability that the item will be used. It follows that accurate information regarding the state of affairs in the stricken area (e.g., extent of damage and number of fatalities and injury) will improve the priority scheme developed by local decision-making groups emerging after the disaster.

Value of Information

To illustrate the concepts determining a priority scheme, consider two items, A and B, both of which may be needed during the emergency period. If community officials know that the arrival time between an initial and a second shipment of outside aid will be x hours then they must estimate the shortage/storage cost ratio per unit of A and B based on this delay, as well as the probability that the jth unit will be needed. For simplicity, consider the case in which item B is twice as large as A so that its storage cost is double that of A. Assume that capacity is limited by space rather than weight and that initial transportation is provided by only one plane which can hold either four units of A, two units of B, or some combination of the two items. The only other meaningful combination would be two units of A and one unit of B. Any other package (e.g., one unit of both A and B) could be improved upon without violating the space constraint.

In determining priorities it is not necessary to estimate costs explicitly since the only critical figure is the shortage/storage cost ratio. This should immediately become clear if we recognize that an item whose storage cost is twice that of another item would be required to have a shortage cost twice as high, for it to be valued equally (assuming the probability of each item being used was the same). To further illustrate this point, suppose the storage cost of B is twice that of A, but B's shortage cost, based on the outlined considerations, is initially estimated to be six times as high as A's. We could arbitrarily set shortage/storage cost at 1 for A and note that this same ratio would be $6/2 = 3$ for B. To calculate the relative value of the jth unit of any item, we would have to multiply the shortage/ storage cost ratio by the estimated probability that the jth unit will be used in the disaster area. Assume that the decision-making group is forced to make comparisons using haphazard initial first impressions. Relevant data based on this imperfect information are assembled for items A and B in Table 3-1.

In arranging priorities he will choose units with the highest relative value as shown in column 4 for item A and column 7 for item B. In this particular example one unit of item B (relative value = 2.1) and two units of A (relative value = 1.4) would be chosen for the first plane shipment.

Suppose that by making a more systematic search, better information could be assembled on both the shortage cost of each item to be ordered from outside and the probability of its use. For example, assume that item B was found to be more critical in relation to item A than had been originally anticipated. The new shortage/storage cost ratios, as well as the possible revised probabilities of uses, are listed in Table 3-2 along with the computed relative value for the jth unit of each item. Two units of B should now be ordered for the initial shipment. The relative value of this new information can be computed from Table 3-2 by taking the difference between ordering the second unit of B instead of the two units of A as before $(2.0 - .9 = 1.1)$. Of course, if one wanted to calculate the value of this information in dollar terms, it would be necessary to estimate explicitly the actual cost of shortage and storage. Furthermore, if any extra expense were incurred in making the more systematic search, this

$Table$ 3-1	INITIAL VALUES FOR ITEMS A AND B

		ITEM A			ITEM B	
(1)	*(2)*	*(3)*	*(4)* Relative Value of jth Unit	*(5)*	*(6)*	*(7)* Relative Value of jth Unit
Number of Units (j)	Probability of Use	Shortage/ Storage Cost	$(2) \times (3)$	Probability of Use	Shortage/ Storage Cost	$(5) \times (6)$
$j = 1$	.8	1	.8	.7	3	2.1
$j = 2$	.6	1	.6	.1	3	.3
$j = 3$	.3	1	.3			
$j = 4$	.1	1	.1			

cost would then have to be subtracted from dollar savings to obtain a net value of information.

We are not suggesting that the community officials actually sit down and calculate shortage/storage cost ratios and probability of use for the many items that they must order immediately following a disaster. For their actual behavior to be optimal, however, they must be putting implicit values on each of these critical figures. If they had more accurate information on the damage and postdisaster needs, they would change the weights that they had originally used and hence alter their decisions. This is what is meant by the concept *value of information.* By preparing a postdisaster plan in anticipation of an extreme event, search procedures can be considerably improved over the makeshift operations that generally exist today. More accurate data should be obtained at very low, if any, extra search cost since community residents are more than anxious to offer their services freely during the emergency period. In fact, frequently a problem exists in knowing what to do with volunteers who mill around the emergency "nerve centers"; thus, a makeshift approach will likely be more expensive than having prescribed tasks for these people to follow. Since this chapter is primarily a theoretical one, we will reserve discussion of some methods for improving postdisaster activities until Chapter 4. Our purpose here is to indicate that substantial improvement may be forthcoming by alleviating the information crisis immediately following unexpected crises.

▷ SUPPLY AND DEMAND PROBLEMS

Prices of emergency goods such as food and shelter do not always conform to economic intuition during the time when the community must rely entirely on its own resources. This problem normally exists because the percentage destruction of physical resources from a disaster is usually much greater than the

Table 3-2

REVISED VALUES FOR ITEMS A AND B

		ITEM A			ITEM B	
(1)	*(2)*	*(3)*	*(4)*	*(5)*	*(6)*	*(7)*
		Shortage/	*Relative Value of jth Unit*		*Shortage/*	*Relative Value of jth Unit*
Number of Units	*Probability of Use*	*Storage Cost*	*(2) × (3)*	*Probability of Use*	*Storage Cost*	*(5) × (6)*
$j = 1$	.6	1	.6	.9	4	3.6
$j = 2$	.3	1	.3	.5	4	2.0
$j = 3$	.2	1	.2			
$j = 4$	.1	1	.1			

percentage loss of human life, as we have shown in Chapter 1. The prescribed period may last anywhere from a few hours to several weeks depending on the location and magnitude of the disaster. For example, swift action on the part of outsiders occurred following the Topeka, Kansas, tornado (June 1966), for the city was easily accessible. On the other hand, several California communities could receive only limited supplies during the first few weeks following the West Coast floods of December 1964. Some resources, such as emergency first aid supplies, are forthcoming almost immediately from outside sources because of the high priority of these items; the short-run period in these cases will last for only a few hours. Other goods, such as canned juices, may have a longer delay time until external aid is made available; if the water supply is contaminated the emergency period could be several days or weeks.

At first glance, a theorist might view these short-term problems as trivial applications of the basic laws of supply and demand, thus concluding they are not worth special study. He might claim that if the disaster decreases the stock of a certain commodity, while demand remains either the same as before the event or increases, then price should rise, other things being equal. Because the *ceteris paribus* conditions might not hold in these extreme situations, the supply and demand curves may shift in unexpected ways. We wish to explore these possibilities.

Assume that an island has just been severely damaged by an earthquake. Three assumptions about economic behavior will be introduced to see how prices are likely to change. First, we will hypothesize that *no* outside aid is expected and that each individual acts as a pure economic man (i.e., altruism does not enter into the utility function of either producers or consumers). This self-help no-sympathy situation will be labeled Case I. If residents do expect help from other countries in the form of emergency supplies, then the price of these commodities should reflect these expectations and consequently differ from the situation in Case I. This type of behavior, Case II, will then be analyzed. If the disaster arouses strong altruistic feelings, prices may differ somewhat from those depicted in the other two cases even if the island has to survive on its own resources. These changes in supply and demand due to a special concern for one's neighbors will be analyzed in Case III. A diagram illustrating the range that prices can take during the short-run postdisaster period will tie together the theoretical discussion.[1]

---

1. Rather than postulating that there is a structural change in the utility function induced by the disaster, it is possible to attribute the sympathetic behavior of

No Outside Aid—No Sympathy (Case I)

If the island receives substantial damage from an earthquake and sees no prospect of outside aid, it is not difficult to depict its short-run economic behavior if all survivors with existing resources are not motivated by altruistic feelings. Consider the effect of the disaster on the price of an emergency item M. Point A in Figure 3-1 represents the market situation immediately preceding the catastrophe, when good M has an equilibrium price of p_0. Assume we are looking at the stock available for sale at a moment in time, so that it is completely inelastic at q_0, as shown by S_0. Some destruction of the commodity will decrease the stock from q_0 to some quantity q_1', depicted by S_1'. If the demand curve to hold item M remains stable, the new price would be expected to rise to p_1 (point B). Even if the stock of M is not affected by the disaster, the price

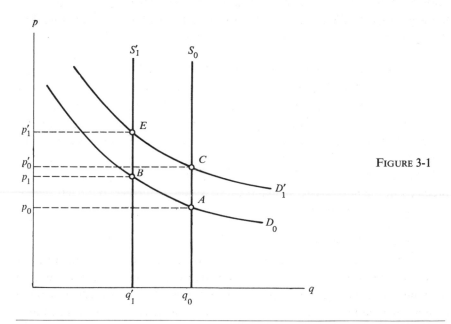

FIGURE 3-1

residents entirely to a change in the value of charity to them. For example, after a disaster there is an opportunity to offer personal aid to victims that may yield more utility per dollar spent than the impersonal contributions made to some general fund in normal times. This higher return from charity may be primarily responsible for the large contributions by outsiders; however, we feel it plays a minor role in determining the behavior of residents in the stricken area. This argument is pursued in more detail by Louis De Alessi in "The Utility of Disasters," *Papers On Non-Market Decision-Making, Volume III*, Fall 1967.

could rise to p_0' following the event if demand for the commodity increased from D_0 to D_1' (point C). Such a situation might occur under severe losses to a substitute commodity N that has some positive cross-elasticity with M. The zero expectation of outside aid may lead residents to pay more for a unit of M in anticipation of future needs, thus shifting the demand curve even further to the right. Naturally if the stock were decreased to q_1' and the new demand curve simultaneously shifted upward to D_1' then p_1' would be higher than any of the other three preceding prices.

In this analysis, the demand for commodity M was assumed to be the same or greater after the disaster than before. Other goods may have a lower demand following the quake because of the decreased wealth position of the consumers and their increased desire to purchase special commodities like M. The new short-run equilibrium value for these lesser-valued goods would depend on both the shift in the demand curve and the destruction caused by the disaster. Some products could thus have a lower price after the quake than before, but these would not be classified as emergency items.

Expected Outside Aid—No Sympathy (Case II)

Residents of the island anticipating aid from other countries will be less concerned with storing large quantities for future needs. Short-run–period behavior will thus differ from the self-help situation analyzed in Case I because the post-disaster demand-to-hold curve would not shift as far to the right as in the self-help case. The extent of the change in demand will be a function of the expected delay in the arrival of outside aid. If a short-time lag is anticipated, one would predict that the postdisaster demand curve would lie further to the left than if longer delays were expected.

No Expectation of Outside Aid—Sympathy (Case III)

Even if the residents in the disaster area do not expect outside aid, the price of M may fall below the level predicted by conventional economic theory because of sympathetic feelings within the stricken region. In other words, a definite change in community feeling (e.g., greater solidarity) occurs following a disaster and leads to altruistic actions that would not be expected during normal times.[2] This emergent altruism brought about by a crisis situation can also be appropriately handled by shifting the supply and demand curves. Using Case I

---

2. For a sociological analysis of this phenomenon, see Charles Fritz, "Disaster and Community Therapy," Institute for Defense Analyses, Arlington, Va., unpublished manuscript, 1960.

as a take-off point, assume that the stock of M has been decreased from q_0 to q_1' because of the disaster, as shown in Figure 3-2a. If the demand curve for the product had remained stable, the expected price would be at a level indicated by p_1'. Suppose, however, that during the emergency short-run period the actual price of shelter is observed to be p_1'', despite no anticipation of outside aid on the part of the residents. If stock and flow concepts of supply and demand are used in a two-part diagram such as Figure 3-2, the reason for this somewhat unusual movement can be better understood.

The curves drawn in Figure 3-2a depict supply and demand relationships using the concepts of stocks. Thus, immediately before the disaster, the amount of commodity M that the community demanded to hold at any given price was represented by D_0; S_0 was the amount of the commodity actually held in stock. The equilibrium price was found to be p_0. We describe market behavior in terms of exchange flows in Figure 3-2b. If at a given price we find $(D_0 - S_0) > 0$ for a particular person, the difference represents his flow demand for M, d_0; when $(D_0 - S_0) < 0$, the residual amount will be flow supply for M, s_0 at the given price. At any given price the horizontal distance between supply and demand will be the same with flow curves as it is with stock curves. The

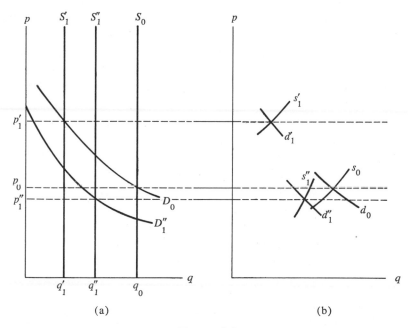

(a)   (b)

FIGURE 3-2

equilibrium price for the two aggregate flow schedules *has* to be the same as when "stock"-analysis is used, in this case p_0.[3]

The equilibrium price of item M just before the earthquake was at p_0, as depicted in Figure 3-2a by the intersection of the demand (D_0) and the stock (S_0) curves for M. This situation can be represented in the flow portion of the diagram, Figure 3-2b, through the appropriate demand (d_0) and supply (s_0) curves, which will also naturally intersect at p_0. If $q_0 - q_1'$ units of M had been destroyed and there were no change in people's utility functions, the implied demand and supply flow curves would be represented by d_1' and s_1' respectively. The price of M would then be expected to rise to p_1', as shown in Figure 3-2b. Empirical data on people's behavior reveals, however, that altruistic feelings play an important role during the short-run postdisaster period. For example, residents with undamaged homes crowd their families into two bedrooms, instead of the normal three or four, so that stranded neighbors can stay with them rent-free while they are looking for a new permanent place in which to live. These actions by individuals will shift both the demand and supply curves for the entire community.

Suppose that sympathetic residents with remaining stocks of commodity M decide to share their wealth with unfortunate disaster victims. By reducing their own consumption, they will make the flow demand for shelter lower than it would be under Case I conditions. At the same time, if these residents offer some of their stored buffer stock to the victims staying with them, then the flow supply curve will be shifted to the right to s_1''. This situation can be viewed in stock terms by the intersection of D_1'', indicating a fall in demand, and S_1'', showing an increase in supply. A similar pattern would have occurred if residents with stocks at home refrained from buying on the market and instead dipped into their reserves. Market demand would again decrease from the earlier cases while the actual stock available for sale would be augmented by the amount of the buffer consumed. Altruism still plays a role here because those with some stored goods make an effort to prevent shortages by consuming what they have on hand.

An intersection of supply and demand curves at the low level of D_1'' still represents a stable equilibrium since no incentive exists to move away from this point so long as the utility functions of individuals remain the same. After several weeks a concern for one's neighbors will likely have decreased to the

---

3. See Alchian and Allen, *University Economics*, Belmont, California: Wadsworth Publishing Company, 1964, pp. 91–92.

point at which a resident will revert to his normal predisaster behavior. This shift will be reflected in the intersection of the flow and stock curves at a higher equilibrium price than p_1'' observed in Figure 3-2, other things being equal.

Range of Short-Run Alternatives

A diagram indicating the range that prices of necessities can take during the short-run period following a disaster can be constructed from the three polar cases analyzed in the preceding section. The shaded area in Figure 3-3 represents this feasible region. When each resident in the community behaves as an economic man without any expectation of outside aid (Case I), the demand curve depicting the upper bound for an emergency item in the short-run will be D_1'. The price of the commodity will lie somewhere between p_0' (when no destruction of the item in question occurs) and p_1' (when a large reduction of the supply is caused by the disaster). Anticipation of outside aid and emergent altruism on the part of residents in the disaster area will tend to shift the demand curve to the left so that it approaches D_1''. Although the disaster initially reduces the actual stock of the commodity to q_1', an increase in the flow supplied by residents who dip into their reserves leads to an effective available stock of q_1'', so that the equilibrium short-run price is p_1'' as shown by point H.

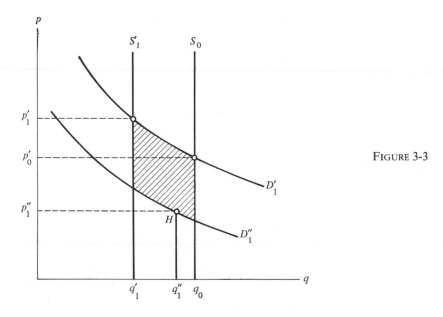

FIGURE 3-3

Conclusions

Most supply and demand problems facing an area hit by a natural disaster are short-run in nature because of the aid forthcoming from outside regions. Even when the threat of shortages does exist, the concern of residents in the community for the plight of others helps to minimize serious problems during the emergency period.

Postdisaster behavior of individuals helps to eliminate a source of demand for some commodities and keeps prices lower than they would be if the same conditions of scarcity arose in a more normal, impersonal market situation. Thus, if people stay with friends and relatives, a large demand for housing is temporarily taken off the market, and pressure on rents is reduced. Possible food shortages are avoided for the same reason; residents respond to urgings not to hoard and, in fact, are likely to dip into their buffer stocks, which are not part of the normal market supply but are held for emergencies. Realtors and store owners are also hesitant to raise rents or food prices during the recuperation period; in fact, selective reductions are often put into effect temporarily. These short-term response patterns indicate that sociological and psychological factors change the utility functions of residents during the short-run period and explain why economic behavior immediately following a disaster appears at first glance to be somewhat peculiar.[4]

LONG-TERM RECOVERY PROBLEMS

▷ GENERAL CONCEPTS

According to our definition, long-term recovery refers to the rebuilding process that brings the community back to its predisaster economic level. This definition implicitly assumes that the community will want to rebuild all structures that were damaged or destroyed by the disaster. Of course, this may not always be the case. For example, if a business had expanded its facilities before

---

4. These positive reactions following a disaster may be triggered by the expectation that substantial outside aid will be forthcoming in the near future. It is possible that altruism would be less prevalent if residents felt that the community would be isolated for a long period of time. Given the prevailing positive reaction to localized disaster by the outside world, it would be hard to rigorously test such a hypothesis unless there were a large-scale catastrophe, such as an all-out nuclear attack.

the disaster in anticipation of future sales that did not materialize, then the destruction may lead to the rebuilding of a much smaller factory afterward. For purposes of this discussion, we will assume that residents desire to be in at least the same position following the disaster as they were before.[5] In contrast to the short-term recuperation phase, which has been studied in some detail by sociologists and psychologists, little attention has been given to the reconstruction problems of a stricken community.[6]

Looking at the economic problems of recovery following a disaster, it is important to distinguish between the stock and the flow effect. Damage to physical and human resources caused directly by the catastrophe itself will naturally decrease the stock of these factors of production at an instant of time. Thus, for example, just before the Good Friday earthquake, the greater Anchorage area had 94,700 inhabitants and an estimated $539 million in real and personal property evaluated at market prices.[7] As a direct result of the disaster, the population was reduced by nine people, but the private property loss was estimated to be more than $42 million. Over time, there is likely to be a flow of resources in the form of capital (funds and equipment) and labor (migration behavior) that will affect the pattern of rebuilding activity. As the magnitude and flow of outside aid is increased, recovery will naturally be more rapid.

Although many disasters in the United States have produced a serious amount of physical damage, all of them have only marginally affected the labor force. In fact, there are few catastrophes on record in which the loss of life has been more than a small fraction of the population.[8] It thus seems reasonable

5. The availability of government grants and low-interest loans will provide more of an incentive for rebuilding and expansion on the part of homeowners and businessmen than if only loans at current market rates were offered.

6. The notable exception is a study on the Waco-San Angelo tornadoes by Harry E. Moore, *Tornadoes Over Texas*, The University of Texas Press, Austin, 1958.

7. This figure is based on a study of overall assessments undertaken by the Governor in January 1964. See "An Economic Profile of Alaska," U.S. Department of Commerce, March 31, 1964, mimeographed, pp. 30–31.

8. The few disasters that have resulted in a large number of fatalities may be classified under two headings: (1) those events that produce severe capital and labor losses (e.g., volcanic eruptions such as the one in Martinique in 1902; the eruption of Mt. Pelee there triggered an avalanche that swept down on the city of St. Pierre completely destroying the town and killing the entire population of 30,000), and (2) bacteriological epidemics such as the Black Plague that destroy human lives without attacking property. For a discussion of recovery following the Black Plague, see Jack Hirshleifer, *Disaster and Recovery: The Black Death in Western Europe*, Rand Corporation RM 4700-TAB, Santa Monica, Calif., February 1966.

to assume that the speed of recovery following a disaster will be determined primarily by the magnitude of the physical damage and of the outside aid made available to the stricken area. To predict the length of time it will take for an area to fully recover, some standardized measure must be utilized. Assume that a tornado causes $10 million damage to a city of 100,000 and then proceeds to destroy the same amount and type of property in a nearby town of 10,000. It would be most unlikely for the small community to recover as rapidly as the large city, since its labor force will be so much less and its per cent destruction of capital will be considerably higher. One way of meaningfully comparing the two communities would be to look at per capita damage figures. In the large city the loss would be $100 per person whereas this figure would rise to $10,000 per person in the smaller village. If one were comparing recovery rates of disaster communities within a given country, one would predict that the lower the per capita damage figures, the more rapid will be the rebuilding process. This point will be elaborated in Chapter 8, when some empirical evidence will be presented. Of course, the type of destruction will play a large part in the length of time it takes for a community to get back on its feet. This problem has been subsumed up to now by lumping all physical damage into the category *capital*. Recovery can be better understood by observing the composition of the loss and the priority scheme for restoring it. After discussing this aspect of the problem in the next section, we will conclude the chapter by analyzing why the speed of recovery following a disaster appears more rapid than might initially be expected.

▷ CAPITAL DESTRUCTION FROM THE DISASTER

Rather than look at the physical stock as just K, we can subdivide losses into the public sector (K_p), the commercial or business sector (K_b), and the residential area (K_r). Public-sector goods comprise such services as transportation facilities, communication networks, and other publicly owned capital. Business capital is composed of plant and equipment as well as inventories on hand. Residential capital includes the value of homes and apartments as well as the land associated with these dwellings.

Clearly, the speed of recovery will be a function of both the composition and magnitude of damage to the capital stock. Losses to the public sector should be most crippling to the community, since such services as transportation and electricity are necessary for the operation of homes and businesses. One has only to look at the Northeast blackout of November 1965 to gain an idea of the paralyzing effects that a power failure can have on an entire region. Moving over to the private sphere, we would expect a community that suffered only residential losses to recover much faster than if it had received equivalent damage to its commercial facilities. As we have noted in the previous section on short-term recuperation, victims can be housed for long periods of time with neighbors or relatives while rebuilding takes place, so the supply of shelter should be extremely elastic.[9] There would, thus, be no reason for residential damage to severely impede the economy. On the other hand, destruction of commercial and industrial plants would deal a crippling blow to the output capability of the area.

Since long-term recovery appears to be a function of the type of capital damaged or destroyed, we would like to analyze this differential effect using basic concepts of economic analysis. Assume that immediately following the disaster a new sector of the economy springs up for rebuilding public capital K_p, business capital K_b, and residential capital K_r. A certain fixed amount of homogeneous labor $\bar{L}$ and outside aid $\bar{K}$ will now be devoted exclusively to this reconstruction work. The remaining factors of production in the community will be utilized in each of the three capital sectors K_p, K_b, and K_r. The allocation problem becomes more complicated if we have to determine how much should be devoted to rebuilding and how much should be allocated to normal production. For purposes of this discussion, we have assumed that $\bar{L}$ and $\bar{K}$ are arbitrarily fixed.

Suppose that following a disaster the stock of capital is reduced to K_p^*, K_b^* and K_r^*. If the inputs $\bar{L}$ and $\bar{K}$ were devoted entirely to rebuilding one sector, we could then draw a curve showing how total output increased as rebuilding proceeded. Thus, for example, the curve $P(K_p, K_b^*, K_r^*/\bar{L}, \bar{K})$ in Figure 3-4 shows the output capability of the economy via some production function, P, for any value of K_p, under the assumption that no restoration takes place in the commercial and residential sectors. Similar functions have been drawn for each type of capital, holding the other two at their *immediate* postdisaster levels. The most efficient process of recovery will be defined as the allocation of

---

9. This was the case following the Dutch floods of 1953 when over 5000 victims were housed by volunteers for over one year. Institute for Social Research in the Netherlands, *Studies in Holland Flood Disaster, 1953*, vol. 2, Committee on Disaster Studies, NAS-NRC, Washington, D.C., 1955, p. 59.

resources over time that maximizes the stricken community's output capability during the reconstruction period. Specifically, we are interested in knowing how labor, $\bar{L}$, and outside aid, $\bar{K}$, should be allocated to the three sectors. By looking at the curves in Figure 3-4, we can determine the priority process during the initial rebuilding stage. Recovery will proceed most efficiently if $\bar{L}$ and $\bar{K}$ are devoted entirely to the public sector, at least for the first instant of time dt following the disaster, since the marginal productivity of K_p, represented by the slope, is higher than for either of the other two types of capital.

From Figure 3-4 it is not possible to say how the allocation process should continue over time since the economy's position is depicted only immediately after the disaster. Once any reconstruction takes place, a new set of curves must be drawn to reflect the revised levels of the capital stock, and only then can a decision be made as to where $\bar{L}$ and $\bar{K}$ should be spent. Because of the importance of public capital and the indivisibilities present in reconstruction work, it appears that, in practice, a sizeable amount of money would be economically justified in restoring community utilities before expenditures would occur in the private sector. If our conjecture about the relative importance of the sectors holds, then we would expect commercial facilities to be rebuilt somewhat more rapidly than homes and apartments. The optimal process of recovery can be determined directly from the marginal productivity conditions. At any moment of time, resources will be utilized in restoring the facilities whose contribution

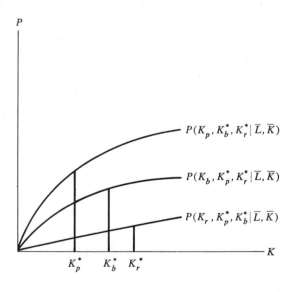

FIGURE 3-4

to overall productivity are the greatest. After the initial emergency period, when all resources are likely to be allocated to the public sector, it would be normal and desirable to expect simultaneous reconstruction of all three sectors.

One way to guarantee an efficient recovery following a disaster is to devise a system of disaster relief that allocates resources to the various sectors of the economy at the appropriate moments of time. In other words, if it is determined from the marginal productivity conditions that restoration should be restricted to the public sector during the first two months following a disaster, then aid to the private sector by agencies such as the Small Business Administration should be delayed for that period of time to prevent any competition for labor, assuming this resource is in limited supply. This recommendation conflicts with the Federal government's stated policy of providing relief as fast as possible to both the public and private sectors. However, the procedure followed in practice unintentionally conforms more closely to the theoretically efficient pattern than to the stated objective. Thus, once an area is declared eligible for Federal disaster relief, a declaration that normally occurs within a week following a severe domestic disaster, work on public facilities begins almost immediately. Activity in the private sector tends to be delayed, partly because of uncertainty as to the future status of the disaster area and partly because of the time-consuming damage analyses necessary for approving loans by the Federal government through the Small Business Adminstration or for issuing insurance payments by private companies. If building-permit data is a meaningful measure of reconstruction activity, then Anchorage figures indicate, as will be shown in Chapter 8, that restoration of the commercial sector occurred much faster than restoration of the residential portion of the city.

▷ SPEED OF RECOVERY

By speed of recovery we are referring to the length of time it takes a community to return to its predisaster capital-stock position. Newspaper reports or magazine articles describing the progress of reconstruction activity frequently comment on the remarkable speed with which the stricken region has got back on its feet again although the opposite phenomenon may also be true in some cases. One reason often given for a rapid recovery is the increased motivation of the people to rebuild their community into a bigger and better place.[10] There appear, however, to be more significant economic factors that should be considered in determining how fast recovery will actually take place.

The amount of aid and the form in which it is supplied from outside sources will play an important role in the recovery process. The disaster-torn area will be best off if resources are provided as an outright grant. The speed of reconstruction activity will then be governed by the rate at which it is feasible to combine the factors of production, with labor normally being the limiting input. If part of the reconstruction cost must be borne by the community itself, then people in the disaster area will have suffered a real and permanent loss of wealth. For example, victims receiving aid in the form of Federal loans must make regular repayments to the government, so they will require more time to accumulate capital than if they had been given a grant. As the flow of outside aid is in time decreased and the community is forced to rely even more on its own resources, the recovery period will be longer. It is thus not surprising to find that Anchorage, which received a substantial amount of funds in the form of Federal grants, was practically fully rebuilt two years after the quake, whereas Skopje, Yugoslavia, with limited outside help, has made a much slower recovery from its July 1963 earthquake. When the required funds for reconstruction represent a sizable fraction of national wealth, as in an underdeveloped nation, we would expect the speed of recovery to be constrained by a limited flow of capital goods (e.g., construction equipment and raw materials) since normal investment projects will compete with postdisaster activities for funds from the national treasury. On the other hand, when the magnitude of damage from a natural disaster is a negligible proportion of national income, as is likely to be the case in industrialized nations, then rebuilding will be constrained by labor rather than capital. In the United States, for example, employees processing SBA loan applications and insurance claim adjustors are often in short supply following a large-scale natural disaster; hence, rebuilding is delayed both by a backlog of paper work and by time-consuming arguments needed to

---

10. See, for example, Charles Fritz, *op. cit.* Fritz claims that the presence of community solidarity over time will be a function of both the magnitude and pattern of the disaster. If the catastrophe is a one-shot affair (e.g., an earthquake), then the residents will probably be linked together for a much shorter period of time than if the area were subject to rapidly recurrent events (e.g., bombings during World War II). The larger the scale of the disaster, the longer should be the expected unity of the community over time. Thus, he would anticipate that survivors of the Hiroshima attack would feel special bonds for each other over a longer time span than residents of a town struck once by a tornado, as Topeka, Kansas, was in June 1966.

reach a mutually satisfactory insurance settlement. If damage from the disaster is extremely severe, then some large-scale studies for rebuilding the community may be undertaken. The formulation and implementation of these studies are frequently time-consuming and extend the recovery period even further. For example, in Skopje a new urban design by the U.N. for the central part of the city was only completed three years after the earthquake. Urban renewal plans for some of the southcentral Alaskan communities were not approved until two or three years after the good Friday earthquake.

Recovery may be shortened if the community utilizes recent technological advances in reconstruction activity. The crisis situation may, in fact, encourage the adoption of these new techniques, which were previously available but had not been adopted by firms because of a normal reluctance to consider innovations when there is no pressure to do so. In Chapter 8 we will illustrate how the earthquake induced certain technological changes in the construction industry in Alaska.

One final factor that may contribute to an unanticipated speed of recovery is the initial overestimates of damage to a stricken area, which lead people to believe that the disaster was much more severe than it actually was. Very frequently the amount of debris and wreckage strewn everywhere tends to paint a much gloomier picture than may actually exist. Damage to underground facilities cannot be estimated with any degree of accuracy until reconstruction begins, and it is thus common to assume the worst initially so that contingency funds by the government will be made available. When a revised estimate is made several months after the disaster, it will generally be considerably lower than the initial figure, as illustrated in Chapter 1. The true value of damage may lie even below this new approximation, although the figure may never be calculated by any group or Federal agency. People tend to remember the initial damage report whether or not there were any future announcements of revisions, so they may be somewhat surprised to find the economy back on its feet in a shorter period of time than they had anticipated.

Summary

This chapter has presented some concepts for structuring short-term recuperation problems following a disaster as well as for understanding the reconstruction pattern during the long-term recovery period. During the aftermath there is great uncertainty as to community needs at a time when information must be transmitted rapidly to the outside. Using concepts from the decision-making process in a firm, we illustrated how a better priority scheme for emergency shipments could be developed with improved information on damage and requirements. Postdisaster needs may thus be met more easily and at lower cost than they are today.

The section on supply and demand problems dealt with price behavior for emergency goods under several contrasting situations. The price of an item will be highest if there is no sympathy between people in the community and no expectation of outside aid. When residents anticipate outside help, then demand for the product will shift to the left, thus lowering the price. If we assume that during the recuperation period a form of altruism exists among individuals in the community, then a positive chain reaction between retailers and consumers is created. Prices of emergency goods are stable or even lower than before the disaster (retailers' contribution), but no hoarding takes place (consumers' contribution). During the emergency period, families frequently utilize some of their stored goods normally reserved for future consumption, so the stock available for sale may be swelled beyond what it initially appeared to be following the disaster. All these actions by residents tend to reduce the immediate pressure on demand during the recuperation period.

Our discussion on long-term recovery was primarily devoted to an analysis of the composition of the capital loss. On the basis of economic intuition, we argued that damage to public-sector facilities will be more serious than losses to commercial or residential capital. For recovery to be efficient, labor and outside aid in the rebuilding sector should be devoted to those capital goods whose marginal productivity is highest. The speed of recovery will be primarily determined by the magnitude and type of outside aid given to the stricken community. It appears that an economy gets back on its feet faster than initially expected both because of overestimates of damage and because of utilization of capital and labor in a more efficient way than when the damaged structures were initially built.

The next five chapters will present some empirical data related to both the recuperation period and long-term recovery. It should be borne in mind, however, that these findings are not being presented in order to confirm the preceding hypotheses; in fact, it was only after examining the evidence from Alaska and other disaster studies that we explicitly formulated the ideas in this chapter.

Part II

SHORT-PERIOD
RECUPERATION:
EMPIRICAL EVIDENCE

| $Chapter\ Four$ | Problems of

Information and

Communication

WHEN DECISION-MAKING problems during the crisis period induced by a natural disaster are discussed, it is helpful to differentiate events with a warning period (e.g., hurricanes, floods), for which some preventive action can be taken to protect individuals, from catastrophes with minimal advance notice (e.g., tornadoes) or with none at all (e.g., earthquakes). In the latter cases it is generally necessary for the community to rely on makeshift organization to undertake emergency measures, unless some well-known Civil Defense plan exists in the area.

The first section of this chapter will briefly look at the different forms of organizational behavior in a disaster with a warning period (hurricane Carla), catastrophes with minimal advance notice (Waco and San Angelo tornadoes), and an unexpected event (Alaska earthquake). We will illustrate the kinds of problems encountered in each situation as well as the effect that predisaster planning had on the decision-making process. Efficient action after a catastrophe is often hindered by the inevitable mass movement of messages, supplies, and people toward the stricken area. A number of examples from the above disasters will illustrate forms of this so-called "convergence behavior,"[1] and suggestions for alleviating the problems will be proposed. In the concluding portion of the chapter, we will analyze the effect that uncertainty, induced by

---

1. The term was introduced into the literature by Charles Fritz and J. H. Mathewson in a study entitled *Conver-* *gence Behavior*, NAS-NRC, Washington, D.C., 1957.

organizational and convergence problems, had on specific actions and decisions in each of the above disasters.

ORGANIZATIONAL PROBLEMS CONNECTED WITH DISASTERS

▷ HURRICANE CARLA (1961)—A DISASTER WITH ADVANCE WARNING[2]

Hurricane Carla followed such a tortuous path that it posed a threat to an area extending from Grande Isle, Louisiana, to Corpus Christi, Texas, with over one million inhabitants. In response to this impending disaster, a mass evacuation took place along the Texas and Louisiana coast on a scale unprecedented in American experience. An estimated 350,000 inhabitants left their homes as a result of the extensive and successful warning system by the U.S. Weather Bureau, thereby keeping the death toll at only forty-five, a negligible figure when pitted against the property damage of over $400 million. We have chosen to concentrate on the behavior of the local organization in Jefferson County, Texas,[3] to illustrate the successful evacuation procedures based on a Civil Defense survival plan and the unexpected organizational problems connected with handling returnees to the area.

On Friday morning, September 8, three days before the hurricane actually hit the Texas coast, the local weather bureau called a meeting at the Jefferson County Airport for officials from Jefferson County and neighboring Orange County.[4] Members of the local division of the state highway patrol, Civil

---

2. Most of the material in this section has been obtained from a study by Harry E. Moore, et al., . . . *And the Winds Blew*, The Hogg Foundation for Mental Health, University of Texas, 1964, pp. 1–85.

3. This county, located in southwestern Texas, has a population of 145,000 (1960 census) including the town of Port Arthur (pop. 67,000).

4. Texas follows a policy of local responsibility so that power to advise, not order, evacuation lies mainly with city and county officials. State agencies still play an important role, of course, by providing services (e.g., state police, health and welfare services), advice, coordination of local efforts, and liason with the Federal government. Moore, et al., *op. cit.*, p. 9.

Defense and Red Cross, Coast Guard and Corps of Engineers as well as representatives from industrial plants in the areas also attended the session.

Everyone present agreed to study and follow a Civil Defense survival plan for the area that had been written under a Federal grant in 1958. This report was unusually detailed, specifying not only appropriate disaster roles but also the exact spots for key equipment, communication channels, and evacuation routes. The county was also fortunate in having one of the coast's few full-time Civil Defense directors to help direct the operations. Knowing that they could act swiftly if necessary, they decided to postpone evacuation measures until Carla's course became more definite.

Several hours later the disaster plan went into effect. All vacations and leaves were canceled for local government employees, equipment was checked, supplies such as gas, food, and water were stored, and patrols surveyed the highways for possible flooding. In Port Arthur itself residents were ready at an hour's notice to barricade store windows and evacuate if necessary. The police chief noted that his entire force of 100 officers and 25 auxiliary policemen were on alert. Around 8 P.M. that evening residents of the small towns of Sabine and Sabine Pass in the southern part of the county were officially advised to evacuate that low-lying area, since it was feared that flooding would cut it off from the mainland.

The next morning a large number of officials assembled at the Jefferson County Airport at the request of the county judge and Civil Defense director. The following bulletin was released to all news media:

> It is the opinion of the mayors of Lake View, Groves, Port Arthur, Port Neches, Griffing Park, and Pearland at a meeting at the Civil Defense office that all persons in these towns should immediately evacuate to the city of Beaumont and north because of extremely high tides now and an anticipated tide of from 10 to 15 feet above normal. It is very important that this advice be heeded and complied with.[5]

The officials also reported that Civil Defense evacuation routes were already marked, except for coastal routes subject to flooding that had to be closed.

Evacuation of the communities proceeded very smoothly. Later in the morning it was reported that all residents from the Sabine Pass region had evacuated the area and had checked into hotels in Houston 100 miles away.

---

5. *Ibid.*, p. 19.

Most of the residents in the Port Arthur area took the advice of their mayors, and automobiles were bumper to bumper on the highway to Beaumont, 17 miles away, by noon. The traffic reached its peak about 3 P.M., according to the highway patrol. Some of the evacuees checked into hotels; many stayed in shelters provided by the Red Cross. A large number of refugees were not stopping at Beaumont as expected but were traveling altogether out of the county. Within six hours, an estimated 200,000 people had been evacuated from the general area without the use of force.

Thus it is clear that with predisaster planning and adequate warnings, the organization set-up in Jefferson County was able to evacuate its inhabitants in an orderly manner. The main difficulties occurred when a number of residents wanted to return early, since no formal organization had been established to cope with this problem. During Monday, the day of the storm, tides in Port Arthur threatened to spill over the eight-foot seawall, but returnees would not stay away, partly because false information and irresponsible rumors had been broadcast from radio and TV stations outside Jefferson County to the effect that the towns were open. The Civil Defense director reiterated that the area was still in a state of emergency and that the all-clear signal would be given at the appropriate times and that until then roadblocks would be established to prevent people from entering the towns.

The following day things were still in a state of confusion, since there was an unofficial all-clear report for the Port Arthur area at 10:45 A.M., although roadblocks were only officially lifted at 1:25 P.M. The absence of any central coordinating group or plan to handle the return problem was the primary cause of these difficulties during hurricane Carla.

▷ WACO AND SAN ANGELO TORNADOES (1953)—DISASTERS WITH MINIMAL ADVANCE WARNINGS[6]

There were distinct differences in organizational behavior between Waco and San Angelo following the severe tornadoes that hit these two towns on May 11, 1953. In the case of Waco there was little predisaster planning and communica-

---

6. The information in this section has been compiled from Harry E. Moore, *Tornadoes Over Texas*, The University of Texas Press, Austin, 1958, Chap. 1.

tions broke down, whereas in San Angelo a tight Civil Defense organization had existed before the storm and there were few problems in transmitting information. Let us consider each of the communities in turn.

Organization in Waco

Although there had been storm and tornado warnings throughout the day for the general area, little attention was given to them in Waco, since the Chamber of Commerce had publicized a couple of years before an ancient Indian legend stating that the city was immune to tornadoes.[7] The only attempt at issuing an explicit warning was made by a local peace officer living some miles to the southwest of town. He had called the office of the county sheriff to report having seen a funnel cloud, but before he could give any details, the telephone connection was broken. As a result there were 114 fatalities and over 1000 injuries, about 145 of them listed as major. Army engineers conjectured that the great majority of the casualties could have been avoided by as little as five minutes' advance notice. This would have given the victims time to take shelter in one of the modern steel-framed buildings in the downtown area that came through the storm with only minor damage. The tornado occurred during a weekday afternoon so that a large number of people was in the downtown area, where the tornado dealt its heaviest blow.

The greatest problem in Waco was lack of organization. Almost simultaneous with the tornado, the switching equipment in the central telephone office jammed so that not even officials there knew what had happened until "a man came pounding at the door shouting that buildings were caving in."[8] A mobile radio unit with a loudspeaker was dispatched downtown one hour after the disaster and was used by the mayor, chief of police, fire chief, and sheriff to issue orders and direct rescue operations. The equipment was of limited usefulness, however, since its audible range was not more than two blocks.[9]

Telephone and electric power lines were snapped, and the two radio stations were off the air for the first few hours after the tornado. During this period of time, the communications center consisted of a mobile telephone car

7. Moore, *Tornadoes Over Texas*, p. 3. The same legend circulated for many years in Topeka, Kansas, so the tornado that whipped through its business section in June 1966 was totally unexpected.

8. *Ibid.*, p. 8.

9. *Ibid.*, pp. 189–190.

parked in front of the First National Bank. By putting a special operator on the switchboard, the mobile unit's calls could be handled. When the two radio stations were again on the air, telephone calls were relayed alternately to them, and they broadcast all requests for supplies.

In general, however, chaotic conditions prevailed in the stricken area, since most persons and groups lacked direction and moved in to tackle whatever problems they saw. Rescue groups often worked at cross-purposes, acting just to "do something" rather than having an overall objective in mind. An attempt to set up some Civil Defense organization in Waco had only reached the paper stage, so that it could not be implemented after the tornado.

Although a meeting was held shortly before midnight at state police headquarters to develop some means of coordination, it was not until the next afternoon that any formal organization took place, with the mayor reluctantly agreeing to take charge. He later explained that he had not known that as the chief city official he was required to direct operations. Personnel work was assigned to the city manager, operations to the city engineer, and equipment and supplies to a man who had sold and serviced heavy equipment. State and city police and the local National Guard unit were asked to divide the patrol and property-protection work among themselves. The city and county health officer was placed in charge of health and sanitation measures, and an employee of the telephone company was asked to assume responsibility for restoring and maintaining communication facilities.

Organization in San Angelo

In contrast with Waco, the city of San Angelo had adequate warning of the tornado not only from the weather bureau but also from two patrolmen of the Texas Department of Public Safety who had reported a funnel over Sterling City, 44 miles to the northwest. Acting on instructions from the officer in charge at San Angelo, they followed the cloud down the valley of the North Concho River as it approached San Angelo. Information on the progress of the cloud was relayed from public safety headquarters to the newspaper, which in turn warned the schools and the city hall of the possible danger. For this reason there were only eleven fatalities from the tornado and just sixty-six people injured seriously. The superintendent of one of the schools estimated that without any warning of the tornado's approach, 300 to 400 pupils could have been hurt or killed; thanks to safety drills, none of the children was seriously injured.

Organizational problems immediately after the disaster were minimal. Although electric power and telephone service in the devastated area were unavailable and commercial radio was not usable for the first few hours, communications were maintained through a radio network embracing the vital agencies in the city—police, fire, state highway patrol, water department, sheriff's office, and funeral homes. Overall coordination of emergency activity was facilitated by the well-developed Civil Defense organization in San Angelo. In fact, only one and a half years before the tornado, on Pearl Harbor Day, a simulated bombing attack had been staged in the city to coordinate the appropriate civilian and military organizations. This drill undoubtedly enabled the groups to function more effectively after the tornado than they might have otherwise.

Almost immediately local and state police, firemen, and National Guardsmen set up patrols to make a systematic search for the dead and injured. They combed the area so thoroughly during the night that only one injured person and one body were found the next day. All three hospitals in the city were prepared to handle all casualties who needed treatment. In order to facilitate the flow of relevant information, a special crew of switchmen and test-board operators was assigned to keep telephone lines open for essential calls. Consequently, it was always possible to get messages through to key personnel except where cables or lines had been broken.

Comparison of Waco and San Angelo

On the whole, the organizational problems in Waco during the period immediately following the tornado were far greater than those in San Angelo. Besides there being no Civil Defense plan in Waco, telephone and radio communications were broken for the first few hours, thereby accentuating the coordination problems. The San Angelo situation offers a direct contrast, since there was no time when messages could not be delivered over the air or via the phone. The adequate warning in the case of San Angelo kept the death toll down to a minimum and enabled city officials to undertake emergency tasks almost immediately. In Waco, on the other hand, there was no indication that a tornado was approaching the city. When it did hit, no one was prepared to act, and there was a temporary lapse of governmental and other forms of social control.

▷ ALASKA EARTHQUAKE (1964)—A DISASTER WITH NO WARNING[10]

At the time of the Good Friday earthquake, there was no explicit local post-disaster plan that could provide organizational guidelines in Anchorage during the emergency period. Although certain utilities, particularly the telephone company, did have standby procedures for handling routine emergencies, they had no instructions for coping with large-scale natural disasters. A local Civil Defense plan for wartime was being drawn up at the time of the quake, but information from this study was not well known to key personnel in the area. At the state level, there was a Civil Defense master plan for wartime situations that was followed by all state agencies having postdisaster responsibility.

During the first few hours following the quake, no one possessed verified information about the total extent of the damage. Although no formal search parties were set up, local police, assisted by teams of volunteers, did make an attempt to gain a very general initial assessment of the destruction in the downtown area through visual inspections of particular streets. While the police were undertaking these informal surveys, unverified reports filtered in that the Turnagain area and other neighborhoods had been severely damaged. However, the lack of direct communication with any section of the city made it difficult for officials to arrive at any quick overall assessment of the damage.

At the local level there was no immediate coordination between the emergency organizations. Each group tended to work separately without extending its activities beyond its normal scope of operations. Of course, there were some tasks created by the earthquake not normally handled by any specific organization. These projects were assumed by several groups in a rather haphazard way, so there was a great deal of duplication of effort. For example, several official and unofficial groups overlapped in search and rescue efforts with the result that some areas were combed intensively numerous times while others were barely scrutinized. Communications became so critical during the evening that the mayor and city manager called a meeting of organization personnel in the Public Safety Building at 3 A.M. Saturday morning. Although there was a

---

10. Most of the material in this section is taken from a working paper by R. R. Dynes, J. E. Haas and E. L. Quarantelli, "Some Preliminary Observations on the Responses of Community Organizations Involved in the Emergency Period of the Alaskan Earthquake," Disaster Research Center, Ohio State University, May 28, 1964.

temporary exchange of information, no attempt was made to develop a communication center and centralized feedback system. The next morning, however, local organizations began to develop tentative cooperative arrangements generally on an informal basis so that such operations as search and rescue work began to be coordinated.

A more formal communication center on the local level finally did develop at the Public Safety Building where Anchorage Civil Defense and city officials—the mayor, city manager, head of the public works department and city attorney—set up shop together. The Kenai peninsula mobile radio and police department cars surrounding the building served as a link in the communications chain between the residents and the officials. Even before this, the state Civil Defense group had established a nerve center in a rather cramped but undamaged Army barracks not far from the downtown area. To aid them in their tasks, RACES[11] ham radio operators parked outside the building and with the aid of emergency power were able to communicate with fellow personnel in other parts of Alaska and the continental United States.

Gradually a system of priorities on action was established. First attention was given to providing emergency supplies and restoring utility services—electricity, sewer, water, and gas. Local Civil Defense personnel were able to forward their requests to state Civil Defense headquarters in the barracks two miles away through a direct field line installed by the Army. Communications with parts of Alaska or the "lower 48 states" could then be established via ham radio requesting the Air Force to ship all urgently needed goods through their Military Air Transport Service (MATS). The secondary phase of the immediate recuperation operations entailed debris clearance, demolition of dangerous structures, and some assessment of damage to buildings.

Convergence behavior

The mass movement of people, messages, and supplies toward a disaster-struck area greatly magnifies and complicates control efforts as well as retarding

---

11. The abbreviation RACES stands for the Radio Amateur Communication Emergency System. It comprises a group of ham operators around the world who help transmit information to and from points where communication is temporarily impaired.

organized relief efforts.[12] In their study of the subject, Fritz and Mathewson distinguished between three major forms of convergence:[13]

1. *Personal Convergence:* The actual physical movement of persons on foot, by auto, or by other vehicle.
2. *Informational Convergence:* The movement or transmission of messages.
3. *Material Convergence:* The physical movement of supplies and equipment.

Although each form of convergence has a somewhat different effect on the recuperation process of the community, they all create communication and information problems, thus increasing uncertainty about the state of affairs. This section will specifically illustrate the different types of convergence problems that occurred during each of the three disasters we have isolated for special study.

▷ HURRICANE CARLA

The convergence problems created by Carla were not so severe as in other natural disasters because of the accurate advanced warnings. In fact, this particular disaster illustrates the presence of both divergence behavior (cars bumper to bumper evacuating the threatened area) and convergence activity (clogged highways upon the return of residents).

According to Moore, few problems in the functioning of mass communication media occurred both before and after the storm. The broadcasts and news media generally performed their reporting job admirably, particularly before the disaster struck. They were able accurately to communicate the need for evacuation so that hundreds of lives were saved in the process. Both before and after the disaster, there was a substantial increase in the number of telephone calls despite the fact that over 165,000 phones were knocked out of service (72,000 in the Houston area alone). Through the use of emergency generators and a large number of extra operators, there were very few difficulties experienced in placing calls where service was available. During the four-day period

---

12. Fritz and Mathewson, *op. cit.*, p. 1. 13. *Ibid.*, p. 4.

of Sunday, September 10th through Wednesday, September 13th, there were almost 3 million calls placed in the Houston area compared to the normal load of 1.2 million.[14] Carla hit the Texas coast on Monday morning, September 11.

One of the problems facing many communities after the hurricane was the arrival of large numbers of sightseers who wanted to survey the damage. For example, tourists arriving in Port Lavaca were so numerous on the Sunday following the storm that streets could not be cleaned. Traffic jams on the Gulf Freeway leading to Texas City and Galveston were also extremely severe.

▷ WACO AND SAN ANGELO TORNADOES

Convergence problems posed much greater difficulties following the tornadoes in Texas than they did after hurricane Carla. In Waco sightseers not only hindered rescue operations but also hampered the treatment of the injured at the hospitals. Large numbers of people streamed into and through the hospitals, seeking families or friends they thought had been injured, thus causing a great deal of confusion. A medical person observing the scene stated that "The hospitals became very quickly a sort of madhouse, with everybody running in to see what was happening. There was just no way to keep them out."[15]

In San Angelo the traffic problems caused by curious people who wanted to view the damage became so serious that on the afternoon of the day following the disaster, a two-hour period was designated during which persons could drive through the area of demolition. Between 5 P.M. and 7 P.M., it was estimated that about 2400 cars and 10,000 persons toured the devastated area.[16] The biggest convergence problem in the form of sightseeing traffic in Waco occurred on the Sunday following the quake, when thousands of cars tried to enter the area despite radio broadcasts urging people to stay away. A police officer reported that "It was worse than a football crowd. Airplanes buzzed over the ruins like buzzards, creating a sky-traffic jam."[17] In the downtown part of town, where the greatest damage occurred, it was impossible to undertake clean-up operations that afternoon since trucks were forced to push their

---

14. Moore et al., ... *And the Winds Blew*, p. 160.

15. Moore, *Tornadoes Over Texas*, p. 22.

16. *Ibid.*, pp. 29–30.

17. *Ibid.*, p. 8.

way through the crowd at a snail's pace. An estimated 10,000 persons were standing idly near the intersection of two main streets in the city.[18]

There were also problems of material convergence in Waco since floods of donated supplies and equipment were forthcoming shortly after the disaster. No provision had been made for a central place where material could be received and dispatched to the points needing them, so most items were more of a hindrance than an aid to recuperation. Even one month after the tornado, shipments of clothing were still arriving for use by the Salvation Army. Many of these were so badly worn that they had to be sent to rag collectors.[19] Food supplies, mainly in the form of sandwiches, rolled into Waco from all over the state of Texas. Although an attempt was made to regulate the flow into the Red Cross canteens set up in the area, there were one or two cases where excess supplies interfered with the movement of workers in the feeding station.[20]

In Waco there was a substantial increase in the number of long-distance phone calls as well as of telegrams handled. Between the day of the disaster, Monday, and Friday evening the telephone company handled 22,400 long-distance calls, about 10,000 more than the normal load despite disruption of service on some trunk lines during this period. The day after the tornado, the central telegraph office handled nearly 15,000 messages compared to the normal weekday average of 1000. San Angelo local calls increased by about 40 per cent whereas long-distance calls from the city almost doubled during the first few days following the disaster. Telegraph service, on the other hand, increased by only about 20 per cent above normal, so there was little problem in handling these messages.[21]

▷ ALASKA EARTHQUAKE—PROBLEMS IN ANCHORAGE[22]

Despite the fact that Alaska is geographically isolated, there were still convergence problems in the Anchorage area. An estimated 20,000 telegrams were

18. Moore, *Tornadoes Over Texas*, p. 18.

19. Harry E. Moore, "Cities in Crisis: A Study of the Tornado Disasters in Waco and San Angelo, 1953, 1954," Department of Sociology, University of Texas, 1956, ms pp. 19, 24–25.

20. Moore, *Tornadoes Over Texas*, pp. 18–19.

21. *Ibid.*, pp. 184–187.

22. Data in this section were obtained through personal discussions with city officials and from reports of such organizations as the Anchorage telephone company.

delivered to Anchorage residents and officials during the first three days after the earthquake. They were immediately brought downtown to the central telegraph office, where personnel read them in order to handle emergencies first. The large number of messages, most of which solely conveyed sympathy to the victims, made it extremely difficult to locate those telegrams requesting direct and immediate action. Following the quake, the Red Cross alone received 70,000 welfare inquiries that had to be routed to Alaska.

Despite frequent radio messages urging residents not to use the telephone except for emergency purposes, lines were tied up immediately after the quake with personal inquiries and requests. The city manager thus found it necessary to disconnect all phones on the central exchange for short periods of time because the overload in calls threatened to blow the 400-amp fuse.

As in other disasters a large number of supplies, notably clothing, was shipped into the damaged area immediately after the quake. Unfortunately, sorting out the worthwhile articles became a difficult and time-consuming process. In fact, the added burden of disposing of the worthless goods even made these gifts costly to the community. In Anchorage the problem was compounded by the arrival of packages earmarked for individuals or families who could not be located. Seward, recently designated an All-American City, received carloads of household goods and clothing from its sister cities in the "lower 48." For example, Allentown, Pennsylvania, shipped trailers full of bedding and linen goods, the large portion of which could not be used immediately.

Complaints were frequently heard in Alaska that if only the "foreigners" would go home "we could get some work done." The comment referred to the many government agencies and private groups visiting the area to study different aspects of the earthquake. Within three weeks after the disaster, more than 700 people had flown into the Anchorage area just for conferences, damage-assessment surveys, and other emergency measures. Residents of Alaska might be more sensitive to this type of intrusion than other U.S. citizens, simply because many of them moved away from the "lower 48" just to lead their own lives. However, these individuals must have soon realized the dependence of the Alaskan economy on the Federal government during normal times and particularly after a disaster. We are skeptical of the alleged difficulties in the normal recovery process caused by the government groups, since geological evaluations and official damage estimates were needed before loans and grants could be authorized.

Speculating that there would be a need for personnel to care for the sick and injured, volunteers from the local communities swamped all the hospitals.

In fact, a group of physicians from Fairbanks chartered a plane on their own initiative and flew into Anchorage only to find that their services were not needed. This type of convergence behavior would have been helpful if the number of people hospitalized had been greater than the ninety-two cases reported in the entire region affected by the quake.

One of the biggest problems faced by Anchorage Civil Defense headquarters during the first few days after the earthquake was a surplus of volunteer manpower. Over 200 people offered their services, but only a few of them could be used for emergency duties; it was difficult to convince the others that Civil Defense efficiency would be improved if they tried to help elsewhere. In fact, many of these individuals posed as Civil Defense personnel by wearing the hastily improvised white arm badges used by authorized members. Some of them caused considerable confusion by tampering with emergency materials to which they now had access by virtue of their assumed status.[23]

▷ SUGGESTED REMEDIES

The above examples illustrate two different types of convergence problems that normally exist after a disaster.

1. A concern for the welfare of residents in the stricken area. This interest manifests itself in the large number of telephone calls, telegrams, and messages about the status of family, friends, and relatives. At the same time, on a more impersonal level, large bundles of clothing, food, and other supplies are shipped to the disaster area because sympathetic outsiders feel these items may be needed during the recuperation period.

2. A morbid curiosity on the part of outsiders who wish to see what damage the disaster actually wreaked. If the community is easily accessible by road or foot, large numbers of sightseers will converge on the area, not so much to help as to view the destruction.[24]

---

23. This information was obtained from the Ohio State University Disaster Research Center. Several members of this group arrived in Anchorage shortly after the quake and were told of these actions while conducting research on organization behavior during the immediate recuperation period.

24. As we have pointed out, this prob-

lem was not acute in Anchorage because of the community's geographic isolation. Those who flew to the area did so for the purpose of engaging in survey work or directly aiding the recovery operations. Had the earthquake occurred in the "lower 48," convergence problems similar to those in Waco and San Angelo would undoubtedly have occurred.

By developing systematic procedures for reducing uncertainty, much of the convergence behavior created by a concern for the well-being of residents can be eased. The establishment of a central office where people may register their names and whereabouts would eliminate many telephone calls. This registration place should be located in a different area from the main communication center or centers so that personal inquiries would not interfere with emergency operations. A telephone line linking the office with the nerve centers and hospitals should permit rapid communication of vital information on fatalities and injuries. The Red Cross has taken a step in this direction through its welfare inquiry program. By providing local chapters throughout the country with as much information as possible on the specific disaster they attempt to eliminate some inquiries which would otherwise have been sent to the stricken area. Even with the establishment of this central exchange, large numbers of telephone calls are bound to be placed. One way of dealing with the heavy overload is to institute a system by which key lines are singled out for special priority. This procedure was adopted in San Angelo following the tornado when connections between emergency groups—fire department, police station, and hospitals—as well as with public officials were continuously kept open. A special crew of operators was set up to explain to residents who could not complete their calls why it was necessary to establish this special procedure.[25] It was impossible to establish any priority system in Anchorage, since the switchboard was not capable of differentiating between lines. As a result there was a peak overload that caused great difficulty during the emergency period.

The problems created by the deluge of clothing and unsolicited supplies arriving in a disaster area can be greatly alleviated through the creation of a central supply clearinghouse. Not only would information and communication problems be greatly improved, but a large amount of unnecessary pedestrian and vehicular traffic would be prevented. The Red Cross frequently establishes central warehouses and tries its best to discourage the huge volume of clothing and unsolicited supplies, but the effort is frequently unsuccessful. If the clearinghouse activities were coordinated with the central nerve center or centers, then once requests for material assistance were received, action could be determined on the basis of overall requirements and available supplies.[26] The problems of surplus clothing in Waco and Anchorage during the emergency period would

---

25. Moore, *Tornadoes Over Texas*, p. 186.

26. Fritz and Mathewson, *op. cit.*, p. 85.

have been greatly reduced if some clearinghouse had existed. In fact, it is quite likely that some victims who needed supplies could not utilize surplus donations from outsiders because they did not know they existed.

An argument can be raised that it may be beneficial to delay public announcement of a disaster to the rest of the nation for several hours so as to avoid convergence problems from curious outsiders. In the case of Waco, the inadequate functioning of communications may have been a partial blessing in disguise, particularly with regard to potential traffic problems. Although numerous people crowded into the area immediately after the disaster, many others did not know anything unusual had happened until the next morning. It is almost certain that if the local radio stations had been broadcasting right after the tornado, large numbers of people would have rushed to the area, thus creating an even worse traffic jam than actually occurred. Evidence on this speculation may be found in the behavior of people who jammed into the city a year earlier when a report of an industrial accident was broadcast immediately after it had happened.[27]

In general, verbal warnings appear to be ineffective in preventing curious outsiders from converging on the stricken area. One possible solution would be to set up a series of roadblocks permitting only authorized emergency vehicles to pass through the gate. Unfortunately, evidence from other disasters indicates that even state police trained in this technique lack both the criteria and means of identifying those who have reason to enter the disaster area.[28] Another difficulty encountered in the use of roadblocks is that they do not keep pace with the ever-widening circles of convergence. Since outsiders arrive from more distant places as time progresses, it is usually necessary to establish control points at a further distance from the disaster area (e.g., 50 or 100 miles away). To supplement the use of this restricting device, some attempt should be made to patrol arterial routes leading to hospitals, medical centers, and other key points. Through the use of cruising police vehicles, guided and controlled wherever possible by observer aircraft, these arteries can be kept partially clear for emergency traffic.[29]

These suggestions appear to be the most important means of helping to stem the tide of convergence activity.[30] It should be clear that all the measures

27. Moore, *Tornadoes Over Texas*, p. 82.

28. Fritz and Mathewson, *op. cit.*, p. 81.

29. *Ibid.*, p. 85.

30. For a more detailed discussion of control methods, see *ibid.*, Chap. 4, "Methods and Techniques for Controlling Convergence Behavior," pp. 61–87.

discussed here can be viewed as part of a systematic program for handling and channeling information and communications in disasters.

DECISION-MAKING UNDER UNCERTAINTY

Organization problems and convergence behavior during postdisaster emergency operations impede the flow of information on which to base decisions. As a result, certain actions that could be justified at the time they were undertaken appear, in retrospect, to be unnecessary. If better data had been available through improved communications (e.g., a well-developed postdisaster organization plan or reduction in convergence behavior through a more systematic program for coordination), then these orders might never have been given. We will conclude this chapter by detailing some specific decisions made immediately following the three selected disasters because of the imperfect information that existed at the time.

▷ HURRICANE CARLA

1. One of the decisions that had to be made following hurricane Carla was when it would be safe for the evacuees to return home. In order to prevent them from entering their towns too early, roadblocks were placed across highways at key points. During the first few days following Carla, several misleading reports were issued regarding postdisaster conditions. For example, the highway department would report roads "open," meaning they were passable, and this information was relayed to listeners who thought that "open" meant that they could return. On the basis of this misinformation, they would drive for hundreds of miles only to encounter a roadblock outside their city limits. Local officials also contributed to the confusion by raising, lowering, and raising roadblocks again within a few hours. Even reports from such normally authoritative sources as the Department of Public Safety and the National Guard did not always agree as to which cities were open for return.[31]

---

31. Moore et al., ... *And the Winds Blew*, p. 101.

2. The control center at the Texas state Department of Health received numerous requests for help and because quick action was often required, the validity of most reports could not be investigated. For example, in the evening after Carla, a message was delivered requesting water, anti-snake-venom serum, and vaccine for fifty people who were isolated in Port O'Connor. Earlier information had stated that this town had been completely wiped off the map and that there were no inhabitants there. Another request for anti-snake-venom serum and typhoid vaccine for nearby Matagorda City also came into the control center about this time. Since the shortage cost of *not* delivering these items was so much higher than the unnecessary shipping expense if the relayed information was false, a helicopter pilot was requested to fly physicians and supplies to the two cities at dawn the next day. Later that night a telephone call was received from a state Department of Health official in Port Lavaca who had personally inspected the entire area of Port O'Connor and categorically stated that there was no one there except the National Guard. On the basis of this new information, the trip to Port O'Connor was canceled, but a physician did fly to Matagorda City. Upon his return he reported that he could find no one in the town who had made a request for help and that in fact they did not need any supplies.[32]

3. A radio report announced that the 1200 refugees in the Galveston courthouse had been buried when the building collapsed. Immediately teams were organized in Beaumont to dig for the victims. Fortunately, the falsity of the report was established before any of the volunteers drove to Galveston.[33]

▷ WACO AND SAN ANGELO TORNADOES

1. The civilian rescue teams in Waco were at first an unorganized group. Any member lacking some article called out his need, which was picked up and amplified by loudspeaker trucks. The requests for aid were then broadcast by radio, connected to a statewide hookup. During the early stages of recovery in Waco, demands for aid were made without checking as to whether the supplies were actually needed. For example, an officer in command of some 18,000 soldiers asked what aid he could contribute. He was told to "send everything

---

32. Moore et al., . . . *And the Winds Blew*, pp. 100–101.

33. *Ibid.*, p. 101.

you've got," but later discovered that only 200 of his men could actually be used.[34]

2. Since there was no information as to the conditions of hospitals in the area, taxi and ambulance drivers took most of their injured to the downtown hospital, which was swamped, whereas hospitals at greater distances were not even filled.[35]

3. There was no central clearinghouse for information and manpower needs in Waco during the emergency period, so that many people just rushed to the scene of rescue operations to see if they could lend a hand. When they arrived and found it already overcrowded, they left and returned home under the assumption that they could not be used. Twelve hours later, when the first volunteers were exhausted, no replacements could be found.[36]

4. Although there may have been a few examples of actions in San Angelo based on imperfect information, Moore has not singled out any in his book. We can therefore assume that the decision-making process in that city was a good one. The adequate warning, the Civil Defense Plan, and the intact communications enabled the emergency organization to function rapidly and efficiently after the tornado.

▷ ALASKA EARTHQUAKE

Several specific decisions made in Alaska very shortly after the earthquake were based on imperfect information.

1. The Alaskan Air Command was asked to fly six 36-bed mobile hospitals from Juneau to Anchorage, although the number of persons needing medical treatment was not known. The action was taken because the cost of a possible shortage (needing the hospitals in Anchorage but not having them) was obviously considered much greater than the holding expense (shipping the units unnecessarily). There were actually fewer casualties than anticipated, so the units were flown back to Juneau without ever being used.[37]

---

34. Moore, *Tornadoes Over Texas*, p. 13. Fortunately the officer did not take the reply literally and only sent limited manpower.

35. *Ibid.*, p. 23.

36. *Ibid.*, pp. 24–25.

37. "Operation Helping Hand," Headquarters, Alaskan Command, 1964, p. 2.

2. Governor William A. Egan of Alaska announced several days after the quake that Anchorage had more than enough construction workers to handle the repair work and erection of new buildings in the area.[38] In making this statement, the governor was aware that a large proportion of summer construction is done by individuals migrating from the "lower 48," and that much more work could be expected than in past years because of the extensive damage to both public and private dwellings. However, construction could not begin until geological tests were made, SBA loans approved, and building permits issued. During this interim period, there would even be an excess of local construction workers in the area so that the problem of migration would compound the unemployment problem. Assuming that there would be no difficulty in obtaining workers when they were needed,[39] Governor Egan's warning, although misleading, could be justified if the probability of a high storage cost (having unemployed individuals in the area) was considered far greater than the probability of shortage costs (the necessity of raising wages or using other inducements to gain needed construction workers later). In actuality, construction activity began later in the summer than usual, so it was difficult to obtain qualified workers when they were finally needed.

3. A rationing scheme, limiting each automobile owner to only five gallons of gasoline, was undertaken not because of shortages in petroleum but out of fear that many residents would leave the state by road. At the time the rationing decision was made, there was incomplete information on the conditions of the roads; it was later discovered that every highway leading out of Anchorage was impassable. It could be argued that even if the roads were passable and Anchorage officials were not concerned about out-migration, a rationing policy would still be meaningful. If they desired to keep the highways free for critical traffic, then one way of keeping motorists off the road would be to limit their purchase of gasoline.

4. About six hours after the quake the military ordered four mechanized platoons with accompanying bulldozers to attempt to reach Seward by road. Although several radio reports indicated impassable fissures in the 140-mile Anchorage–Seward highway, there was no official confirmation of these announcements. At the same time, no definite word had been heard from

---

38. *Anchorage Daily Times*, April 1, 1964.

39. Immediately following the quake,

Senator Bartlett's office received numerous letters and phone calls from people who offered to help Anchorage dig out and rebuild.

Seward, but it was feared that the town was severely hit; in fact, inability to establish radio or telephone contact with Seward heightened the suspicion that the town had been badly damaged. With planes unable to fly until morning, a relatively high shortage/storage cost ratio dictated the mission despite the small probability of its succeeding. When it was discovered that a number of gaps would have to be filled so that it might take quite a few days to reach Seward, the platoons were ordered to clear the road so that they could evacuate residents from the nearby villages of Girdwood, Alyeska, and Portage.[40] Therefore, despite the inability of the military to reach its original destination, the mission still managed to serve a worthwhile purpose. In fact, if knowledge of the plights of these three small hamlets had been known in advance, the same platoons might have been sent along the road even though there was complete certainty that they would never arrive at Seward.[41]

These examples illustrate the difficulties faced by people required to act with incomplete information at hand. A disaster often implies the need for rapid action even though decisions may only be determined by a combination of guesswork, informed opinion, and intuition.

---

40. They had to span two gaps in the road to Portage with Bailey bridges, clear a dozen snow and rock slides, make numerous road fills, deck a railroad bridge for vehicle use, and cross countless fissures before reaching Portage on Tuesday, April 2.

41. "Operation Helping Hand," pp. 60–61.

| Chapter Five | Short-run

Supply and Demand

Problems

OUR INTEREST in this chapter is focused on the short-run problems of resource allocation following a serious disaster, when the community is likely to be faced with food and housing shortages. During this period it appears that behavior by residents is governed more by a sympathetic concern for others than by normal self-interest. Although long-run profit considerations may be partly responsible for the absence of short-run price increases, the different frame of reference affecting postdisaster actions during the immediate recuperation period is worth stressing.

The bulk of the chapter deals with the housing and food problems in Anchorage and in other disaster areas during the recuperation period. The concluding portion discusses the derived disaster demands caused by the Alaska earthquake, indicating whether the resources were available in the Anchorage area or had to be imported from outside regions. The reader may then be in a better position to appreciate the advantages of stockpiling items to handle emergency problems.

HOUSING PROBLEMS

▷ GENERAL CONCEPTS

A disaster that damages dwellings upsets the equilibrium, which we will assume existed before the event, between supply and demand for housing. It is reasonable to assume that the demand for shelter will cause rents to rise above their predisaster levels, unless everyone whose home was destroyed left the area immediately. It would also theoretically be possible for rents to remain stable even without any out-migration, if people's wealth fell sufficiently as a result of the disaster. The necessary decline in income for this situation to exist would depend upon the number of dwellings destroyed and the elasticity of housing demand with respect to income.

Following extensive destruction of dwellings in a community where no rental vacancies had previously existed, shelter for the homeless must be found. Although public buildings such as schools and churches may serve as uncomfortable emergency quarters for a few nights, the victims will either migrate thereafter to an outlying area where vacant units are available for rent or use part of another family's dwelling either within or outside the disaster zone. Owners with undamaged property will either continue to use their homes entirely for themselves or free some of their space for others by crowding their families into fewer bedrooms. It would be reasonable for them to charge rent for the newly available space under normal economic conditions. Yet disasters, by their nature, seem to generate a different set of motives in the short run from those that would be expected to exist according to the economic theory of an impersonal market. It is not surprising, therefore, to find people going out of their way to aid those who are stricken and homeless without receiving or demanding any monetary compensations from them. It still may be argued that these altruistic actions are economically motivated because the individuals are rewarded by a feeling that they are being useful to the community.

▷ OTHER DISASTERS

Empirical studies of housing problems following limited disasters have concentrated primarily on the means of providing sufficient temporary shelter for evacuees. Data from the disasters to be described indicate the following pattern of behavior:

1. Evacuees generally resist the use of mass public shelters and normally resort to them only when no other alternative is available.
2. Evacuees prefer to reside with families or friends but will choose to stay with complete strangers rather than go to a public shelter.

3. Large numbers of people, unaffected by the disaster, are willing to take in homeless strangers without charging any rent.

4. A majority of the homeless in most disasters can find shelter on their own, even for the first night following the event.

Dutch Floods (1953). The floods affecting coastal regions of Holland in February 1953 required a gradual evacuation of 72,000 persons.[1] It was not unusual for evacuees to have neither friends nor relatives with whom they could stay outside the affected area. Nevertheless, within one or two days, they were able to find shelter with one of the thousands of Dutch citizens volunteering to house flood evacuees. In many communities, more homes were made available than there were displaced persons to fill them. The number of people wanting to house such families is especially significant, for it was known that the arrangement would last for at least a few weeks and perhaps even months; in fact, over 5000 evacuees did not return home for over one year. Because of the length of time necessary to house the flood victims, the Dutch government provided some relief to the host families. All evacuees received a weekly allowance out of which they were expected to compensate their hosts for gas, electricity, food, and so on.[2]

Waco and San Angelo Tornadoes (1953). Following the severe tornadoes that devastated portions of Waco and San Angelo, Texas, in May 1953, many persons were forced to seek emergency housing. Sample data on fifty families who resided temporarily with friends or relatives indicate that in only one case was rent actually paid for makeshift quarters.[3]

Worcester Tornado (1953). On June 9, 1953, an unusually severe tornado swept across the northeast section of Worcester, Massachusetts, leaving in its wake approximately $52 million in damaged property and 1200 individuals homeless.[4] Because the tornado struck Worcester about 5 P.M., officials believed that many of the homeless would require mass shelter for at least the first night until

---

1. Institute for Social Research in the Netherlands, *Studies in Holland Flood Disaster*, 1953, Committee on Disaster Studies, NAS-NRC, Washington, D.C., 1955, p. 8, vol. 1.

2. *Ibid.*, vol. 2, p. 59.

3. Harry E. Moore, *Tornadoes Over Texas*, The University of Texas Press, Austin, 1958, pp. 116–117.

4. Anthony F. C. Wallace, *Tornado in Worcester*, Committee on Disaster Studies, National Academy of Sciences–National Research Council (NAS-NRC), Washington, D.C., November 1954, p. 52.

they were able to make other arrangements. A report on the disaster[5] indicates that about 99.5 per cent of the displaced people found their own accommodations, moving in with friends, relatives, or complete strangers who opened their homes to victims. Of the few who did remain in shelters during the first night, almost all left on the following day to stay in more pleasant surroundings.[6]

▷ ANCHORAGE EXPERIENCE

Vacancies Before the Earthquake

In contrast to the other disaster areas, where few vacancies seem to have existed before the event, Anchorage had a large number of unsold housing units at the time of the quake. According to a survey taken by the FHA at the beginning of 1964, the city had a six-month supply of new units on hand; of the 311 units put in place, only 4 had been sold or rented before construction, and 118 still remained unsold after they had been completed.[7]

A survey sampling approximately 25 per cent of the number of housing units in the Anchorage area happened to have been taken two weeks before the

| *Table 5-1* | VACANCIES IN SELECTED RENTAL PROJECTS IN ANCHORAGE, PRE-EARTHQUAKE (MARCH 1964) |

VACANT UNITS

Type of Project	Total Units	Number	Per cent of Total
FHA-Insured	2152	407	18.9
Conventionally Financed	400	17	4.3
Alaska State Housing Authority	472	1	0.2
TOTAL	3024	425	14.1

Data Source: Charles Ball, economic consultant to Alaska State Housing Authority.

5. Irving Rosow, *Public Authorities in Two Tornadoes*, NAS-NRC, Washington, D.C., November 1954, unpublished manuscript, p. 143.

6. Wallace, *op. cit.*, p. 95.

7. The FHA bases its estimate of oversupply on the percentage of unsold speculative houses. For example, if only 10 per cent remained on the market this would represent a one-month supply of housing; 24 per cent is a three-month supply, and 38 per cent is equivalent to a six-month supply. The 118 unsold units of the 307 that were constructed on speculation represent 38 per cent of the total.

quake. The results in Table 5-1 indicate that nearly one in every seven units was unoccupied as of that date.

This figure is deceiving, however, because it does not distinguish vacancies by type. According to Elmer Gagnon, director of the FHA in Anchorage, very few two-, three-, and four-bedroom apartments have been vacant during the last fifteen years. Since 1952, most multifamily construction has been in the form of efficiency and one-bedroom apartments. Because Anchorage has been a growing area with a larger average family size than that of any other community in the United States, such a building program has produced far too many small units and not enough larger ones.[8]

The rents on apartments are considerably higher in Anchorage than in the "lower 48,"[9] and most of the vacancies are in relatively low-rent classes, a fact that suggests these dwellings are unsatisfactory for living. For example, the walls may be so thin that heating is a problem;[10] therefore, the actual cost during the winter would be considerably higher than the rental price. For these reasons, the high number of vacancies in such units might not necessarily have satisfied all the demand after the quake. On the other hand, in addition to the listed vacancies, several apartments were within one month of completion at the time of the quake. These buildings, located in the western part of Anchorage, were unaffected by the disaster and therefore proved to be an extra source of supply. A number of the units were rented out to earthquake-displaced persons searching for new facilities.

Damage to Houses

Damage to houses was confined primarily to areas within the Anchorage city limits. Following the event a block-by-block external inspection was undertaken by the city in order to estimate future needs. Table 5-2 details the results of this survey by classifying dwelling units according to the extent to which they were damaged. All units needing 60 per cent or more repair were classified as heavily damaged since they were considered either totally destroyed, economically unfeasible for restoration, or unfit for occupancy within a two-year period.

---

8. Personal communication with Elmer Gagnon, February 1965.

9. According to the Census of Housing, the median monthly rent for Anchorage in 1960 was $146 compared to $71 for the continental United States.

10. Thin walls may also increase the noise factor; however, this problem would be minimized if many of the neighboring units were vacant.

Although units with less damage may not have been immediately repaired and hence remained vacant for some time after the quake, they were still considered to be restorable within a one-year period.

Of the 971 heavily damaged units (60 per cent or greater damage), almost half of them, 480, were in apartment houses with more than 40 units. The 219 private homes destroyed were located mainly in the Turnagain area, the high-rent district of Anchorage. It is thus not surprising to find that over three quarters of them were worth more than $30,000, as shown in Table 5-3. These figures are undoubtedly underestimates, for they are based on 1960 census data for blocks most severely affected by the quake. Houses built in the Turnagain area after that date and subsequently destroyed by the earth slides were priced even higher than in 1960.

| *Table 5-2* | EARTHQUAKE DAMAGE TO ANCHORAGE HOUSING STOCK |

Number of Units[a]	Per cent of Damage
921	80–100
50	60–80
26	40–60
35	20–40
11,715	0–20
12,747	

Data Source: Land-use maps, Anchorage City Planning Commission.
[a] Includes 518 trailers, only 5 of which were severely damaged.

| *Table 5-3* | DISTRIBUTION BY VALUE OF PRIVATE HOMES DESTROYED IN ANCHORAGE |

Value of Home in Dollars[a]	Per cent of All Homes Destroyed
Under 15,000	2.3
15,000–19,999	3.8
20,000–24,999	5.0
25,000–29,999	12.3
30,000–34,999	58.6
35,000–39,999	13.8
40,000 and over	4.2
	100.0

Data Source: Federal Housing Administration.
[a] Based on 1960 Census figures.

Relocation of Residents

Most of the homeless stayed with friends for several days while deciding what to do. Those forced to vacate apartments were able to resettle themselves fairly easily because they did not have mortgage problems. Homeowners had a more difficult problem, for they were confused about the government's disaster policy regarding old unpaid mortgages and new ones. Therefore, they remained in the homes of friends or relatives for several weeks until the Federal groups clarified their intentions. A few typical examples will illustrate some of the problems faced by residents who lost their homes as a result of the quake.[11]

One family had worked for seven years on their home while living in the basement and were all set to move upstairs during April 1964 when the earthquake changed their plans. After living with friends in a nearby section of town for several weeks, they were able to find an apartment that satisfied their needs temporarily. A large portion of their old home could still be salvaged and was relocated on property declared geologically sound. By October, the family could move into their newly restored home, which had a thirty-year mortgage instead of the original five-year one.

Another family moved four times before finally resettling in the Anchorage area again. After staying in a room at their local church for several days, they spent a week in an empty house that was still waiting to be rented. During the next several months they used the homes of vacationing friends, and then, in the early fall, they obtained an SBA loan to build their own house. By October, they had moved into the completed basement where they were able to remain during the winter, thanks to the help of friends who loaned them a portable stove to prevent their pipes from freezing. After a year of makeshift living, this family was able to move into the upstairs portion of their new dwelling.

A third family spent the first five days with friends and then moved in with relatives for about one month. During that time, they searched for new quarters and were able to locate a small house in town where they lived until Christmas. They then moved to a place in the area where they had lived; there they intended to stay until they could rebuild their own house.

These incidents illustrate the importance of friends and relatives in alleviating housing difficulties in Anchorage following the earthquake. Practically all

---

11. *Anchorage Daily Times*, March 26, 1965, pp. 41–42. This issue of the newspaper, entitled "The Incredible Year," described the state of recovery in Anchorage and the surrounding area one year following the Good Friday earthquake.

residents faced with shelter problems utilized private homes until they could calmly decide on a future course of action.

Changes in Rents

An unofficial survey of postquake rents by the FHA and real estate dealers showed that only slight changes occurred during the recovery period. Real estate agents claimed that in many cases the rents decreased after the quake, though they also noted several examples of slight increases. The FHA in their analysis claimed that no change in rents took place after the disaster. At first sight, these facts may be surprising to the economist. Certainly vacancies existed, but the units were generally inferior in quality to the dwellings destroyed and therefore did not satisfy the needs of persons seeking new residences. Normally an increase in demand would have increased the price of the better dwellings. This in turn would have induced some tenants to leave their homes and move into the smaller or inferior units, whose rents would then also have risen. This did not occur in Anchorage, partly because most displaced residents stayed temporarily with friends and relatives. Thus immediate pressure on rents from the dispossessed was less than it would have been otherwise. At the same time, real estate offices were generally reluctant to list any property or rental units priced substantially above predisaster figures. Immediately following the earthquake, local realtors spontaneously pooled sources of information on available space where people could relocate. These agents attempted to keep the lid on prices during the recuperation period both because they did not want to charge high rents to the unfortunate residents and because they felt that any shortage in housing would be short-lived. In a sense, real estate agents were attempting to impose informal short-term rent controls in the area.

*F*OOD PROBLEMS

▷ OTHER DISASTERS

Existing literature on other disasters than the Alaska earthquake has generally not dealt with food problems during the emergency period, except to refer briefly to meals offered hungry residents by Red Cross and Civil Defense

groups. This is not surprising since the psychological and sociological orienta-
tion of these studies precludes much interest in such economic considerations
as food prices, not to mention the fact that, unlike Alaska, almost all domestic
disaster areas have been close enough to other food markets that supplies could
easily be provided. In fact, the Red Cross claims that in its entire history of
disaster experience it has rarely faced a problem of actual food shortages in this
country and, in fact, has noted only two recent cases of potential shortages: one
following hurricane Audrey (1957) and the other, after the California floods
(1964). By shortage of a particular commodity, we mean an actual demand for
the good when its stock is depleted. Some perspective may be gained by looking
at how these and several other disaster areas handled their food problems.

San Francisco Earthquake (1906).[12] Even after the severe San Francisco earthquake and fire in April 1906, food shortages never occurred. In that catastrophe,
San Francisco was isolated from nearby communities, more because transportation facilities were lacking than because they had been disrupted. The city
had very little food on hand, for it normally received supplies on a daily basis;
any available stocks were destroyed during the fire, which burned the entire
wholesale-retail section of the city. Although over 300,000 homeless residents
needed food, the Citizens' Relief Committee and the Army jointly were able to
round up enough vehicles to meet all needs.

Waco Tornado (1953).[13] During the first few days following the severe tornado
that hit Waco, many retailers freely distributed their goods to disaster victims
to meet their needs. Merchants took this action without even asking for any
assurance that they would be reimbursed by the persons receiving items or by
any governmental or private agency. These store owners were obviously not
motivated by their ordinary goal of selling merchandise for a profit; rather,
they operated in the role of citizens aiding other citizens in an effort to meet a
grave emergency.

Hurricane Audrey (1957).[14] The experience of Cameron, Louisiana, following
hurricane Audrey is interesting since potential shortages did exist. All stores in
the town were actually blown down, and until electricity was restored to the
area nine weeks later, there was no refrigeration in homes or restaurants. It was
thus necessary for the Army and Air Force to set up mass feeding centers during

---

12. Maj. Gen. A. W. Greely, *Earthquake
in California: April 18, 1906,* Government Printing Office, Washington, D.C.,
1906, pp. 25–27.

13. Moore, *op. cit.,* p. 43.
14. Personal discussion with Mona
Murphy and Vernon Zimmerman of the
American Red Cross, May 1965.

the emergency period.[15] Local store owners still continued to order food from their normal suppliers 50 miles away though, in fact, the owners did not actually handle the goods. Instead, the Red Cross acted as a middleman by reimbursing the local merchants and distributing the items to the feeding centers. In this way the owners remained in business despite the unusual disruption of their market and the physical destruction of their stores. The merchants' margin was their normal mark-up on wholesale prices.

Skopje, Yugoslavia, Earthquake (1963).[16] The earthquake that destroyed most of Skopje only slightly damaged the surrounding areas. Peasants from the small outlying villages continued to bring their produce to the sites of the former market places in Skopje and deposited the goods on the ground. No prices were charged; all food was free.

California Floods (1964).[17] In December 1964, the small town of Orleans, California (population 500), was threatened by a potentially serious food shortage when floods isolated it from the rest of the state. The flooding severed the access highway to Orleans at both ends of town, and all supplies had to be carried in by helicopter for almost nine weeks. The Red Cross handled the distribution of food supplies for the entire period because the sole local merchant was unwilling to go back into business, even with Red Cross help. An actual food shortage never did develop, but serious potential threats occurred whenever bad weather prohibited helicopter flights. Because food was obtained by means of written purchase orders enabling those in need to buy supplies from local merchants, prices did not operate to equilibrate supply and demand. This is the normal Red Cross method of handling food problems.

▷ ANCHORAGE EXPERIENCE

Transportation Pattern

Transportation considerations are much more vital to the Anchorage economy than to any city in the continental United States, for the distance between its

---

15. The food service teams moved into the area at Red Cross request. Red Cross not only provided all the food but reimbursed the military for the out-of-pocket costs of maintaining troops in Louisiana.

16. Agency for International Development, "Disaster Information Memo: Yugoslavia—1963 Skopje Earthquake," July 1966, mimeographed, p. 2.

17. Personal discussion with Mona Murphy and Vernon Zimmerman of the American Red Cross, May 1965.

nearest source of supply, Seattle, is over 1500 miles. Before the quake, practically all nonperishable items were carried by boat to the port of Seward or Whittier and transported by the Alaska Railroad into Anchorage, 160 miles away. Perishable items such as fresh vegetables and meat were generally brought up by truck or plane; items in short supply were often rushed by one of these faster carriers. It usually takes eight days from Seattle to Anchorage by ship, four days by truck, and three hours by jet aircraft.

For the first few weeks following the quake, the bulk of food shipments to Alaska was transported by either truck or plane. Not only was speed essential to minimize shortages, but water transportation facilities had been damaged. Seward's waterfront was totally destroyed, and broken sections of the Alaska Railroad prevented the ice-free port of Whittier from being used during the first two weeks of April, even though its harbor was unscathed. However, the port of Anchorage, despite some damage to facilities, could still handle a limited number of vessels after the ice was broken.

Safeway stores report that during the first seven weeks after the quake all produce, cheese, eggs, butter, and margarine were carried over the highway rather than by water. Shipments of frozen food and ice cream were sent by truck rather than ship during the first two weeks of April, after which normal water shipments were restored. The same pattern seems to have been true for the smaller Anchorage stores that had received goods from Seattle.

Shortages After the Quake

Because the warehouse of only one of the two wholesale grocers survived serious damage, he was the only effective supplier of dry and canned goods to the area after the event. The other firm was able to salvage some of its dry stock, such as baby food and frozen food, which it stored in several empty refrigerated trucks that had made deliveries to Anchorage stores just before the disaster. Other perishable items were brought to warehouses at Fort Richardson and at Elmendorf Air Force Base.

Despite a number of emergency plane shipments of groceries, potential shortages still existed in the area. This deficiency resulted from both the destruction of large quantities of goods and an unusual demand for certain items. However, the community appeared to respond positively to advertisements in the Anchorage newspapers and verbal warnings not to hoard necessities but to purchase instead the minimum quantity they would need. Cigarettes were apparently not considered a necessity in the context of survival because individuals did not hesitate to stock up on their favorite brand, thus creating a temporary shortage during the immediate postquake period. Because families were content with substitute products (e.g., apple juice instead of orange juice) when the store ran out of their initial choice, supplies on hand proved adequate. Table 5-4 lists certain groups of items that were in high demand following the quake and, consequently, in relatively short supply.

Table 5-4	ITEMS IN HIGH DEMAND IN ANCHORAGE AFTER THE EARTH-QUAKE

Item	*Reason for Increased Demand*
Main Meals	
Beef stew	Limited cooking facilities were available
Corned beef hash	after the disaster, and these dishes could,
Canned spaghetti	if necessary, be eaten cold
Canned luncheon meats (e.g., Treat, Spam)	
Vienna sausage	
Pork and beans	
Canned Juices	
Orange juice	Contamination of water supply necessitated drinking substitutes
Grapefruit juice	sitated drinking substitutes
Apple juice	
Blend	
Pineapple juice	
Hawaiian juice	
Presweetened Dry Cereals	
Frosted flakes	Easy to prepare, no sugar needed
Sugar flakes	
Cold-water All	Hot water shortage. All was the only detergent that advertised that it could clean clothes in cold water
Bleaches	
Clorox	Decontaminates the water supply and makes it potable.
Purex	makes it potable.
Flashlights and Batteries	Substitute for electric lights
Paper Items	
Plates, cups, forks, spoons	No washing facilities for dishes
Charcoal	Utilized for cooking since stoves could not be used
Cigarettes	Possible fear that shortages would result after several days. Some hoarding.
Snack Items	
Cookies, candies, crackers	No preparation needed, satisfies hunger pains
Electric Light Bulbs	Needed four to five weeks after the quake when electric power was restored

Data Source: J. B. Gottstein and Company, wholesale grocers.

Changes in Prices

During normal times, an increase in demand for an item accompanied by a decrease in supply would lead to some increase in the item's price. Yet the prices remained stable following the earthquake, despite the apparent existence of these two conditions.[18] A combination of factors may have been responsible for producing price stability.

1. MERCHANTS KNEW THAT ANY SHORTAGES IN GOODS WOULD BE TEMPORARY

Because the Federal government was prepared to fly emergency supplies by military or commercial air transport and because the Alcan highway with its extension to Anchorage was only slightly damaged and there would be little difficulty in hauling goods up by truck, merchants knew that it would be senseless to create ill-will among the residents by temporary price increases for the first few weeks.

2. ACCURATE MARKET INFORMATION MAY HAVE BEEN UNAVAILABLE OR TOO COSTLY TO OBTAIN

Sellers on the market may have kept their prices stable during the period immediately following the disaster because they had little information on either the existing supply of goods in the community or a change in patterns of demand caused by a loss in wealth. In the absence of these data and because of the high cost of obtaining it, they may have preferred not to take any action at all.

3. STORE OWNERS FELT THAT ANY PRICE INCREASE WOULD TEND TO ACCELERATE EMIGRATION FROM ANCHORAGE

People who had suffered extensive damage to home and business were in no position to accept higher food bills with equanimity, particularly when they were uncertain as to what role the Federal government would play in helping

---

18. In theory it is impossible for prices to remain stable if demand increases and supply declines, unless some form of rationing is instituted. In effect, that process is exactly what occurred after the quake but on a voluntary basis: people bought only the minimal quantity needed and were willing to purchase substitute products when the desired one was not available, rather than bidding prices up through the black market.

them to recoup their losses. From a long-run point of view, the stores would want to keep as many Anchorage customers in town as they could.

4. A COMMITTEE ON ECONOMIC STABILIZATION WAS ESTABLISHED UNDER THE OFFICE OF EMERGENCY PLANNING TO MONITOR WAGE AND PRICE CHANGES

Surveys were made of pre- and postquake differences in food prices to determine whether any inflationary trend had developed because of shortages. Stores may have feared that government controls would be introduced if they permitted food prices to get outside normal lines, and, in fact, evidence supporting this point has been obtained through discussions with persons from the Office of Emergency Planning.

5. AFTER THE EARTHQUAKE THERE WAS A FEELING IN THE COMMUNITY THAT EVERYONE HAD TO MAKE SOME SACRIFICES IN ORDER TO HELP ANCHORAGE REBUILD

The natural disaster brought individuals in the community closer together than they had ever been before, and as a result, normal impersonal market phenomena were colored by personal feelings.

Although the first four factors undoubtedly influenced price behavior, we would argue that the fifth reason was largely responsible for the noninflationary trend, particularly during the first few weeks in April. As we have pointed out from studies on other disasters, community feelings largely dominate individual actions during the immediate recovery period. Store owners with largely undamaged stocks were willing to sacrifice some profit on these goods to help those who had suffered losses.

Evidence to support this point was gleaned from talking with a Safeway manager in Anchorage who was given the authority to change prices as he saw fit. On some items for which there was great demand following the quake and a potential shortage, he even lowered prices rather than raise them as economic logic would dictate. For example, a can of orange juice normally selling for $.55 was reduced to $.34 during the first two weeks of April.[19] No advertising announced these reductions; the housewife simply saw the new price on the item as she took it from the shelf. In normal times, the consumer would have purchased large quantities of such goods, knowing that the low price would be

---

19. Personal discussion with Howard Trombley, manager of Spenard Safeway Store, Anchorage, February 1965.

temporary. From talks with Anchorage residents, it seems that, despite the absence of direct controls, hoarding never did occur, primarily because of a concern for other people's needs.[20]

During the first two months after the disaster, the trucking companies in Seattle also cooperated by lowering their freight charges so that they were the same as rates for water transportation. These reductions were only for items that could not be shipped by boat because of space limitations or the need for rapid delivery.

Table 5-5 presents the Safeway prices of items both in high postdisaster demand and comprising the normal marketbasket used by the Bureau of Labor Statistics in computing the food component for the Consumer Price Index. Prices are listed for the Monday preceding the earthquake, for the two consecutive Mondays following it, and for biweekly periods thereafter through the middle of June.[21] During the month of April, Safeway refrained from raising its Anchorage prices when normal market advances were suggested,[22] by May, when management decided that the city was no longer in an emergency state, increases were put into effect on these items.

Conclusions from Short-Term Food Experience

Several conclusions can be drawn from this study of food problems in the Anchorage area after the Good Friday earthquake.

1. Despite emergency plane shipments, the threat of shortages of certain goods existed in the area during the first few weeks following the disaster. Not only were large quantities of food destroyed, but certain items experienced unusual demand because of damage to public utilities; for example the need arose for canned juice as a result of a contaminated water supply.

---

20. An interesting contrast to this post-disaster attitude may be found in the large amount of sugar hoarding following World War II when fear of a potential shortage existed. In that case, each individual was concerned with his own needs rather than with what his large purchases of sugar would do to the aggregate stock. See *Congressional Record*, 66th Congress, First Session, p. 6762 and Second Session, pp. 943–44.

21. The Bureau of Labor Statistics and the Agricultural Experiment Station undertook a series of surveys on food prices in five Alaskan cities (Anchorage, Fairbanks, Kodiak, Seward, and Valdez) from April through September, 1964. They found that prices remained relatively stable except in the outlying towns of Kodiak and Seward, where higher transportation costs led to increases for some items during the immediate post-quake period.

22. A normal market advance represents a price increase resulting from changes in market conditions for the item throughout the country; market declines (i.e., lower prices) were *never* discontinued after the quake.

| Table 5-5 | PRE- AND POSTEARTHQUAKE RETAIL FOOD PRICES IN ANCHORAGE FOR SELECTED ITEMS, MARCH 23–JUNE 15, 1964 |

PRICE IN DOLLARS[a]

Food Item	Unit	March 23[b]	March 30[c]	April 6[c]	April 20	May 4	May 18	June 1	June 15
Normal Marketbasket Goods									
Bread, Mrs. Wright's White Standard Large Loaf	22½ oz.	0.47	0.47	0.47	0.47	0.47	0.47	0.47	0.47
Milk, Fresh, Lucerne	qt.	0.45	0.43	0.43	0.43	0.43	0.43	0.43	0.43
Eggs, large, Grade AA Cream of the Crop	doz.	0.77	0.77	0.75	0.75	0.75	0.75	0.75	0.74
Coffee, Edwards	lb.	0.83	0.83	0.83	0.83	0.83	0.87	0.87	0.87
High-demand Goods									
Canned beef stew	24 oz.	0.65	0.65	0.65	0.65	0.65	0.69	0.69	0.69
Pream	7 oz.	0.65	0.65	0.65	0.65	0.65	0.65	0.65	0.65
Grapefruit juice, Townhouse	46 oz. can	0.63	0.63	0.63	0.63	0.69	0.69	0.69	0.69
Cigarettes	Carton—all brands and sizes	2.79	2.79	2.79	2.79	2.79	2.79	2.79	2.79

Data Source: Safeway stores.
[a] Underscored numbers indicate price changes.
[b] Monday preceding quake.
[c] Successive Mondays following quake.

2. The public responded to advertisements and public warnings not to hoard necessities and were willing to use substitute products if the store ran out of their initial choices.

3. Retail stores kept food prices stable and even lowered a few of them during the first month following the quake. A feeling of community responsibility and the knowledge that any shortage would be temporary seem to have been largely responsible for this action.

*D*EMAND FOR SPECIFIC ITEMS IN ANCHORAGE[23]

It is highly likely that physical damage to an area will trigger an increase in demand for specific items. This section will detail these so-called "derived disaster demands" caused by the Alaska earthquake and specify whether the resources were available in the Anchorage area or had to be imported from regions outside the disaster zone.

Auxiliary Generators. Destruction of power lines in many parts of Anchorage necessitated the use of emergency generators at several of the local hospitals. Elmendorf Air Force Base used over forty auxiliary power units to restore electricity and light despite crumbled masonry, shattered light fixtures, and broken glass. In practically all the outlying towns electric power was either completely cut off or drastically curtailed during the first few days after the quake. The one major exception was the port of Whittier, where electricity was restored in six hours and water was running in ten. On the other hand, on Easter Sunday nine 30-kilowatt generators were flown into Seward to provide emergency power for its hospital, and two smaller 1.5-kilowatt generators were furnished for the airfield control facilities.

Flashlight Batteries. Since the sun set within an hour after the quake, flashlights and extra batteries were needed almost immediately. One Anchorage resident volunteered 2000 batteries that he was able to salvage from his store, but more still had to be flown up from Seattle.

---

23. The information in this section was obtained from "Operation Helping Hand," Headquarters, Alaskan Command, 1964, and from articles in the *Anchorage Daily Times* and *Anchorage Daily News*.

Heat. With many houses badly damaged, heat became a scarce commodity in most areas. Therefore, it is not surprising that a number of space heaters were ordered from the "lower 48." The Navy and Red Cross also flew over 1000 blankets from Seattle to Kodiak the day following the quake.

Bulldozers. Highway destruction spurred the demand for bulldozers and snow cats to clear the debris and make the roads passable. The most pressing need for this equipment was on the Anchorage-Seward highway, where the military was attempting to reach Seward by road six hours after the quake.

Water. Sewer facilities were severely damaged in almost all areas, thus contaminating the water supply. In Anchorage, as many as thirty-three water trailers at hospitals, in school yards, and at major public buildings provided water for the residents. This equipment was obtained from the Fort Richardson water purification plant. Similar trailers and purification units were flown from Anchorage to the outlying villages.

Typhoid Protection and Water Purification. Fear of contamination from the damaged sewers necessitated typhoid shots to 24,000 Anchorage residents, with the serum and injection needles shipped from Fairbanks. The need for safeguarding the drinking water also induced an increase in demand for halazone and other purification tablets.

Pipe. Serious damage to underground sewerage facilities in the Anchorage area triggered a large order of aluminum piping from the "lower 48." To provide water to the residents, large sections of this piping (9 miles) coupled with garden and fire hosing (12.5 miles) were laid directly on the ground. Although the system served its purpose well during the summer, it was necessary to restore the underground facilities by September to prevent freezing of the pipes when winter set in.

Toilet Facilities. Damaged toilet facilities necessitated an emergency order of 1000 folding camp stools and 100,000 plastic refuse bags. To many people, these two items became the symbol of postquake Anchorage, since there were so many of the portable outhouses around the town.

The availability of military supplies (e.g., generators, water trailers, and bulldozers) greatly facilitated emergency operations during the immediate recovery period. However, the localized nature of the disaster made it easy to import demanded items that were not available, although there was some delay between the recognition of the need for certain resources and their actual arrival.

RECAPITULATION

Most problems of supply and demand facing an area hit by a natural disaster are short-term in nature because of the aid forthcoming from outside regions. Even when the threat of shortages does exist, the concern of residents in the community for the plight of others helps to minimize serious problems during the emergency period.

From the economic point of view, it is important to note that postdisaster behavior by individuals helps to eliminate a source of demand for some commodities, thereby tending to keep prices lower than they would be if the same conditions of scarcity arose in a more normal, impersonal market situation. For example, if people remain with friends and relatives, a large demand for housing is temporarily taken off the market, thus minimizing any pressure on rents. Possible food shortages are avoided for the same reason: residents respond to urgings not to hoard and are easily satisfied with substitute products when their first choice is out of stock. Realtors and store owners are also hesitant to raise rents or food prices during the emergency period; in fact, selective reductions are often put into effect temporarily.

Naturally, the restraining actions on the part of both consumers and merchants are affected by future expectations. Because the availability of outside aid tends to make supply very elastic, shortages of resources are felt to be short lived. This promise of support by nonaffected regions is yet another element in the pattern of disaster response indicating that economic behavior during the recuperation period is influenced by sociological and psychological factors.

Part III

LONG-TERM RECOVERY:
EMPIRICAL EVIDENCE

Chapter Six | Planning for Recovery:

The Special Problem

of Damage Assessment

ONE OF the most difficult problems following a major disaster is assessing the value of physical damage to the stricken area. Both the variety of the losses and the initial uncertainties as to the actual needs for reconstruction, which are based on necessarily peripheral observations make it very difficult to arrive at accurate figures. And yet dollar values must be quoted, not only to satisfy newspaper reporters but also to determine if the region qualifies as a Federal disaster area and thus is eligible for aid under PL 875, which authorizes Federal funds for temporary repair of Federal facilities damaged in a disaster.

Unfortunately, little information is available on what cost criteria are the bases of such damage estimates, so that it is difficult to meaningfully interpret the published figures. If the estimate is based on the original cost of a building, it will normally be lower than if replacement cost is used. In the case of the earthquake in Alaska, most estimates made after April 1964 represented current restoration costs since Federal aid was allocated with this criterion in mind; however, some inconsistencies in damage and expenditure estimates over time may still exist.

The unit of analysis also becomes critical in interpreting damage reports and understanding the meaning of the word *disaster*. A figure of $100 million destruction from an earthquake may be highly significant for the towns suffering losses, but will appear to be relatively small when viewed from a broader economic scale. Specifically, although several communities in Alaska received severe damage on a per capita basis and the losses cut sharply into the state's economic base, the destruction was only a fractional portion of national income. Thus the Federal government did not hesitate to extend generous aid to the state, particularly as Alaska depended so heavily on Federal expenditures for its economic survival in normal times.

At the outset of this chapter we may distinguish between three categories of losses following a disaster. The first is losses to the public sector, which include impaired utilities (e.g., sewer, electricity, and telephone) as well as damaged Federal, state, and local structures and roads. Normally, preliminary estimates of damage to the public sector are revised several times because the Federal government must determine how much money to allocate for specific reconstruction projects. The second is losses to the private sector, which include not only physical damage to homes and businesses caused in the disaster but also the indirect economic injury reflected in the abnormally low operating levels of businesses whose facilities are being restored.[1] Although some crude initial gross estimates are made for the private sector, they are rarely revised over time because the Federal government is specifically concerned with individual rather than with aggregate expenditures. The third category of losses can be labeled *shortfall of revenue*, or the decline of state and Federal government receipts from various taxes and levies.

Damage can be broken down in a number of different ways depending upon the interest of the study. The above classification of losses most clearly reflects the role of Federal, state, and local agencies in postdisaster operations and is particularly relevant to Alaska because of the large number of Federally owned or operated facilities there. If one wished to examine the composition of industrial losses, damage from a disaster could be classified by structure, contents, and economic injury.[2]

This chapter will focus on damage figures and actual expenditures resulting from the Alaska earthquake of 1964. Estimates of losses to the public sector and the forthcoming Federal aid for restoring these facilities will first be

---

1. Of course, industrial concerns who are spared any damage to their facilities may have a higher level of production immediately after the disaster than before. Therefore, to obtain the net economic injury to the community, such gains must be subtracted from other firms' losses.

2. For a description of this type of classification see Robert Kates, "Industrial Flood Losses: Damage Estimation in the Lehigh Valley," *Department of Geography Research Paper No. 98*, University of Chicago, 1965, Chap. 1.

discussed. An analysis of losses to the private sector and available aid to individuals through agencies such as the Small Business Administration will follow. We will then briefly present figures on shortfall of revenue incurred by the state with the resulting aid provided by Washington. The concluding section will relate the pattern of estimates and expenditures in Alaska with the figures from other natural disasters in the United States.

LOSSES AND AID TO THE PUBLIC SECTOR

▷ DAMAGE ESTIMATES

Gross Figures

After observing the magnitude and duration of the Good Friday earthquake in Alaska, seismologists noted that it was almost a miracle that the damage and loss of lives were so small. Since the disaster occurred at low tide, the seismic seawaves generated by the quake produced far less damage to certain areas than they might have. Potential fires were also kept to a minimum. In Anchorage, for example, there were no fires fueled by oil tanks, so that destruction in the area was limited almost exclusively to the direct effect of the shocks. The small communities of Seward and Valdez, on the other hand, did suffer substantial losses from fire and seismic sea waves triggered by the quake.

Although there was no doubt that losses were large enough for the region to be declared a Federal disaster area, it was still necessary to produce some estimates to substantiate this classification. In early April the Office of Emergency Planning (OEP), the disaster coordinating group of the Federal government, indicated that total state and local property damage might be as high as $244 million. By June, gross totals had been revised to $149 million after detailed surveys and soil tests revealed that the land was more stable than had been originally thought. Estimates on replacement cost to damaged Federal facilities, on the other hand, remained relatively stable over this period, only dropping from $74 to $71 million.

Federal Facilities

Table 6-1 presents a more detailed breakdown of estimates of losses to facilities operated by the various Federal agencies in Alaska made approximately six weeks after the quake. The Department of Defense estimated destruction of barracks and other property at Fort Richardson, Elmendorf Air Force Base, and Kodiak Naval Station to be about $35.6 million. Within several weeks after the quake, battered structures were being rebuilt or restored, cracked runways at Elmendorf were being repaved, and the shaky docks at Kodiak Naval Station were reinforced.

Damage to the Alaska Railroad accounted for over $30 million of the loss estimate provided by the Department of Interior.[3] Before the quake, most goods from Seattle arrived by ship at Seward, the terminus of the railroad, and were shipped by train along the 411-mile line to a number of communities, including Anchorage and Fairbanks. Primary damage to the railroad was incurred on the 64-mile stretch between Seward and Portage, where restoration work took almost one and one half years. Because the track from Whittier to Anchorage (62 miles) was only partially damaged, it was reopened to full tonnage at slow speeds a little over three weeks after the quake. Similarly, the disaster caused

Table 6-1	ESTIMATED DAMAGE TO FEDERAL FACILITIES IN ALASKA, MAY 1964

Federal Agency	Primary Loss	Estimated Damage ($Million)
Dept. of Defense	Barracks and other facilities at Fort Richardson, Elmendorf Air Force Base, and Kodiak Naval Station	35.6
Dept. of Interior	Alaska Railroad	31.5
Dept. of Commerce	Damaged facilities	1.8
Federal Aviation Agency	Facilities at Anchorage International Airport	1.3
Dept. of Health, Education, and Welfare	Public Health Service, Native Hospital	.6
General Services Administration	Office supplies and equipment	.4
TOTAL		71.2

Data Source: Office of Emergency Planning, May 11, 1964.

3. The remaining estimated expenditures by the Department of Interior were for the repair and restoration of Indian villages damaged by the quake as well as for the restoration of the Federally owned Eklutna hydroelectric power dam. At the time the initial figures were being compiled by the OEP (May 1964), the Bureau of Reclamation had not conducted any detailed survey of the damage to this dam. For this reason it initially thought that repair work would cost only $230,000; more detailed investigations made during the next two months revealed that restoration expenses might run as high as $4 million.

little damage to the Anchorage–Fairbanks portion of the line, which was operational within days. Repair of the railroad involved not only laying new tracks and restoring bridges but probing underwater for salvageable equipment as well.

The other major items in Table 6-1 refer to the Federal Aviation Agency estimate on damage to its own facilities at Anchorage International Airport and the Bureau of Public Roads figures on expenditures for repairs to structures damaged by the quake.

State and Local Facilities

Figures broken down by community on changes in estimates of damage to state and local public facilities are shown in Table 6-2. The initial estimates, made by the state within one week after the quake, project both the minimum and maximum costs of the disaster to each of the affected towns.[4] These initial ranges are seen to lie surprisingly close to the more accurate June figures except for the early inflated highway damage total. A closer look at the data indicates that, although Anchorage suffered the largest physical loss, its per capita damage

$Table\ 6\text{-}2$	CHANGES IN DAMAGE ESTIMATE TO STATE AND LOCAL PUBLIC FACILITIES AND PER CAPITA FIGURES BY COMMUNITY

DAMAGE ESTIMATE (*$Million*)

Community and Environs	Population[a] (1964)	April 4[b] Max.	April 4[b] Min.	June 10[c]	Per Capita Damage[d] in Dollars
Anchorage	94,700	80.7	56.7	63.6	670
Homer	1,500	.1	.1	.2	130
Kodiak Island	8,200	5.6	3.8	2.3	280
Seward	1,600	6.8	4.7	9.6	6,000
Valdez	1,000	4.1	2.5	3.2	3,200
Other	—	2.0	1.0	1.6	—
State of Alaska					
Public Buildings	—	16.1	16.1	14.8	—
Highways	—	111.1	111.1	55.0	—
TOTAL		226.4	195.9	150.3	

a NAS-NRC Committee on the Alaska Earthquake.
b "Alaska Earthquake Disaster Damage Report," State of Alaska, Office of the Governor, April 4, 1964.
c Office of Emergency Planning.
d Based on June 10 damage estimates.

---

4. It should be noted that the maximum damage to state and local facilities estimated by the state several days after the quake, $226 million, is still $18 million less than the OEP figure presented earlier in this chapter.

was considerably less than that of either Seward or Valdez. In line with the discussion on per capita losses in Chapter 3, it is not surprising that Anchorage recovered far more rapidly than either of the other two villages, both of which had to be rebuilt practically from scratch.[5]

▷ ACTUAL EXPENDITURES

On the basis of the damage estimates, Federal groups were allocated funds for repairing and restoring their public facilities. Some changes from normal post-disaster procedures were implemented through special amendments to the Alaska Omnibus Act, passed in 1959 after Alaska assumed statehood.[6] For example, the expenditures for repair and reconstruction of damaged state highways outside the national forest under the Federal-aid program had normally been equally divided by the Federal and state governments. The amended act authorized that funds for repairs be allocated on the same basis as for new

| *Table 6-3* | COMPARISON OF ESTIMATED AND ACTUAL EXPENDITURES TO REPAIR PUBLIC FACILITIES IN ALASKA |

Agency	Use of Funds	*Estimated Expenditures, August 1964 ($Million)*	*Revised Expenditures, May 1966 ($Million)*
Dept. of Defense	Repair of damaged military facilities	35.6	35.6
Office of Emergency Planning	Expenditures under PL 875	82.0	58.0
Dept. of Housing and Urban Development	Urban renewal projects in various communities	27.4	27.4
Bureau of Public Roads	Repairs of highways in Federal-aid system	65.0	37.5
Alaska Railroad	Restoration of railroad to pre-quake standards	30.5	27.0
Bureau of Indian Affairs	Repair and rebuilding of Indian villages	1.4	.4
Bureau of Reclamation	Repair of Eklutna Dam	4.0	3.0
TOTAL		245.9	188.9

Data Source: Individual Federal agencies.

---

5. For a discussion of the reconstruction patterns of Anchorage and the outlying villages, see Chap. 8.

6. This act amended certain laws of the United States and provided for transition grants over a five-year period to assist Alaska in accomplishing an orderly transition from territorial status to statehood.

roads.[7] Therefore, in Alaska the Federal share of highway reconstruction jumped to 94.9 per cent.[8]

The Department of Housing and Urban Development was authorized by another Alaska Omnibus Act amendment to provide grants, not exceeding $25 million, for urban renewal projects in the various communities in south-central Alaska severely damaged by the quake.[9] If additional funds for this work were needed, they could be provided by the Office of Emergency Planning under PL 875.

In Table 6-3 we have compared the estimated expenditures as of August 1964 with the actual expenditures by May 1966, when all reconstruction except for urban renewal projects was completed. The OEP used PL 875 funds not only to restore state and local public facilities but also to repair structures owned by some Federal agencies such as the FAA and HEW. Some agencies, such as the Bureau of Public Roads, were given funds for rebuilding Federal facilities to meet current rather than prequake standards. For this reason, the August figure with respect to projected highway expenditures is $10 million above the June damage estimate in Table 6-2. The figures indicate that every agency involved with public projects spent either the same or less than they had originally anticipated. Perhaps the best explanation of this phenomenon is that reconstruction needs cannot be estimated with certainty before a great deal of work has been completed; accordingly there is an incentive to overestimate costs, for it is much easier to return unused funds than to obtain more aid.

▷ PUBLIC LAW 875—ALLOCATIONS AND EXPENDITURES

The most detailed breakdown of postdisaster relief in Alaska may be obtained from the expenditures under PL 875. This legislation authorizes the Federal government to provide funds "to repair essential public facilities in major disasters, and to foster the development of such State and local organizations

---

7. "1964 Amendments to the Alaska Omnibus Act," Public Law 88-451, 88th Congress, August 1964, S. 2881, Sec. 3.

8. Bureau of Public Roads expenditures on new Federal-aid highways as a proportion of total costs increase directly with the number of Federal facilities in the area and indirectly with the state's population. Because the U.S. government plays a prominent role in sparsely populated Alaska's economy, it is clear that the state would have to spend only a small fraction of the funds required to build these highways.

9. "1964 Amendments to the Alaska Omnibus Act," Sec. 4.

and plans to cope with major disasters as may be necessary."[10] The severity of the quake led the OEP to interpret the provisions of this legislation rather broadly in making allocations under the act. Rather than simply authorize funds for temporary restoration of public facilities, as was the intent of the act, the OEP went two steps further: They permitted not only permanent repair or

Table 6-4

DAMAGE ESTIMATES, ALLOCATIONS OF FUNDS, AND ACTUAL EXPENDITURES UNDER PL 875 FOR RESTORATION OF PUBLIC FACILITIES IN ALASKA BY TYPE OF PROPERTY

	Damage Estimate, June 1964 ($Millions)	Allocations of Funds, June 1964 ($Millions)	Estimated Expenditures, May 1966 ($Millions)
Public Utilities	41.4	27.0	12.6
Public Buildings	14.2	11.4	9.3
Education Facilities	10.4	10.4	7.8
Transportation Facilities[a]	25.4	22.0	19.4
Debris Clearance	3.6	4.7	3.8
Other[b]	.3	6.5	5.1
TOTAL	95.3	82.0	58.0

Data Source: Office of Emergency Planning.
[a] Does not include damage and expenditures for highways.
[b] Includes emergency measures, and damage and planning surveys.

Table 6-5

DAMAGE ESTIMATES, ALLOCATIONS OF FUNDS, AND ACTUAL EXPENDITURES UNDER PL 875 FOR RESTORATION OF PUBLIC FACILITIES IN ALASKA AND PER CAPITA EXPENDITURES BY COMMUNITY

	Population (1964)	Damage Estimate, June 1964 ($Millions)	Allocations of Funds, June 1964 ($Millions)	Estimated Expenditures, May 1966 ($Millions)	Per Capita Expenditures in Dollars
Anchorage and Environs	94,700	63.6	48.4	18.3	190
Homer	1,500	.2	.3	.5	330
Kodiak	8,200	2.3	2.7	2.7	330
Seward	1,600	9.6	10.3	6.7	4,200
Valdez	1,000	3.2	3.4	7.0	7,000
Other	—	1.6	1.1	2.1	—
State of Alaska (Public Buildings)	—	14.8	15.8	20.7	—
TOTAL		95.3	82.0	58.0	

Data Source: Office of Emergency Planning.

10. "Federal Disaster Act" (as amended), Public Law 875, 81st Congress, Sec. 1.

replacement of damaged facilities but even some modernization of those buildings and utilities.

Table 6-4 compares the PL 875 allocations as of June 1964 for reconstruction work based on damage estimates and the actual dollar expenditures. In all cases, the restoration costs were considerably less than the allocations made several months following the quake, which indicates that needs were overestimated even after detailed surveys had been undertaken.

A breakdown of damage estimates and expenditures for public facilities by community in Table 6-5 reveals a slightly different picture. In the outlying towns of southcentral Alaska the expenditures by May 1966 generally were larger than the estimates made in June 1964. Part of this upward shift over the two-year period may be attributed to an Alaska Omnibus Act amendment permitting the Corps of Engineers to increase expenditures on previously authorized civil works projects, if additional changes were needed to overcome the adverse effects of the earthquake.[11] The amendment was specifically geared to permit PL 875 allocations for the expansion and modernization of damaged small-boat harbors. The community of Valdez required additional funds when a decision was reached in July 1964 to rebuild the entire town on more solid ground about 4.5 miles from the prequake location. Not surprisingly, expenditures in May 1966 were over twice as large as the original allocation in June 1964. Anchorage on the other hand, required much less money to restore public facilities than had originally been anticipated. Consequently its per capita expenditures were far below original estimates and much less than those of the smaller communities.

LOSSES AND AID TO THE PRIVATE SECTOR

▷ DAMAGE ESTIMATES

Information on disaster-caused damage to private property is particularly difficult to assemble because, at present, there is no agency set up to coordinate the assistance program of loans and grants to the private sector as the Office of

---

11. "1964 Amendments to the Alaska
Omnibus Act," Sec. 4.

Emergency Planning does for the public sector. The separate organizations that assist are primarily concerned with individual cases and therefore have only a peripheral interest in the total loss figures. Consequently, the only available estimates on real property damage in Alaska were made during the first six weeks after the quake. Table 6-6 shows the initial figures issued by the state one week after the quake and the revisions by the Housing and Home Finance Agency (HHFA) five weeks later. Total damage estimates for the private sector were initially assumed to fall somewhere between $177 and $257 million, with the Anchorage area accounting for the bulk of the losses. During early May, the Alaska State Housing Authority and HHFA undertook a property-by-property damage appraisal in order to determine more accurately the amount of private loss. Its survey estimated a total of $77 million in private real property damage with Anchorage still accounting for most of the losses. These revised figures are still the latest and perhaps final official estimates, for the OEP in its concluding progress report still uses the $77 million total as the loss to the private sector.[12]

It should be observed that both the initial and revised estimates of damage to the private sector are restricted to real commercial and residential property, including land. Personal losses (e.g., for contents and furnishings of a home) and economic injury (e.g., reduction of income due to the quake) would augment the totals.

Table 6-6	**CHANGES IN ESTIMATES OF DAMAGE TO PRIVATE REAL PROPERTY AND PER CAPITA FIGURES BY COMMUNITY**

DAMAGE ESTIMATE ($MILLION)

Community and Environs	Population[a] (1964)	April 4, 1964[b] Max.	April 4, 1964[b] Min.	May 8, 1964[c]	Per Capita Damage[d] in Dollars
Anchorage	94,700	208.9	143.2	42.6	450
Homer	1,500	1.2	.7	1.3	870
Kodiak Island	8,200	27.7	20.7	10.5	1,280
Seward	1,600	7.8	5.4	5.5	3,440
Valdez	1,000	8.5	6.0	3.5	3,500
Other	—	3.0	1.5	13.5	—
TOTAL		257.1	177.5	76.9	

[a] NAS-NRC Committee on the Alaska Earthquake.
[b] "Alaska Earthquake Disaster Damage Report," State of Alaska, Office of the Governor, April 4, 1964.
[c] Housing and Home Finance Agency Damage Survey.
[d] Based on May 8 damage estimates.

12. Office of Emergency Planning, *The Alaska Earthquake: A Progress Report,* Washington, D.C., December 29, 1964, p. 19.

▷ SOURCES OF AID

A large number of government agencies and organizations provide long-term recovery aid following a severe disaster. We are using the term *long-term recovery aid* to distinguish this form of relief from the food and shelter provided by such groups as the Red Cross, U.S. military, and community organizations during the recuperation period. Table 6-7 presents the principal sources and uses of funds offered to Alaskans who suffered damage from the quake. This section will analyze the role of each of the listed groups who helped residents get back on their feet again.

The first item in Table 6-7 refers to the forgiveness provisions applied to mortgages held by financial institutions on severely damaged homes. Soon after the earthquake, the Federal National Mortgage Association (FNMA) passed an unprecedented ruling forgiving indebtedness on uninsured outstanding mortgages that they held. Homeowners suffering severe damage were permitted to pay $1000 to be relieved of all obligation; naturally they surrendered equity

| *Table 6-7* | SOURCES AND USES OF RECOVERY FUNDS TO THE PRIVATE SECTOR IN SOUTHCENTRAL ALASKA |

Source	Use	Approximate Amount ($Million)
Federal National Mortgage Association, Farmers Home Administration, VA, SBA, and 1964 Alaska Omnibus Act, Amended	Forgiveness on mortgage and other indebtedness	6.5
Red Cross	Grants to restore homes and businesses or replace furnishings and equipment	.8
Small Business Administration	Loans for repair and reconstruction of homes and businesses	82.2
Farmers Home Administration	Loans for repair and reconstruction of farm dwellings	.3
Bureau of Commercial Fisheries	Loans for repair and replacement of fishing vessels	1.0
Internal Revenue Service	Tax refunds and offsets on property losses	15.0
Rural Electrification Administration	Loans for repair of cooperative electric power facilities	2.7
TOTAL		108.5

Data Source: Estimates from Federal agencies providing aid to public and private sectors, September 1966.

on the home if it still existed.[13] The FNMA's action spurred other agencies such as the Small Business Administration and Farmers Home Administration to make similar arrangements. One of the amendments to the Alaska Omnibus Act formalized these terms by permitting uncompensated victims holding mortgages with private institutions to pay $1000 for retiring their outstanding debt on the home if it did not exceed $30,000. As a criterion for this forgiveness, damage to the property had to be greater than 60 per cent of its market value. The state and Federal government would share equally the cost of reimbursing the financial institutions who held these mortgages.[14] By the July 1, 1966 deadline, 350 applications were received. The latest estimate by the State of Alaska on the total cost of this forgiveness provision is $6.5 million.[15]

Besides providing mass care during the recuperation period, the Red Cross also offered individual assistance to families in the form of grants for long-term recovery purposes. For example, aid was provided to self-employed workers or small-business operators who needed tools or equipment; lost home furnishings and possessions were replaced, and building repair costs were supported in special cases. The Red Cross normally provides assistance only to families who cannot obtain low-interest loans from the appropriate government agency. These agencies—SBA, Bureau of Commercial Fisheries, or Farmers Home Administration—would normally refuse a loan if they thought the individual was such a poor credit risk that he would not be able to make repayments even at low interest rates. The Red Cross also contributed about $400,000 to help rebuild and furnish the Indian villages of Chenega and Old Harbor, which were almost completely destroyed by the quake.

The Small Business Administration provided the major portion of relief to the private sector with low-interest loans to restore homes and businesses destroyed by the quake, *except in rural areas*. SBA relief under the category "Economic Injury Loans" was also given to firms whose income was reduced by the disaster. Because of the magnitude of the earthquake and the vast rebuilding program it necessitated, SBA modified its policy by making broader and more liberal loans than it had granted following other disasters.

---

13. The FNMA took over the mortgages of twenty-five homeowners whose residences were totally destroyed or irreparably damaged. Although the total value of the debts incurred was $475,000, FNMA kept its expenses down to $410,000 through receipts of the token $1,000 payments and some slight re-covery on the property which it took over.

14. "Amendments to the Alaska Omnibus Act," Sec. 4.

15. "Fifth Semiannual Report: Alaska Omnibus Act," Washington, D.C., March 1967, p. 4.

Before the quake the agency provided 3-per cent loans with a maximum repayment period of twenty years to cover the exact amount of physical damage. After the Alaska earthquake, SBA permitted the authorization of loans to retire old debts that may have had nothing to do with the disaster itself as well as loans to repair the damaged structure. Thus, instead of continuing to pay conventional 6- or 8-per cent rates on outstanding claims, the borrower could now retire them at a subsidized 3-per cent rate. A further reduction in the size of the victim's monthly payment was achieved by permitting a thirty-year amortization period instead of the normal twenty years. If the property owner requested it, the agency would waive any payment on both principal and interest during the first year of the loan and on principal up to an additional four years. Thus the victim's burden was minimized; in fact, in quite a few cases, particularly for businesses, the borrower was financially sounder after the disaster than before.

In similar fashion, the Farmers Home Administration greatly liberalized its policy by offering 3-per cent emergency housing loans, instead of the usual 4 per cent, for a maximum of thirty-three years to rural residents who had to rebuild or repair earthquake-damaged dwellings. Following the precedent set by the FNMA, the agency forgave loans on destroyed homes, in a few cases requiring no payment on indebtedness. Since the agricultural areas were only mildly affected by the quake, only thirty-nine loans totaling $259,000 were made, mostly in the Valdez area.

The Bureau of Commercial Fisheries was extremely helpful in getting fishermen back on their feet by making loans for repairing vessels or purchasing new ones. Within two weeks after the quake, the Senate passed a special statute (PL 309) permitting fishermen to borrow funds to charter vessels so that they would not miss the season's catch. Primarily because of a lack of available boats for charter, only one person took advantage of this provision.

Alaskan businessmen and homeowners obtained further relief through the deduction of uninsured property losses from their Federal income tax payments. The Internal Revenue Service permitted taxpayers to include in their 1963 returns losses sustained during the earthquake so that they could benefit immediately from the provisions of the law. The size of the write-offs naturally depended on the kind and amount of property damaged and the tax bracket of the owner. Individuals suffering nonbusiness losses could only write off the portion exceeding $100; businessmen could deduct the entire business loss. Estimated tax refunds and offsets due to the quake are approximately $15 million.

The function of the Rural Electrification Administration (REA) was to help those of its private cooperative associations with damaged facilities resume operations as soon as possible. The Chugach Electric Association, for example, lost its Anchorage transmission line, thus curtailing service to the entire Anchorage area. Outside supplies were immediately shipped to Alaska to temporarily repair the damage so that two weeks after the quake 90 per cent of the electric power customers in Anchorage were again receiving service.[16]

REA made a loan of $1,188,000 to Chugach for repair of earthquake damages, and, in order to ease the cooperative's financial position, the Agency deferred payments on the principal of all previous loans for a 4-year period. This extended the maturity of the loans by the same period of time. REA loans are self-liquidating, bear 2 per cent interest and are amortized over a maximum period of 35 years.

A $60,000 loan was made to the Kodiak Electric Association of Kodiak enabling it to resume service to its consumers within a short time after the earthquake. Another $25,000 loan, to Copper Valley Electric Association of Glennallen, led to immediate repair of that cooperative's generating plant. After the decision was made to rebuild the town of Valdez in another location in Copper Valley's service area, REA made a loan of $1,167,000 to Copper Valley to finance an electric system in the new location. REA also helped to make possible a new telephone system in Valdez through a $239,000 loan to the Copper Valley Telephone Cooperative.

SHORTFALL OF REVENUE AND EXTRAORDINARY OPERATING EXPENSES

As a result of the earthquake, the State and local governments in Alaska temporarily lost sizable portions of their tax revenues. The decline in these receipts jeopardized the continuation of many State and local services including the ability to match certain normal Federal grant-in-aid funds and to finance capital projects through the sale of State and local bonds. In addition to losses from these normal sources, emergency expenditures were incurred in connec-

---

16. Office of Emergency Planning, *op. cit.*, p. 30.

tion with relief and reconstruction. For this reason, Governor Egan requested an appropriation of $44.7 million from Congress to cover the shortfall in state revenue ($26.8 million) and the extraordinary operating expenses ($17.9 million) that were anticipated through June 1966.[17]

The earthquake occurred at a legislatively propitious time, for it enabled Congress to justify a continuation of the statehood transition grants of 1959 to handle this earthquake.[18] After a series of estimates based on available data and prior disaster experience had been made, a grant of $23.5 million to cover the period through June 1966 was approved by Congress (PL 88-311). Estimated state losses in revenue as a result of tax write-offs from casualty damage were $4.8 million. Reduced taxes from unemployment and a decline in business caused by the earthquake (economic injury losses) accounted for another $4.4 million. Local governments in southcentral Alaska estimated losses of $4.8 million in property and other taxes during the coming two years. A detailed set of calculations on projected extraordinary operating expenses and FAA operation of certain intermediate airports in Alaska indicated a total expense of $9.5 million for this category.

Despite the fact that the grants covered a two-year period, an initial appropriation of $17 million was made to Alaska immediately after PL 88-311 was passed by Congress. This relatively high proportion of the total grant could be justified because practically all casualty losses could be expected to be written off retroactively because of the higher tax rates that had prevailed in 1963. Even if there was an overestimate in the required funds for the two-year period, the Federal government still had $6.5 million to handle cutbacks for 1966. Based on revised data available in April 1965, a request for the remaining funds was made. The total shortfall of revenue and extraordinary expenditures were estimated at $23.1 million, thereby indicating that additional grants of $6.1 million would be needed. Of that amount, the state of Alaska was given only $4.5 million, with the understanding that final appropriations would be determined after actual revenue data for fiscal year 1965 were available.

---

17. Statement of Honorable William A. Egan, Governor of the State of Alaska in support of the Passage of H.R. 11039 and H.R. 11038, May 1964.

18. Shortly after the territory had been admitted as a state in 1959, grants had been authorized for a five-year period to help Alaska assume responsibility for public services (e.g., highway construction and maintenance, administration of justice, and the management of fish and wildlife resources) previously provided by the Federal government. This authority expired on June 30, 1964.

At the close of the fiscal year 1965, Governor Egan assembled figures on state revenue for various categories on the basis of a comparison of estimated and actual losses. He received a final Federal grant of $.9 million, bringing the total authorization through June 1966 to $24 million. Table 6-8 presents these changes in estimates on tax losses and extraordinary expenses from the original tally of June 1964 through the final revision in July 1965. As one can see, the discrepancies are slight.

Conclusions

From the maze of figures reflecting damage estimates and expenditures following the Alaska earthquake, a rather clear pattern emerges: There was a tendency to overestimate damage to both the public and private sectors during the initial stages of recovery. Both the Office of Emergency Planning and state officials produced initial estimates of loss that were much higher than the final figures released eight months later. This overestimation pattern in Alaska is consistent with available evidence on other disasters. In fact, the OEP has concluded from an informal analysis of the problem that initial figures are almost twice as high as final damage estimates.[19]

To illustrate this point, Table 6-9 presents summary figures on changes in damage estimates and Federal expenditures for Alaska. The initial estimates on

Table 6-8	CHANGES IN ESTIMATES OF STATE AND LOCAL SHORTFALL IN REVENUE AND EXTRAORDINARY EXPENDITURES ($MILLION)		
	June 1964 Estimates	*April 1965 Estimates*	*July 1965 Estimates*
State Tax Losses	9.2	11.3	11.5
Local Tax Losses	4.8	2.9	3.0
State and Local Extraordinary Operating Expenses	9.5	8.9	7.9
TOTAL	23.5	23.1	22.4

Data Source: Bureau of the Budget.

---

19. Personal communications with OEP personnel.

damage to the public and private sectors were made by the Office of Emergency Planning several days after the disaster;[20] figures for shortfall of revenue and extraordinary operating expense were presented by Governor Egan in congressional testimony early in May 1964. The latest official damage estimates[21] indicate clearly that losses were much lower than originally anticipated, particularly with regard to the private sector, where the initial figure was more than three times as large as the final one.

Of the expenditures listed, we see that the Federal government provided $190 million in grants to cover public sector losses. That allocation falls below the $234 million damage figure not only because of lower state and local expenditures but also because of damage estimates revised since December 1964. For example, the Alaska Railroad damage was assumed to be $30.5 million in December 1964, but the final estimate was only $27 million. We can thus conclude that the Federal government covered practically all losses to the public sector through grants.

For the private sector, Table 6-9 indicates that Federal aid was somewhat larger than the latest damage estimates. This difference can be attributed primarily to the Small Business Administration special policy of providing low-interest loans for retirement of debts having nothing to do with the disaster itself. We will have more to say on this subject in Chapter 9, which discusses the

$Table$ $6-9$	CHANGES IN DAMAGE ESTIMATES OVER TIME AND ACTUAL FEDERAL EXPENDITURES ($MILLION)

DAMAGE FIGURES

	Initial Estimate (April 1964)	Latest Estimate[a] (December 1964	Federal Expenditures[b] (September 1966
Public Sector	318	234	190
Private Sector	257	77	109
Shortfall of Revenue	27	14	14
Extraordinary Operating Expenses	18	10	8
TOTAL	620	335	321

[a] Office of Emergency Planning.
[b] Individual Federal agencies.

20. The public-sector total is simply the sum of estimated damage to state and local property ($244 million) and Federal facilities ($74 million). The private-sector figure represents the maximum estimated loss ($257 million).
21. Office of Emergency Planning, *op. cit.*, pp. 18–19.

role of the SBA in disaster relief. Federal aid to cover shortfall of revenue and extraordinary operating expenses was only slightly less than that initially approved. Appropriations were revised downward because balance-sheet figures assembled at the end of 1966 indicated that operating expenses related to the disaster were less than originally anticipated. The exact toll of the Alaska earthquake will never be known, for so many intangibles affecting human and physical losses defy assessment. Our careful review of the fragmentary data would place the total figure for all tangible losses at slightly over $300 million.

The Federal government made it very clear at the outset that enough aid would be provided in the form of grants and low-interest loans so that Alaska could recover completely. Congress passed special legislation to accomplish this aim, such as amending the Alaska Omnibus Act of 1959, which liberalized disaster relief on several fronts. This extended role of the Federal government in disaster relief has not been confined to the forty-ninth state, however. A series of catastrophes has occurred in all parts of the country since the earthquake, and after each, special legislation has been introduced in Congress modeled on the Alaska example of Federal relief.[22] The discussion in this chapter of Federal expenditures in Alaska should therefore give the reader some feeling for the government's new role in aiding stricken areas today.

---

22. For a description of this special disaster legislation, see Chap. 2, pp. 31–57.

Chapter Seven

Population

Migration: The

Supply of Labor

CHAPTER 1 INDICATED that in recent years the number of fatalities due to natural disasters has been only a fraction of the population of the stricken community. Alaska proved no exception in this regard—only 115 persons were killed out of the 150,000 living in the entire southcentral region.[1] This small percentage tells only part of the story with regards to manpower available for postdisaster reconstruction work. The labor force was also determined by the size and composition of people moving in and out of the area following the catastrophe. This chapter will attempt to characterize normal migration patterns based on studies of both foreign and domestic disasters, and we will then look more specifically at data from Alaska to see if there were any notable differences in behavior generated by the earthquake.

OTHER DISASTERS

▷ GENERAL PATTERNS

Evidence from many other disasters[2] indicates that postdisaster migrations follow a common pattern.

---

1. American Red Cross, "Alaska Earthquake Disaster," March 1964, p. 12, mimeographed.

2. Fred C. Ikle et al., *Withdrawal Beha-* *vior in Disasters: Escape, Flight, and Evacuation Movements*, Committee on Disaster Studies, NAS-NRC, Washington, D.C., April 1957, unpublished report.

1. If families leave the area, they insist on remaining together as a unit while they are in temporary quarters.
2. Whenever possible, families reside with close friends or relatives in the same community and if it is at all feasible, will attempt to restore or repair their own dwelling rather than look for a new one.
3. Residents leave the area voluntarily only when strong warnings indicate possible destruction, and even then many remain.
4. Convergence problems in the disaster area are often caused by the large numbers of immigrants seeking work or just viewing the damage.

▷ SPECIFIC EXAMPLES

Halifax Explosion (1917).[3] One of the few times a record has been kept of migrants entering a disaster area was following the Halifax explosion and fire of 1917, which damaged $35 million of property and resulted in 8000 casualties (15 per cent of the population). Immediately after the disaster, the Red Cross and other relief groups entered the community to coordinate relief and rehabilitation operations. By establishing a thorough system of personal identification, they were able to unite family members and announce the names of victims with a minimum amount of delay. Gradually, this system was extended to cover all incoming personnel. The relief organizations' figures show that approximately 3500 individuals entered Halifax within the first three months following the explosion, and at least 2300 of these actually found jobs in the city during this time.[4] No migration records were kept beyond that period; however, population statistics indicate that approximately 2000 new residents were living in the city one year after the disaster.[5]

White County, Arkansas, Tornado (1952).[6] The Arkansas tornado of March 1952 destroyed and damaged a number of homes in the White County area.

---

3. Samuel H. Prince, "Catastrophe and Social Change," *Studies in History, Economics and Public Law*, vol. 94, no. 1, Columbia University, New York, 1920. The Halifax catastrophe will be discussed in more detail in Chap. 8 in the section on economic improvements following a disaster.

4. Though there undoubtedly were more than 2300 in-migrants who were employed in the city, the figure represents only those who were actually registered as working.

5. Prince, *op. cit.*, p. 129.

6. Eli S. Marks and Charles E. Fritz, *Human Reactions in Disaster Situations*, University of Chicago, University National Opinion Research Center, Report no. 52, June 1954.

Despite cold and inclement weather during the night following the disaster, residents preferred to remain in their own dwellings, which may have lacked windows, heat, gas, or electricity. They "took shelter elsewhere only when their own living quarters were completely unlivable."[7] Of those forced to leave their own homes, only five traveled out of the county and only one left the state; the others remained close to their original residences. Of the latter group, over half stayed with relatives and another 20 per cent with friends. Practically no one chose to live in hotels, with strangers, or in mass shelters. We may assume that the remaining group of evacuees found apartments or homes somewhere in town, although it is not stated in the study. Less than 1 per cent of all displaced families were forced to separate; some of them actually refused shelters because they could not be accommodated together. Each resident desired to reoccupy his old home just as soon as it was made livable again. Several families even returned before their dwellings were repaired, preferring to live in tents or trailers on their land rather than to remain in more distant shelters.

Disasters with Warning Period. In disasters predicted beforehand through explicit warnings or when there is a strong likelihood of their recurrence in the near future, a different migration pattern prevails.[8] Voluntary migration to a safer region is not unusual, with husbands often remaining while wives and children depart. In the wartime bombing experiences of England, Germany, and Russia, many wives and children were sent away before the attacks reached their peak intensity. The number leaving Great Britain alone reached 3.5 million during the months of July to September 1939.[9] Following the Winstead, Connecticut, flood (1955), many parents, fearing a typhoid epidemic, sent their children to stay with relatives in other areas.[10] In many health disasters, such as polio epidemics, children are also sent to safer communities. The distance that migrants must travel naturally depends on the size of the danger zone. In the cases of localized floods and epidemics, it is not necessary to travel very far. On the other hand, during the London bombings, many families fled to Canada or even Australia, the choice of area being often based on the possibility of staying with friends and relatives.

As we have already seen in Chapter 4, entire areas were evacuated

---

7. *Ibid.*, p. 168.

8. Tornado warnings do not fall in this class because the storms are so erratic that people would not know where to move.

9. Richard M. Titmus in *Problems of Social Policy: History of the Second World War, United Kingdom Civil Series*, ed. by W. K. Hancock, H. M. Stationary Office, London, 1950, p. 102.

10. Ikle et al., *op. cit.*, p. 52.

preceding hurricane Carla as a result of accurate warnings by the weather bureau and the efficient use of mass communication media. An estimated 350,000 inhabitants left their homes before the storm reached the Gulf Coast, thereby limiting fatalities to forty-five persons.

*e*ANCHORAGE EXPERIENCE

▷ MIGRATION FROM ANCHORAGE

The record of other natural disasters suggested that there would be little out-migration from an area unless prolonged warnings of possible recurrent destruction had been issued. The movements from Anchorage following the quake conformed largely to that pattern. The main stimulus triggering the outward flow seemed to be the series of severe aftershocks that occurred in the area during the first few weeks after the big quake.[11] This voluntary out-migration can be compared with the evacuation of certain areas of Europe during World War II in anticipation of future bombings.

In general, the emigrants from Anchorage were wives and children who decided to stay temporarily with relatives in the "lower 48" while rebuilding took place; husbands remained in the area to aid recovery operations. Because the earthquake covered such a wide area, the closest safe places to which residents could migrate were Fairbanks (435 miles away) or Juneau (510 miles away). Therefore, most of the Anchorage emigrants preferred to make the longer trip into the continental United States where they could stay with close friends or relatives. The vast majority of the evacuees from Valdez, however, drove to Fairbanks (370 miles away) immediately following the disaster.

---

11. An analysis of seismographic readings on the Richter scale indicates that there were at least three shocks having a reading of 6.5 or over following the Good Friday quake, which had a record-breaking 8.5 magnitude. In an unpublished report by Dr. Rodman Wilson and Dr. William J. Rader, "A Study of Reactions of Alaskans to the 1964 Earth- quake," February 19, 1965, the authors claim that there was a significant relationship between the magnitude of the after-shocks and the out-migration from Anchorage. The only statistical analysis performed with the data, however, was a graph relating out-movements from the city to the size of the aftershock.

Transportation Data

To estimate the outward movement we obtained figures from the Canadian border station on the monthly automobile traffic for a three-year period, 1962 to 1964. These totals of the number of cars heading south along the Alcan Highway, when coupled with data from Anchorage International Airport, would indicate the ordinary flow of residents from the city during the spring months.[12] However, following the quake there were so many government officials and survey teams flying into and out of Anchorage that it is impossible to isolate the local departures from the total figures. Nevertheless we have presented the monthly figures for both outbound automobile and airplane traffic for the years 1962 to 1964 in Table 7-1 to depict the overall increased movement. Discussions with Anchorage residents indicate that the vast majority of those leaving the area departed by car during the first month following the disaster; by using only automobile data, we still find that passenger traffic in April 1964

| *Table 7-1* | TRAFFIC LEAVING THE ANCHORAGE AREA BY PLANE AND AUTO-MOBILE, FEBRUARY 1962–DECEMBER 1964 (FIGURES IN THOUSANDS OF PASSENGERS) |

Month	ANCHORAGE INTERNATIONAL AIRPORT DEPARTURES			ANCHORAGE AUTOMOBILE DEPARTURES		
	1962	*1963*	*1964*	*1962*	*1963*	*1964*
Jan.	—	9.0	10.3	—	1.1	1.3
Feb.	7.5	8.3	9.7	1.0	1.1	1.3
Mar.	9.1	10.0	11.2	1.4	1.5	1.4
April	9.8	10.7	14.2	1.5	1.6	3.0
May	13.5	13.7	18.6	4.1	5.2	5.8
June	17.0	16.6	18.8	4.7	8.4	7.1
July	14.6	18.1	20.2	9.6	10.8	11.0
Aug.	18.2	20.0	22.3	8.6	10.3	10.1
Sept.	13.2	15.1	18.3	4.6	4.6	4.8
Oct.	11.3	12.4	15.1	3.2	3.1	3.5
Nov.	8.3	10.7	13.1	2.4	2.4	2.4
Dec.	10.0	11.3	13.5	2.1	2.1	2.4

Data Sources: *Automobile traffic:* Beaver Creek, Canada, Customs Office.
Airplane traffic: Division of Aviation, Anchorage International Airport.

12. A few tourist departures may have occurred during these months but these would have a negligible effect on the total since the tourist season really begins in June.

(3000 passengers) was about double the figures for the same period in 1962 (1500) and 1963 (1600), despite no discernible change in pattern for the first three months of the year. By May, the traffic had become only slightly higher than normal. A conservative estimate of the number of out-migrants would therefore be the additional 1500 passengers that left Alaska by car.

School Enrollment Statistics

For the Alaskan postdisaster situation, monthly enrollment changes in the Anchorage public schools are more meaningful indicators of out-migration. These data, presented in Table 7-2, for the end of February through May during the four-year period from 1961 to 1964, detail both cumulative totals and monthly changes for all twelve grades. One can easily observe the significant change in the pattern following the earthquake. For the three years preceding the disaster, school population remained relatively stable through April and then declined slightly in May because early-vacationing families took their children out of classes shortly before the end of the school year.[13] During the month of April 1964, a substantial decline in school population occurred, although May seemed to follow the normal pattern. It is therefore safe to assume that the bulk of outgoing traffic occurred during the first month following the quake, as would have been expected from the record of other disasters. We can supplement the figures on Anchorage public school population during

| *Table 7-2* | TOTAL MONTHLY SCHOOL ENROLLMENT, 1ST THROUGH 12TH GRADES, ANCHORAGE INDEPENDENT SCHOOL DISTRICT (FEBRUARY 28–MAY 31, 1961–1964) |

Date	1961[a]	1962[a]	1963[a]	1964[a]
Feb. 28	12,740	14,044	15,281	16,392
	+12	−9	+48	+29
Mar. 31	12,752	14,035	15,329	16,421
	+14	−28	+34	−555
Apr. 30	12,766	14,007	15,363	15,866
	−124	−85	−79	−105
May 31	12,642	13,922	15,284	15,761

Data Source: Division of Records, Anchorage Independent School District.
[a] Numbers between entries indicate change between the two months.

13. Because the school totals are compiled on the last day of each month, the May 31 figure represents the enrollment at the end of the school year. This explanation for the drop in May totals was given to us by Gerald Marquees, Director of Records for the Anchorage public schools, who assembled all these figures.

April with data from a survey made of school enrollment changes on military posts one month after the quake. The Army and Air Force have schools for children of military personnel at Fort Richardson and Elmendorf Air Force Base, respectively. In Table 7-3 the relevant statistics have been listed for both types of school, together with the combined totals.

School enrollment figures show a 3.5 per cent decline in the month following the earthquake. The Census Bureau estimates that the total population in the Anchorage school district just prior to the earthquake was 59,000. Using the same figure (3.5 per cent) for estimating the decline in total population, the outmigration estimate would be approximately 2070 persons. This figure undoubtedly overestimates the flow from the city because in most cases only wives accompanied their children while the husbands remained in Alaska to help with the rebuilding.

Rather than trying to pinpoint an exact total from the limited data available, we will simply postulate that out-migration from Anchorage lay somewhere between the 1500-passenger increase in automobile traffic for April 1964, as against the normal passenger rate of the previous two years, and the 2070-person ouflow obtained by using school enrollment changes.

▷ MIGKATION INTO ANCHORAGE

Estimates of the number of people migrating to Alaska following the disaster can be obtained from inbound traffic data and school enrollment statistics.

Automobile Traffic

Despite a request by Governor Egan several days following the quake that outsiders stay away from the disaster area, a large increase in automobile traffic

Table 7-3	CHANGE IN ANCHORAGE PUBLIC AND MILITARY SCHOOL ENROLLMENT CAUSED BY GOOD FRIDAY EARTHQUAKE

	Prequake Enrollment (March 27)	*Postquake Enrollment (April 30)*	*Change*
Public Schools	16,421	15,866	−555
Military Schools	4,797	4,606	−191
TOTAL	21,218	20,472	−746

to Alaska still occurred, as shown in Table 7-4. These data, listed monthly for the six-year period 1959 to 1964, indicate that traffic during April and May of 1964 was higher than usual. Although weather conditions play a role in determining the flow of cars along the highway, there was no substantial change in temperature or condition of the road over the previous years to account for this pattern, according to Immigrant Inspector William Craig at the Tok border station.[14]

The difference in traffic between April 1964 and the prequake month of March 1964 indicates a much larger percentage increase than for any of the previous five years. From 1959 to 1963 volume from March to April never rose by more than 26 per cent; this figure increased to 69 per cent in 1964. After April the monthly differences were not abnormally high, but the absolute totals (except for June) were somewhat above previous years' movements.

Table 7-4	MONTHLY PASSENGER TRAFFIC BY AUTOMOBILE INTO ALASKA, 1959–1964 (FIGURES IN THOUSANDS OF PASSENGERS)

Months	*1959*	*1960*	*1961*	*1962*	*1963*	*1964*
January	1.4	1.2	1.8	.9	1.6	1.9
February	1.3	1.3	1.6	1.1	1.7	1.8
March	2.7	2.1	2.3	1.6	2.4	2.2
April	3.1	2.8	3.0	2.1	2.7	3.7
May	4.1	3.7	3.4	3.1	3.8	4.6
June	9.1	8.8	7.8	7.2	9.9	10.0
July	11.2	11.3	11.0	12.1	13.4	15.6
August	8.1	8.0	9.0	10.5	11.0	12.3
September	2.9	3.1	3.8	4.5	4.6	6.5
October	1.2	1.7	1.4	1.9	1.8	2.8
November	.8	1.2	.8	1.3	1.2	1.8
December	.7	1.0	.7	1.2	1.1	1.7
Total	46.6	46.2	46.6	47.4	55.2	64.9

Data Source: Tok, Alaska, Immigration and Naturalization Service.

14. Inspector Craig organized these figures and described changes in the composition of incoming traffic as a result of the quake. Automobiles crossing the Tok border have the option of branching off to either Anchorage or Fairbanks. Before the quake about 65 per cent headed for Anchorage; after the disaster this percentage increased to approximately 75 per cent for the next two months and then dropped down to normal again.

Inspector Craig attempted to analyze the migration pattern in the post-disaster months by checking on the reasons for travel into Alaska. According to his observations, the increased traffic during the months of April and May represented men seeking employment in Anchorage. Many of these individuals had done construction work in the area during previous summers and decided to return earlier than usual; during normal times, summer employees arrive toward the end of May and early in June for the start of the construction season. Others, who were unemployed in the "lower 48," hoped to find work up north. During the summer months, the increased traffic can be attributed to Alaskans returning either to resettle or rejoin members of their families who had remained after the quake.

School Enrollment Data

Further confirmation of the immigration of a large number of Alaskan families during July and August may be obtained from Anchorage public school data. Enrollment figures for September 30 in Table 7-5, adjusted to eliminate the difference between outgoing twelfth grade and incoming first grade, confirm this trend.[15] The number of students enrolled on September 30, 1964, was considerably higher than the enrollment one month after the quake and even surpassed

Table 7-5	**TOTAL ANCHORAGE PUBLIC SCHOOL ADJUSTED ENROLLMENT, SEPTEMBER 1961–SEPTEMBER 1966**

Date	*Unadjusted*	*1st Grade (Sept. 30)*	*12th Grade (March 30)*	*Adjusted*[a]
Sept. 30, 1960	12,475	1,656	567	—
Sept. 30, 1961	14,019	1,815	657	12,771
Sept. 30, 1962	15,166	2,009	693	12,566
Sept. 30, 1963	16,351	1,955	886	12,489
March 30, 1964	15,866	1,955	886	12,004
Sept. 30, 1964	17,704	2,076	1,047	12,652
Sept. 30, 1965	20,436	2,195	1,095	14,236
Sept. 30, 1966	21,374	2,233	—	14,036

Data Source: Division of Records, Anchorage Independent School District.
[a]Adjusted data eliminate trend due to differential between incoming 1st grade in year *t* and outgoing 12th grade in year *t* − 1.

15. The adjustment for the first and twelfth grade differential may be calculated as follows. Assume in a base year *t* the school population is p_t. Let the difference s_t represent the incoming first grade in year *t* minus the outgoing twelfth grade in year *t* − 1. Then the adjusted school population p_t^* is simply $p_t - s_t$.

Expressing the enrollment of future years in terms of the base year *t* to make valid migration comparisons, we must calculate as follows for each year *t* + *n*

$$p_{t+n}^* = p_{t+n} - \sum_{m-t}^{t+n} s_m.$$

the total for September 1963 by more than 150 students. School officials indicated that the increase could be attributed primarily to families who had temporarily left the area after the disaster and were resettling. A further influx of residents during the following year is reflected by the September 1965 adjusted school figures, which show an increase of more than 1500 children over enrollment of the previous year. The relatively small decline in adjusted school enrollment figures between September 1965 and September 1966, indicates that practically all these new arrivals became permanent residents.

▷ LABOR MARKET TRENDS

The effect of migration on the composition of the work force can be understood from labor market figures in Table 7-6 for the Anchorage area. The only two sectors that experienced a noticeable rise in employment during the month following the quake were contract construction and government. The construction totals increased by 55 per cent in April as against a rise of 12 per cent and 15 per cent in 1962 and 1963, respectively. The industry continued to utilize more men each month through September. Federal employment in Anchorage rose by over 6 per cent immediately following the quake as personnel in the area were utilized to cope with the disaster. In the previous two years, the number of workers in that sector between March and April had remained stable or even fallen.

The unemployment rate in Anchorage declined from 8.8 per cent in March 1964 to 7.3 per cent in April 1964, despite new arrivals into the area. According

| *Table 7-6* | LABOR MARKET STATISTICS FOR ANCHORAGE, MARCH–APRIL 1962–1964 |

Year	Total Labor Force	Total Unemployment	Total Employment	Contract Construction	Government	Other
1962						
Mar.	28,290	2,660	25,630	1,080	11,380	13,170
Apr.	28,630	2,480	26,150	1,210	11,230	13,710
1963						
Mar.	29,240	2,550	26,690	860	11,940	13,890
Apr.	29,590	2,450	27,140	990	11,950	14,200
1964						
Mar.	29,990	2,640	27,350	1,150	12,090	14,110
Apr.	31,270	2,290	28,980	1,760	12,850	14,370

Data Source: "Monthly Labor Market Newsletter (Anchorage)."

to the Anchorage "Labor Market Newsletter" of April 1964, "much of the Anchorage area unemployment was among in-migrants, who were far more numerous than in 1963."[16]

▷ SUMMARY AND CONCLUSIONS

1. As in other natural disasters a number of wives temporarily left the area with their children after the Good Friday quake, while the men remained behind to aid in clean-up and reconstruction.

2. After a disaster outgoing residents normally remain relatively near the stricken area and return as soon as possible. In the case of Anchorage, families who left generally decided to stay with relatives in the "lower 48." Since distances traveled were far, they tended to remain away longer than if they were living in temporary quarters nearby. By the end of the summer, however, most of these families had returned to Alaska. A further influx of new inhabitants occurred during the spring and summer of 1965 as shown by a rise in the adjusted school figures for September 30, 1965, over the previous year. In light of the September 1966 adjusted enrollment data this in-migration seems to have been permanent.

3. As would be expected from other disasters, workers did arrive in Anchorage seeking construction jobs, despite discouraging announcements by Governor Egan on the possibility of finding employment. According to the Anchorage "Labor Market Newsletter," these in-migrants constituted a large percentage of the unemployment in the area during the month following the quake.

---

16. Alaska Department of Labor, "Labor Market Newsletter (Anchorage)," Employment Security Division, Anchorage, April 1964, p. 1.

| Chapter Eight | Reconstruction

and Economic Developments

Following a Disaster

THE RECOVERY period was defined in Chapter 3 as the interval during which facilities were being restored to their predisaster position. To explicitly measure progress within this period, it is necessary to sort out disaster projects from overall construction activity. In the United States this problem is a particularly thorny one for the private sector, where building permit records are the only available source of data. Unless specific information on each permit is compiled it would be impossible to isolate postdisaster work within the overall totals. Even if this separation could be made, one would still need to formulate a building-progress curve to gain a measure of the speed with which recovery took place.

Activity in the public sphere provides a more useful guide, since special reports are likely to exist on the progress of postdisaster work performed by Federal agencies. Another advantage of using this reconstruction work as a measure of the speed of recovery is that it offers the possibility of making meaningful comparisons between the rebuilding pattern in the United States and in foreign communities that have been severely damaged by a disaster. In fact, the only figures likely to be available from foreign sources are the national government's expenditures in the damaged region. We would expect recovery to be painstakingly slow in a relatively poor nation that could not afford to divert large amounts of capital at one point of time for rebuilding a disaster-torn community; in a highly industrialized nation such as the United States, aid for rebuilding should flow more freely and rapidly.

The first section of this chapter will describe the recovery process in Skopje, Yugoslavia, following the disastrous earthquake of July 1963. By then looking at the restoration rate for public facilities in Anchorage, differences in the two recovery patterns should become clear. Anchorage building-permit data on private construction will also be introduced to estimate crudely the length of time for rebuilding damaged structures in the commercial and residential sectors. A section will also be devoted to problems faced by the outlying Alaskan communities that suffered relatively high per capita damage. The Federal government rescued these communities with urban renewal projects, but the time delay in getting formal plans and approval for this work lengthened the recovery period. The concluding portion of the chapter will describe post-disaster economic improvements due to technological innovations as well as social and political factors.

RECOVERY OF SKOPJE

The earthquake that struck Skopje on July 26, 1963, left 170,000 residents, three quarters of the population, with their homes either destroyed or very badly damaged.[1] Following the quake there were no hospitals, clinics, schools, or public buildings in operating condition. Of the forty-five industrial enterprises in the city, fourteen were totally or almost totally destroyed by the initial quakes and all others were damaged by the eighty-four aftershocks of various intensities that occurred during the remainder of the summer.[2] Damage has been estimated at approximately $600 million.

Except for a U.S. grant of $25 million to repair 8500 damaged homes and a $25 million U.S. loan for reconstructing utilities and preparing an urban plan, most of the contributions from nations were utilized for short-run recuperation purposes.[3] Thus the Yugoslavian government has been forced to cope with

1. Final estimates indicate that 30,000 out of 36,000 dwelling units in the city were unfit for habitation. *The New York Times*, October 9, 1966, p. 31.

2. *Ibid.*

3. Over $15 million were donated by seventy-seven nations for relief in the form of medical, food, and housing needs during the first few weeks following the quake. "Yugoslavia—1963 Skopje Earthquake," AID Disaster Information Memo, July 5, 1966, p. 8.

long-term recovery problems practically on its own. The lowest cost of reconstruction according to an initial plan formulated by a government council would have required drawing 1 per cent of Yugoslavia's national income for ten years. This plan fell through since the country could not supply the required funds.[4] As a result, progress has been slow. Even three years after the quake, little permanent rebuilding in Skopje itself had taken place. A large proportion of the damaged structures were simply propped up and plastered together, very frequently by the individual owners themselves, thus creating the impression of a masterpiece in patchwork. On the outskirts of the city eighteen new settlements have sprung up, each consisting of rows and rows of neat prefabricated houses complete with shops and other facilities. The layout is in the conventional Yugoslavian style of neighborhood units,[5] where each settlement is supplied with essential daily services. Since the layout conformed with standard housing practice, it allows for the integration of the emergency units into some subsequent regional plan.[6] There is one large international complex made up of groups of houses donated by many different countries shortly after the quake, so that a variety of national styles is represented. Most of the other settlements were contributed by the republics and towns of Yugoslavia, and these, too, reflect the various architectural styles found in different parts of the country. Thus the new Skopje is more than twice as long and nearly twice as broad as it was before the earthquake.[7]

By the end of 1964 approximately $240 million had been spent on the restoration of the town. The Yugoslavian government plans to spend another $540 million by the end of 1970 on rebuilding alone and a further $210 million on economic recovery.[8] If government expenditures are used as a basis for judging the speed with which rebuilding has taken place, we thus find that only 25 per cent of the capital stock was restored one and a half years after the quake.

---

4. Eric Larrabee, "Letter from Skopje," *The New Yorker*, vol. 40, October 17, 1964.

5. The neighborhood unit is a self-sufficient independent association that has the authority to look after local affairs. The development of these housing projects occurred in Yugoslavia because of an increasing tendency toward administrative decentralization. For a further discussion of this concept, see Jack L. Fisher, "Planning the City of Socialist Man," *Journal of the American Institute of Planners*, vol. 28, November 1962, pp. 251–265.

6. Jack L. Fisher, "The Reconstruction of Skopje," *Journal of the American Institute of Planners*, vol. 30, February 1964, p. 46.

7. "Skopje after the Fall," *The Economist* (June 19, 1965), p. 1390.

8. *Ibid.*

The slow pace of recovery can best be depicted through a few statistics. Two years following the disaster 6000 to 7000 more apartments and houses were needed for the town to reach its prequake housing capacity. By October 1966 the United Nations reported that units had finally been constructed to house the current population of 190,000.[9] Sizeable areas of the city still lay beneath the debris deposited by the earthquake even three years after the quake. Many buildings, including factories, still stood but were uninhabitable and irreparable because of fundamental structural damage.[10] The design of a new urban plan for the central part of Skopje under the direction of the U.N. was begun in December 1964 and was finally completed during the spring of 1966 so that permanent rebuilding only recently got under way. Under this program, a large part of the U.S. loan of $25 million will be utilized to build a principal thoroughfare in New Skopje and to construct a main water line from the reservoir to the city.

By 1971 Skopje is expected to be an industrial center with a population of 260,000. Reconstruction goals include a steel mill in full production, a complex of chemical industries, modernized metalworking plants, a number of light industries, and a cement plant with double the capacity of the present one. Work has already begun on building larger railroad yards than existed before the quake to be able to handle the city's anticipated industrial needs. The center of Skopje will be the last part of the city to recover. It will eventually house a city hall, museum of modern art, university center, and a central park.[11]

Skopje's slow recovery can partially be attributed to the relatively high per capita damage, approximately $3000. However, the primary cause for rebuilding delays is undoubtedly the limited capital that could be provided by the central government. When the rebuilding activity of the small Alaskan communities suffering even higher per capita losses than Skopje is detailed later in this chapter, the contrast with the Yugoslavian city will be obvious. We now turn to reconstruction activity in Anchorage, whose per capita losses were smaller than most of its neighboring towns, whose absolute damage was higher and whose recovery was unusually rapid.

9. *The New York Times*, October 9, 1966, p. 31.

10. " Yugoslavia—1963 Skopje Earthquake," p. 5.

11. *The New York Times, loc. cit.*

PROGRESS IN ANCHORAGE

▷ PUBLIC RECONSTRUCTION OF STATE AND LOCAL FACILITIES

The Corps of Engineers undertook the reconstruction of all public facilities in Anchorage with the exception of the International Airport, which became the responsibility of the FAA. A large amount of the work done by both these agencies was covered by PL 875, which provided funds for debris clearance, the restoration of public utilities, and the repair of docks and other community facilities. Because of the unprecedented amount of Federal aid, the Corps prepared detailed monthly reports indicating the value of each contract awarded, the estimated completion date, and the percentage of the contract completed at that point of time. By combining these data with FAA activity at the International Airport, some measure of the speed of recovery in the public sector can be obtained. Figure 8-1 depicts the cumulated percentage of the overall $15 million of public contracts that were awarded and completed at the end of each month following the quake.[12] Within a year and a half after the quake, practically all the reconstruction contracts had been awarded and 98 per cent of the total value had been completed. This rapid recovery occurred despite the fact that there was a delay of several months before any awards were made for permanent restoration of facilities, since relocation sites depended on the results of soil studies showing where it was safe to build.[13] During the immediate postdisaster period, reconstruction was confined to the emergency repair of utilities such as water, sewer, telephone, and electricity. In other words, the first order of business was to restore these facilities to a level of operation that would eliminate any possible health hazard (e.g., the contamination of the water supply by broken sewers). The Corps was also initially involved in demolition and other work for protecting public health and safety, including debris clearance and the razing of irreparable structures.

---

12. The only public construction contracts in Anchorage not included in these figures are the urban renewal projects undertaken by the Corps. These contracts had nothing to do with state and local facilities but were related to commercial redevelopment in the downtown area.

13. The Corps of Engineers awarded two contracts totaling over $950,000 for soil studies in the Anchorage area immediately following the quake.

To gain some idea as to the effect of the quake on *new* public construction in Anchorage, monthly figures on the values of awards in 1964 are compared with the previous two years in Table 8-1.[14] The unusually high total for April 1964 is primarily due to an $11.4 million award for troop housing at Fort

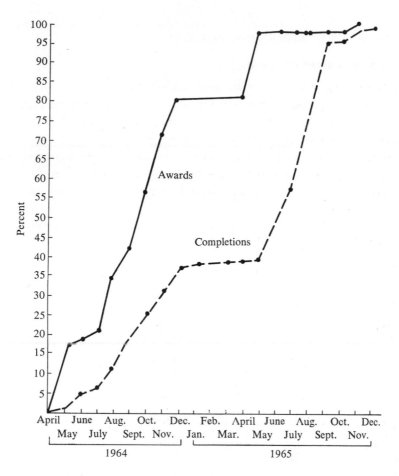

FIGURE 8-1. *Cumulated percent of public construction awards and completions in Anchorage at the end of each month, March 31, 1964– November 30, 1965 (based on dollar value).*

14. No comparative figures on repairs to public facilities in the area are available, so only data on new construction could be presented.

Richardson. The Corps of Engineers did not include this figure in their post-quake construction awards to public facilities since it was not related to damage and therefore did not qualify for PL 875 funding. However, even after subtracting this figure from the 1964 totals the difference between pre- and postquake activity is still substantial.

▷ PRIVATE CONSTRUCTION ACTIVITY

Limitations of the Data

In theory, any person or contractor undertaking private construction is required to hold a building permit for the value of anticipated expenditures. According to the Census Bureau, however, these permit figures should be interpreted with caution when used as an index of construction activity. Because the building fee is based on the value stated on the permit, there is good reason to assume that individuals registering with the city office will underestimate the cost of construction.[15] This practice is reinforced by a feeling that the tax assess-

| *Table 8-1* | MONTHLY VALUES OF NEW PUBLIC CONSTRUCTION AWARDS IN THE ANCHORAGE AREA, 1962–1964 |

VALUE OF AWARD ($THOUSAND)

Month	*1962*	*1963*	*1964*
January	26	—	32
February	—	48	451
March	2,336	—	430
April	—	102	14,417[a]
May	418	—	1,379
June	665	1,461	1,235
July	3,013	2,365	5,814
August	442	216	969
September	182	171	2,678
October	543	442	498
November	102	1,446	1,418
December	38	—	1,438
TOTAL	7,765	6,251	30,759

Data Source: U.S. Census Bureau.
[a] This figure includes an $11.4 million award for troop housing at Fort Richardson, not related to earthquake reconstruction.

15. Unless the policing system in the area is inefficient, very few individuals will engage in construction work without obtaining a permit, except in the case of minor alterations and repairs.

ment of property will somehow be based on the permit figure.[16] On the other hand, there are generally a few permits issued that are not actually used.[17] In spite of these forfeitures the Census Bureau feels that consolidated permit data still underestimate actual construction activity.

For the purpose of yearly comparisons this bias is of no consequence if it is consistent. In the case of Anchorage, however, the earthquake appears to have induced more accurate permit figures than for earlier years. Before the disaster the borough assessor, Glen McKee, claims that there was a tendency to underestimate by as much as one-third the value of the proposed structure. Contractors engaged in residential work were the worst offenders since industrial estimates were normally based on the architect's figures. Following the quake, all permits for repairs were given free so there was no need to undervalue work. In fact, there was an incentive to report the cost of reconstruction accurately since residents thought that the size of SBA loans was influenced by the value stated on the building permit. This concern about accurately estimating the value on the building permit to obtain a requested loan from the SBA proved unfounded because the agency did not actually inspect these figures. Permit fees were still charged on new structures, however, and only a portion of post-quake construction was financed by the SBA. Thus, there is still an aggregate underestimation bias in the reported figures, although much less than before the disaster. The data presented in the next sections must be interpreted in this light.

Residential New Construction

Despite liberal financial terms offered by the SBA, there was no pronounced rush to build new dwellings in Anchorage following the Good Friday disaster. Building-permit figures assembled in Table 8-2 indicate that projected new construction for 1964 was somewhat below the requirements necessary to re-place the 219 private homes and 752 multiple units that were heavily damaged.[18] The high vacancy rate at the time of the quake undoubtedly accounts for the

---

16. In actual fact, the tax assessor is given a copy of the building permit just to indicate that a new structure is being put in place. He will eventually make his own estimate of the value of the property.

17. The average default rate for the entire United States is only 2 per cent; however, there is a large variance between communities.

18. For a description of damage to Anchorage residences, see Chap. 5, "Anchorage Experience, Damage to Houses."

relatively small number of multiple units scheduled for construction during 1964.[19] Practically all the homes destroyed were in the Turnagain area, which was condemned by the government until thorough soil tests on the stability of the land had been undertaken. Most homeowners preferred to take temporary quarters until they knew what the final zoning regulations would be. Even with these delays, by the end of 1965 the number of postquake permits issued for single-family and multiple-unit dwellings equaled the number of units destroyed in each of these categories as shown in Figure 8-2. Most of these structures were expected to be completed within one year after the permit was issued. It is thus safe to say that recovery within the residential sector was completed around two and a half years after the disaster.

Nonresidential New Construction

Table 8-3 clearly shows a definite increase in the *total value* of permits for new nonresidential construction during the first few quarters following the disaster when compared with a similar period for 1962 and 1963. On the other hand, the *number* of permits issued during this period declined significantly from previous years since new building activity was limited almost entirely to replacing business establishments that were damaged beyond repair. The consequent increase in the average value of the permit is due to a combination of factors. The severe damage to the main street in Anchorage, Fourth Avenue, enabled many business establishments to modernize and expand their new

$Table\ 8\text{-}2$	NEW PRIVATE HOUSING UNITS IN ANCHORAGE COVERED BY BUILDING PERMITS, 1960–1966

Period	Single	Multiple	Total
1960	214	45	259
1961	140	61	201
1962	157	214	371
1963	217	411	628
Postquake, 1964[a]	170	342	512
1965	141	468	609
1966	125	120	245

Data Source: U.S. Census Bureau.
[a] There were only two building permits for new housing construction issued during the first quarter of 1964 before the earthquake, both for duplex structures.

---

19. As pointed out in Chap. 5, an FHA survey taken just before the quake revealed that approximately 1 in every 7 units was vacant.

facilities; they could afford to spend more on reconstruction than they might have normally contemplated because the SBA offered low-interest long-term business loans. The average value of all permits was also affected by a few extremely large dollar figures such as J. C. Penney's ($2.2 million) and the Captain Cook Hotel's ($1.75 million). An increase in the cost of construction may have slightly raised the average permit value above that of previous years, though this effect would be minor compared to the other two factors.

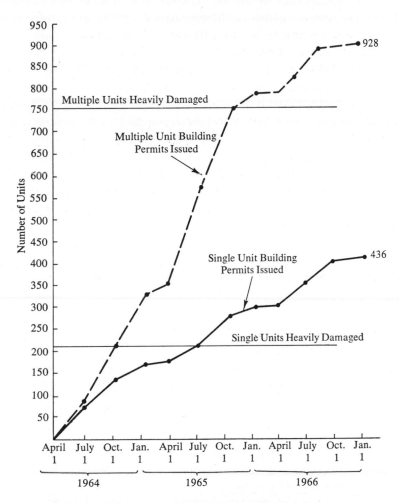

FIGURE 8-2. *Speed of recovery for single and multiple unit homes in Anchorage based on building permit data.*

RECOVERY: RECONSTRUCTION AND ECONOMIC DEVELOPMENTS

To demonstrate their confidence in Anchorage, the board of the First National Bank unanimously agreed, one week following the quake, to proceed with the construction of their proposed new building. At about the same time, Walter Hickel and his associates decided to start building the $1.75 million Captain Cook Hotel, which had been in the planning stage before the quake. These two positive actions, indicating faith on the part of business leaders in the future of Anchorage, came at a time when firms were still undecided as to what future actions they would take. Owners of businesses now committed themselves to rebuilding their establishments shortly thereafter, with most of them obtaining a permit during the 1964 season. In fact, with the major exception of the J. C. Penney store, which took out a permit to rebuild its store only in December 1964, practically all other damaged establishments had been restored or modernized within a year following the Good Friday disaster.

The rapid postdisaster reconstruction activity triggered new developments in the area during 1965. A look at specific permit data for the year reveals that the relatively high value, particularly for the third quarter, is due to construction contracts for erecting three new retail stores ($638,000) and several storage tanks and warehouses ($1,125,000) for the oil and shipping industries. None of these structures was a replacement for a building in Anchorage destroyed by the quake; rather, they represented optimistic feelings regarding the future development of the area.

Table 8-3	NUMBER AND VALUE OF BUILDING PERMITS FOR NEW NON-RESIDENTIAL CONSTRUCTION ($THOUSAND)[a]

| | YEAR | | | | |
QUARTER	1962	1963	1964	1965	1966
First	2,683[b]	—	157	708	184
	(14)	(—)	(3)	(10)	(5)
Second	1,948	1,988	3,362	1,954	1,956
	(47)	(32)	(23)	(31)	(29)
Third	1,730	1,184	4,375[c]	4,164	2,541
	(42)	(72)	(37)	(50)	(26)
Fourth	896	185	3,065[d]	652	1,270[e]
	(24)	(23)	(16)	(12)	(15)
TOTAL	7,257	3,357	10,960	7,473	5,959
	(127)	(127)	(79)	(103)	(75)
AVERAGE VALUE	57	26	134	73	79

Data Source: Anchorage Building Permit Data.
[a] Figures in parentheses indicate number of permits.
[b] Includes permits for a Shell Oil Refinery tank ($1,275,000) and a J. C. Penney Store ($1,078,000).
[c] Includes 5 separate permits issued from July through October to rebuild the Captain Cook Hotel ($1,750,000).
[d] Includes a permit to rebuild J. C. Penney ($2,200,000).
[e] Includes a permit for a parking ramp at J. C. Penney ($1,250,000).

Repairs, Additions, and Alterations

Partially damaged buildings were restored either through repair work or additions and alterations, so comparative permit data on these categories have been combined in Table 8-4 for the period 1963–1966. Permit data on repairs were not available for 1962, so the postquake period could be compared only with data from the previous year. Second-quarter figures for 1964 on value and number of issued permits show a substantial increase over the same period during the previous year in both the residential and nonresidential spheres. The response of businessmen was particularly rapid, with over 65 per cent of the value of all permits in 1964 issued during the quarter immediately following the quake. Homeowners were a bit slower in their response as can be seen from

Table 8-4		NUMBER AND VALUE OF BUILDING PERMITS FOR REPAIR, ADDITIONS, AND ALTERATIONS ($THOUSAND)[a]		

	RESIDENTIAL			
Quarter	*1963*	*1964*	*1965*	*1966*
First	116	196	284	95
	(64)	(40)	(79)	(46)
Second	438	1478	717	357
	(186)	(459)	(232)	(154)
Third	256	1671	837	180
	(173)	(421)	(169)	(113)
Fourth	122	693	125	102
	(91)	(175)	(65)	(52)
TOTAL	932	4060	1963	734
	(514)	(1114)	(545)	(365)
AVERAGE VALUE	1.8	3.6	3.6	2.0
	NONRESIDENTIAL			
First	89	156	231	82
	(48)	(44)	(53)	(36)
Second	425	2478	1011	492
	(68)	(309)	(103)	(75)
Third	251	733	568	382
	(63)	(87)	(84)	(48)
Fourth	73	434	299	311
	(30)	(52)	(47)	(59)
TOTAL	838	3808	2109	1267
	(209)	(496)	(287)	(218)
AVERAGE VALUE	4.0	7.7	7.3	5.8

Data Source: U.S. Census Bureau.
[a] Figures in parentheses indicate number of permits.

the figures in Table 8-4. This pattern jibes with economic reasoning: business-men are much more likely to suffer losses and economic injury by not rapidly restoring their damaged facilities than are homeowners, who have the option of temporarily renting existing vacant units or residing with friends and rela-tives.

Comparisons of residential and nonresidential repairs and alteration figures on an annual basis indicate that for 1964 the total and average value of permits as well as the number taken out was considerably higher than during the previous year. The totals for the next year were also substantially above the prequake levels but considerably lower than in 1964. By 1966, activity had dropped substantially, particularly in the residential sphere. The somewhat higher value of permits for 1966 compared with 1963 in the nonresidential sphere may be due to a systematic component having nothing to do with the quake (i.e., increased construction costs) as well as purely random variation. Note that the number of permits issued during that year is approximately the same as in 1963.

RECONSTRUCTION OF OTHER ALASKAN COMMUNITIES[20]

Although the outlying villages suffered substantial damage, an early decision to rehabilitate these towns was reached by the Federal government. The Urban Renewal Administration (URA) and Office of Emergency Planning (OEP) were jointly assigned the task of developing large-scale plans for rebuilding, using PL 875 funds for the purpose. Under Alaska state law the responsibility for the planning and administration of urban renewal programs lies with the Alaska State Housing Authority (ASHA). Unfortunately, there was a notice-able lack of coordination of recovery activity, with decisions made at the top levels frequently not filtering down to the lower echelons.[21] Personnel involved

---

20. The Department of Housing and Urban Development was extremely help-ful in critically reviewing the material in this section and providing up-to-date information on recovery operations in the outlying villages.

21. Specific examples of these problems

as well as recommendations for improv-ing the urban renewal program following future disasters appear in a paper on "The Role of Urban Planning in the Recon-struction of Alaska," (Committee on the Alaskan Earthquake), NAS-NRC Washington, D.C., 1967, mimeographed.

in the implementation of programs were often not aware of decisions that had been made by higher officials. Confusion was compounded when a number of teams of planning consultants were hired to work on different phases of development within some of the smaller villages (e.g., Kodiak and Valdez), a practice that led to inconsistencies and unnecessary delays. Reconstruction of the villages even after plans were drawn up was further delayed because loans for residential and commercial rebuilding had to be provided by agencies such as the SBA, Farmers Home Administration, and Federal Housing Authority, all of whom had no direct connection with ASHA. For all these reasons a slow recovery rate was inevitable. This section will briefly describe some problems faced by each village with the exception of Seward.[22]

▷ CORDOVA

The city of Cordova, located in southcentral Alaska, is primarily dependent on the fishing industry for its economic activity. In contrast with all the other towns in Alaska, whose land masses subsided, the quake produced a tectonic uplift in Cordova, thus causing it to rise approximately seven feet and leaving the city dock and other harbor facilities high and dry. Public utilities, particularly the sewer system, were also severely impaired. Dredging of the harbor began soon after the quake so that a new channel for accommodating ocean-going vessels was completed by the fall of 1964. The initial urban renewal activity occurred early in 1965 when the Renewal Assistance Administration approved a land acquisition application in connection with the Corps of Engineers reconstruction of the small-boat harbor. One of the major problems, however, in connection with the Cordova Project was that only $170,000 was available from the Alaska Omnibus Act appropriation for Alaska urban renewal projects at the time Cordova's application was submitted. Thus, the development of a financing plan for the Cordova Project utilizing regular Title I urban renewal capital-grant funds resulted in a substantial delay of this project. Actual construction and rehabilitation activity on the waterfront and within the town finally got under way early in 1967, so that the $1.6 million project is not expected to be completed until December 1969.

---

22. Discussion on the rebuilding of Seward will be reserved for the next section to illustrate how sociological factors influence economic considerations in recovery operations.

▷ KODIAK

Kodiak is the largest city and principal harbor of Kodiak Island, with a population of 6300, approximately 3000 of whom are connected with either the naval or coast guard stations on the island. Since the city is built on solid rock, which makes an excellent foundation, only minor damages were caused by the earthquake shocks; however, the tsunami, or tidal wave, that followed destroyed 80 per cent of the downtown area. Moreover, the entire Kodiak Island land mass subsided 6.5 feet, thus exposing the city to future tidal inundation.[23] Rather than moving the entire city to higher ground, the Federal agencies involved in disaster relief decided to build fill and seawalls in the lowest portion of the downtown area and develop a breakwater system to prevent future tidal flooding. In this way the fishing and commercial activities of Kodiak could continue during the rebuilding process. Through the OEP-URA joint efforts and the cooperation of other Federal agencies (e.g., Bureau of Yards and Docks), a plan was developed for simultaneously rebuilding the boat harbor, raising lowland elevation, repairing utilities, and installing new facilities. In essence, an entire new commercial district was superimposed on the old one without any one business having to shut down for more than twenty-four hours. Initial private redevelopment under the urban renewal plan began toward the end of August 1965; subsequent revisions in the program have been made to handle problems of land acquisition and residential relocation. Completion of the redevelopment plan is expected by August 1969, with estimated expenditures of $6.3 million.

▷ SELDOVIA

A small picturesque town in a protected inlet on the Kenai Peninsula, Seldovia is accessible only by sea or air. Aside from the tourist trade, the community depends primarily on the fishing industry for its income. Prior to the quake, Seldovia had a relatively solid economic position because of its strategic location with respect to one of the king crab fishing areas.[24] Although the town did

---

23. "The Role of Urban Planning in the Reconstruction of Alaska," p. 23.
24. The commercial market for king crab has only been developed on a large scale since 1960.

not suffer major physical damage, the subsequent lowering of the land mass by 3.7 feet subjected all waterfront facilities to inundation at high tide. Built on wooden pilings, these structures had been high enough to be protected from tidal flooding before the land mass subsided. This inundation meant that almost the entire business district and approximately half the residential area were seriously affected by the land movement. The URA developed a plan by the summer of 1965 to rehabilitate the waterfront and move the industrial and commercial areas to a safer location on higher ground. During the construction period a large temporary building was erected to house some of the displaced businesses; twenty house trailers were also brought in to provide temporary residential accommodations. The 4000-foot boardwalk, which had provided access to the waterfront commercial area before the quake, became unusable and dangerous afterwards. It was therefore removed and replaced by broad, stable, rock and earth fill, thus placing the entire waterfront on a safe and permanent foundation. A new city dock is presently under construction at a cost of $800,000, financed by an Economic Development Administration loan and grant. When completed, this dock will be able to handle any ship that presently sails in Alaskan waters. The urban renewal and related projects were completed during the summer of 1968 at a cost of $3.8 million. To further implement these postquake changes, a general plan for the community and its immediate vicinity will be formulated by the Alaska State Housing Authority. Concern will be with the need for a capital improvement program, better use of existing resources and preparation of zoning regulations to permit orderly development consistent with the urban renewal projects.

▷ VALDEZ

Since the epicenter of the Good Friday quake was only 50 miles west of Valdez, damage to the town was massive. A submarine slide was triggered by the shocks, destroying the harbor and nearby facilities. Waves generated by this slide caused structural damage to all buildings in the business district and destroyed the sewer and water systems. Although the residents of Valdez attempted to return to their homes almost before these tidal waves subsided, geological surveys during the next few weeks indicated that the town's subsoil was sliding into the bay and could not be stabilized. As a result, it was decided to move the entire town with its businesses, homes, schools, streets, and utilities to more solid ground at Mineral Creek 3.5 miles away. Ironically enough, this location had been seriously considered as the original site for Valdez when it was decided to build a community in that area. Two urban renewal programs were thus initiated: a project for moving the old village of Valdez ($3.1 million) and a plan for developing the new town at Mineral Creek ($1.6 million).[25] By August 1964 the Urban Renewal Administration had approved the proposal for rebuilding Valdez on its new site, and one year later almost all outside utilities and streets were laid down. During 1966 the new city dock, small-boat harbor, city hall, as well as the elementary and high school, were completed under PL 875 funds. The substantial amount of Federal reconstruction has acted as a catalyst for the erection of private residences and businesses on the new townsite. Relocation of the community should be completed by September 1969.

ℰCONOMIC IMPROVEMENTS FOLLOWING A DISASTER

Despite the large amount of destruction caused by a disaster, we have shown that recovery can be rapid if capital in the form of loans and grants is readily available. In fact, a disaster may actually turn out to be a blessing in disguise. Aside from the economic boom that often follows because of the large amount of reconstruction, there is an opportunity for commercial establishments and homeowners to improve their facilities. Two interrelated factors play a role here.

1. The availability of grants and cheap loans for reconstruction and replacement.
2. The destruction of old business establishments that permits rapid modernization to replace gradual renovations.

The unusual challenges frequently triggered by disasters may also accelerate the normal process of technological change within the affected community.

---

25. These figures represent urban renewal capital grants for the respective projects. The townsite for the new community was donated, thus eliminating one of the major costs of carrying out an urban renewal project. The major costs in moving the old town to Mineral Creek were acquisition of property and relocating the residents and businesses.

In this sense, the forthcoming innovations represent a step forward in economic development. The pattern may be partially marred, however, if the allocation of funds to some areas is based on social and political factors at the expense of economic considerations. This section will touch on the positive and negative aspects of long-run recovery, primarily using examples from the Alaska earthquake for illustration. Of course, every disaster induces unique economic problems, but the phenomena observed in Alaska provide some indication of the benefits and costs associated with recovery after a crisis situation. To provide some perspective on the subject we will first look briefly at the long-run economic and social charges in Halifax, Nova Scotia, induced by a bomb explosion in the port during World War I.

▷ THE HALIFAX EXPLOSION (1917)

The record of economic, political, or social changes following a major disaster is generally incomplete simply because most studies are concerned only with immediate events following the catastrophe rather than long-term developments. Among the few studies discussing these far-reaching changes, the Samuel H. Prince examination of the Halifax explosion is perhaps the most thorough.[26]

The city of Halifax, on the southeastern coast of Nova Scotia, had developed into one of the most important British seaports during World War I. Virtually all the American munitions destined for the European front passed through its harbor. Despite the dangers inherent in handling such vast amounts of explosives, the city had never passed any precautionary regulations. On the morning of December 6, 1917, a heavily laden French munitions ship collided in the harbor channel with an empty Belgian relief freighter, setting off an explosion that killed 2000 persons and seriously injured another 6000. The explosion was the largest known to man at that time. Over 10,000 were left homeless—more than one fifth of the entire population of Halifax. Damage was estimated at about $35 million.

After a long period of rescue and relief operations conducted primarily by outside organizations, Halifax was faced with the task of rebuilding. It soon became apparent that the new city would hardly resemble the old either in social organization or in physical appearance. "Up to the time of the disaster,

---

26. Samuel H. Prince, "Catastrophe and Social Change," *Studies in History,* *Economics and Public Law,* vol. 94, no. 1, Columbia University, New York, 1920.

Halifax had certainly preserved the status quo."[27] The community was staid, unambitious, conservative, and content to live in the past. People sat back and watched events happen to Halifax; there was no desire or attempt to control the city's future.

In the wake of physical destruction came an equally severe collapse of the old order, since individuals from all social classes were forced to work together. The necessity of planning the future of the city for the first time and the exposure to new ideas introduced by the external relief organizations produced far-reaching changes in community attitudes. The net result was a social consciousness and appreciation of the individual as an essential part of the community. This new outlook was reflected in the many physical changes that were subsequently made in Halifax.

Civic groups were formed to help the government plan the new city; streets were widened, uniform sidewalks installed, store fronts made more appealing, and modern architecture adopted for homes and offices. Zoning laws were immediately passed dividing the city into residential, industrial, and commercial areas. Plans for planting trees and shrubs throughout the city were approved, and, for the first time, areas for parks and playgrounds were reserved. Interest in public health was especially keen due to the number of serious and often permanent injuries, such as blindness, resulting from the explosion. Within two years, the city had expanded its virtually nonexistent public health program to one that was admired as "the finest . . . and most complete public health organization in the Dominion."[28]

Overnight the city became receptive to new ideas and innovations. Trams were installed, telephone lines to major cities in Canada and the United States were made available to the public, and new industries were encouraged. The outlook toward commerce became more receptive and encouraging since residents began to realize that the future of the city lay in its harbor. Consequently, plans were developed for improving port facilities and attracting more traffic. Comprehensive munitions laws were gradually instituted to prevent the occurrence of a similar catastrophe. Additional regulations standardizing relief procedures and assigning postdisaster responsibilities to different organizations were passed for the first time in Canada. There is little doubt that without the stimulus provided by the disaster these changes would have taken at least a generation to accomplish.

---

27. "Catastrophe and Social Change," p. 121.

28. *Ibid.*, p. 133.

▷ THE FISHING INDUSTRY IN ALASKA

The fishing industry in Alaska provides an example of the fringe benefits that any disaster is bound to produce for businesses if large-scale loans and grants are made available from outside sources. Fishing is the most important economic sector in Alaska not dependent on Federal contracts for its income.[29] The industry is highly seasonal, since the entire catch is brought in during the spring and early summer. Early reports of damage to vessels and canneries following the Good Friday earthquake indicated that the losses were in the "millions and millions"[30] but that a thorough check would have to be made before releasing any official figures. The fishing commissioner also indicated that contamination to streams might damage the salmon pack. These official releases tended to convey an impression of a crippled industry, provoking comments that the 1964 output would be seriously affected because the season was so near at hand.

Table 8-5 details the final estimates of damage to both vessels and processing facilities caused by the earthquake and seismic waves. Despite substantial losses to individual fishermen and canneries, these figures conceal the fact that the entire industry actually suffered only minor losses; approximately 15 per cent of the canneries and just 3 per cent of the vessels were either damaged or destroyed. It is therefore not surprising to find that, contrary to initial

Table 8-5	DAMAGE ESTIMATES TO FISHING VESSELS AND COMMERCIAL CANNERIES IN SOUTHCENTRAL ALASKA

	VESSELS		CANNERIES	
Type of Fish Processed	Number	Value ($million)	Number	Value ($million)
King Crab	134	4.14	5	2.10
Salmon	165	3.05	} 13	} 1.95
Dungeness Crab	3	0.12[a]		
Shrimp	1	0.08	—	—
TOTAL	303	7.39	18	4.05

Data Sources: "Post-Earthquake Fisheries Evaluation," Alaska Department of Fish and Game, January 1965; "Earthquake and Seismic Wave Effects on Fish and Game (March 27, 1964–May 15, 1964)," Alaska Department of Fish and Game.
[a] Estimate also includes damage to 800 crab pots.

29. The continental United States, however, is the primary customer for Alaska's catch, purchasing 90 per cent of the salmon, 40 per cent of the dungeness crab, and the entire king crab haul.

30. *Anchorage Daily Times*, April 1, 1964, p. 1.

expectations, the 1964 fishing season was the best in recent Alaskan history. Figures from the Bureau of Commercial Fisheries indicate that the catch for the three principal fish in the area was greater than in any year since 1950.[31] From the point of view of the industry as a whole there obviously existed some over-capacity before the quake, since the loss of facilities in Kodiak enabled the Aleutian Islands to more than double their output of previous years.[32] On the other hand, because of the accelerated growth of the king crab industry in recent years, the 1964 catch might have been even higher if canneries in the Kodiak area had not received any damage.

The loss of the 300 fishing vessels had only a small effect on the industry, particularly as most fishermen were able to replace or repair their damaged craft and equipment through loans from the Bureau of Commercial Fisheries (BCF) or the SBA.[33] In fact, as early as May 15 the commissioner was advising nonresidents that Alaska had plenty of fishing vessels and gear to harvest that year's runs and that an influx of nonresident fishing equipment would only compound management problems and result in greatly reduced fishing time for everyone.

From the point of view of the individuals affected by the disaster, both the BCF loans for replacement of vessels and gear and the SBA loans for restoration of canneries encouraged the expansion and modernization of facilities over their prequake level.[34] Walter Kirkness, Alaska Commissioner of Fish and

---

31. The 1964 catch was a record for king crab and dungeness crab, both relatively new industries in Alaska. Although the salmon catch in southcentral Alaska was larger than the annual haul during any of the previous fifteen years, its peak was reached back in 1935.

32. In 1963 the Aleutian Islands handled approximately 16 million pounds of king crab; this figure jumped to 33.6 million in 1964. The catch of king crab in the Kodiak area decreased from 43 million pounds in 1963 to 29.6 million pounds in 1964.

33. Fishermen ineligible or rejected under the Bureau of Commercial Fisheries program could still apply for an SBA loan. For example, an individual was not entitled to BCF funds unless he actually owned the vessel that was damaged or lost. Many fishermen had conditionally bought a boat from one of

the canneries by making a small down payment but did not officially own the craft until the final installment was made. SBA was willing to make replacement loans under these circumstances. Two months after the quake, sixty-eight loans totaling $1.1 million had been approved by the BCF or SBA. All fishermen, except one, chose to replace their vessels immediately rather than charter a boat for the season. The final number of loans was 133 with a total value of $3.1 million, thus indicating that over half had been approved before the 1964 fishing season got underway.

34. For example, one of the canneries, which suffered approximately $100,000 damage, received an SBA loan for $750,000. $325,000 was used to rebuild and modernize facilities; the remainder of the loan went to debt retirement ($294,000) and working capital ($131,000).

Game, noted that less than one year after the disaster "the crab processing facilities in the Kodiak area have been rebuilt so that their capacity is equal to or greater than that prior to the earthquake."[35]

Damage from the earthquake also offered fishermen the possibility of improving methods of bringing in the catch, but this development was not forthcoming. Groups of fishermen would have had to pool their resources and buy bigger vessels using low-interest loans from the Bureau of Commercial Fisheries that undoubtedly would have been made available for this purpose. The fishing industry in Alaska however, is comprised of small-scale operators using traditional methods; fishermen trying new techniques are normally ostracized from the group. The men thus preferred the old familiar way of life to embarking on an innovational course.[36] Thus we see that disasters may offer the possibility of change but cannot always force the issue.

▷ LENGTHENING OF THE ANCHORAGE CONSTRUCTION SEASON

One of the most beneficial economic effects of the earthquake was the change it induced in the length of the Anchorage construction season. Prior to 1964 building activity was limited to only five or six months, beginning sometime in April and tapering off by October. In order to complete as much work as possible, contractors often had their employees undertake substantial amounts of overtime during the summer months, thereby increasing hourly costs as well as lowering workers' productivity per hour. Winter construction was normally restricted to completing buildings that were closed in by the end of fall and therefore could be adequately heated. The demand for workers was limited to the specialized trades (e.g., electricians and plumbers); common laborers either departed for the "lower 48" or remained unemployed during the winter months.

The soil studies required after the earthquake produced a substantial delay in reconstruction contract awards, and it was not until late July that most jobs were actually underway. Pressure to repair or restore facilities like schools as rapidly as possible thus forced contractors to search for new methods to

---

35. Personal letter from Walter Kirkness, March 19, 1965.

36. Personal discussion with Professor

George Rogers, University of Alaska, May 1966.

continue work on buildings that were not closed in by the end of October. By draping a plastic covering over the partially completed structure, portable heaters were found effective in warming the work area. Although this plastic material had been on the market for several years, contractors in Alaska never bothered using it for this purpose until after the earthquake. The crisis situation forced them to improvise in a way that turned out to have beneficial effects not anticipated beforehand. The plastic covering was so effective in increasing productivity per worker that contractors now feel it is to their advantage to maintain this expansion of winter construction.[37] They prefer to have a more stable labor force working more regular hours throughout the year than to rely quite as much on substantial blocks of overtime from their summer crews. Thus the increased activity that took place during the winter months of 1964–1965 induced a permanent change in the building season.

Statistical evidence confirming the new-construction pattern is presented in Table 8-6. We have computed the total number of hours worked per quarter in contract construction for the Anchorage area for the years 1962–1966 as well as the quarterly hours worked as a percentage of the peak period. The postquake winter quarters are a significantly higher percentage of the peak period than their prequake counterparts. At the bottom of Table 8-6 we have listed the coefficient of variation (i.e., the ratio of standard deviation/mean) for quarterly hours worked during each year since it provides another meaningful statistical measure of this change. For 1965 and 1966 this ratio was much lower than for

Table 8-6 QUARTERLY COMPARISONS OF ANCHORAGE CONTRACT CONSTRUCTION HOURS WORKED, IN THOUSANDS OF HOURS. AND PER CENT OF PEAK QUARTER FOR 1962–1966

Quarter	1962	1963	1964	1965	1966
First	539	405	592	1035	836
	27%	20%	23%	41%	35%
Second	1107	935	1432	1974	1509
	55%	47%	56%	78%	63%
Third	2020	1999	2577	2543	2395
	100%	100%	100%	100%	100%
Fourth	1090	1084	1960	1564	1766
	54%	54%	76%	62%	74%
Coefficient of Variation	.447	.519	.700	.311	.343

Data Source: Alaska Department of Labor (Employment Security Division).

37. Personal discussions with contractors in Anchorage, February 1965.

the previous three years, thus indicating less variability in number of hours worked.

Even with the introduction of the plastic coverings, the first quarter remains a much slower period than the other three. The principal utility of this material has been to allow work to be continued on partially completed structures. Since very little new construction is scheduled after October, when cold weather sets in, it is understandable that there is still a tapering-off of activity during the first quarter of the year, although this drop is not so pronounced today as it was before the earthquake.

▷ THE RECONSTRUCTION OF SEWARD

Background

The decision to rebuild Seward, Alaska, following the Good Friday earthquake is an excellent example of how sociological and political factors can overshadow economic considerations. The town, located about 125 miles, by road, south of Anchorage at the tip of the Kenai Peninsula, was established in 1918 as a potential mining center. When the Alaska Railroad was completed between Seward and Fairbanks in the early 1920s, the town served as the principal port of entry for freight and passengers to south and central Alaska. During World War II the port of Seward assumed increasing importance; most goods from the continental United States arrived there by boat and were then shipped by rail to Anchorage, Fairbanks, and other inland cities. At that time, the port of Whittier was developed and connected to inland areas by an extension of the Alaska Railroad from Portage.[38] This new port could be used as an alternate harbor for receiving military supplies, equipment, and personnel.

Following World War II the Department of Interior recommended that the Portage–Whittier portion of the Alaska Railroad be improved and expanded, while the Portage–Seward section be discontinued. Both ports were ice-free the year round, but Whittier was less than half the distance to Anchorage (62 miles) than was Seward (126 miles). Implementation of this change would have effectively meant a *coup de grace* to Seward. However, pressure from its townspeople

---

38. The town of Portage lies directly on the Seward–Anchorage line about halfway between the two cities. The railroad connection from Portage west to Whittier is about 12.5 miles long.

forced the rebuilding and modernizing of the entire railroad line and the continued use of Seward as the major port in southcentral Alaska. In mid-1961 the modern port of Anchorage started operation, making its bid to supplant Seward as the main point of entry for goods coming to the area. In its fight for economic survival, Seward had two allies. The Alaska Railroad, faced with the loss of substantial freight revenues if shipments from Seward to Anchorage were replaced by direct landings at Anchorage, insisted that the Federal government maintain and improve Seward's facilities. Furthermore, officers of freighters claimed that tide and ice conditions in Cook Inlet on the way to Anchorage constituted serious hazards that could be avoided by using ice-free Seward.[39]

Although Seward attempted to diversify its basic economy through the addition of seafood processing facilities and tourism, these ventures were not successful—manufacturing employment dropped from a monthly average of 135 in 1961 to 123 in 1963.[40] Between July 1, 1960, and the time just prior to the Good Friday earthquake, the population of Seward fell from approximately 1900 to 1600 inhabitants, lending further evidence to its declining position.

Effect of the Alaska Quake

The earthquake dealt a crippling but a potentially merciful blow to the already dying town. The port was hit by three of the elements the night of Good Friday —fire, earth, and water. Almost immediately after the earth stopped shaking, the Standard Oil fuel tanks along the waterfront collapsed and went up in flames. The great seismic waves that followed spread blazing gasoline and oil over most of the community so that utilities were battered, the harbor wiped out, and rail and road transportation lines wrecked. Although only twelve residents were killed, the town was almost completely devastated, with the physical damage estimated at over $29 million, or $19,600 on a per capita basis.[41] Immediately following the earthquake, approximately 90 per cent of the nongovernment labor force was unemployed.[42]

---

39. George Rogers, "Economic Impact of the Alaskan Earthquake," Committee on the Alaska Earthquake, NAS-NRC, Washington, D.C., 1966, p. 30, mimeographed.

40. *Ibid.*, p. 30.

41. The specific estimates assembled by the NAS-NRC Committee on the Alaska Earthquake show state and local property damage at $11 million, private property losses at $5.5 million, and damage to the Federally owned and operated Alaska Railroad (terminal facilities at Seward and the Seward–Portage section of the line) at $13 million.

42. "Local Office Reports from Seward," Alaska Department of Labor, Juneau, June 1964, mimeographed.

Fortunately, the port of Anchorage suffered only minor damage and could effectively substitute for Seward's functions within a few days. Further assistance was provided by the ice-free port of Whittier, whose harbor was relatively unscathed and whose rail connections to Anchorage were temporarily restored by the middle of April.

The cards lay face up on the table: (1) An economically declining town had been almost totally destroyed, and (2) competitive facilities at Anchorage and Whittier were relatively unscathed. Undersecretary of the Interior James Carr saw the handwriting on the wall several days after the quake and raised the possibility of permanently moving the terminal of the Alaska Railroad to Whittier. He reasoned that before the quake there was a duplication between the two ports, and since Whittier could be restored to normal in three weeks with little cost, there was absolutely no sense in spending an additional $29 million to rebuild Seward's facilities. United States Senator E. L. Bartlett of Alaska, however, voiced strong objections to this proposal solely on sociological grounds, asserting that Seward "is dependent upon transportation facilities and would be wiped out by a decision not to rebuild port facilities."[43] In the end Bartlett had his way, with the final decision authorizing the complete rebuilding of Seward. Anchorage and Whittier would serve as substitute ports during the reconstruction period.

Postquake Developments

Once the decision to rebuild Seward was approved, every effort was made to improve the town over its prequake position. Universal Seafood Processors announced in April 1964 that it planned to construct a $500,000 seafood processing and freezing plant in the area that would provide $750,000 in annual income for Seward as well as forty year-round jobs and forty seasonal positions. Interestingly enough, the firm had intended to build this structure in an entirely different location before the quake struck. A few days later, the town learned that they were getting a much more modern dock than the one that had been destroyed; President Johnson also appropriated the necessary funds for rebuilding the Alaska Railroad. By the end of August 1964, the Urban Renewal Administration approved plans for redeveloping land-side facilities along the

---

43. *Anchorage Daily Times*, April 1, 1964.

waterfront area. Table 8-7 provides a detailed breakdown of Federal expenditures for emergency relief as well as long-term recovery. Even without the inclusion of figures on relief to the private sector (SBA loans, FNMA mortgage forgiveness, tax write-offs) for which no specific data were available, it is clear from the overall total that the government met its commitment to rebuild the town of Seward.

Despite the complete reconstruction and modernization of transportation (railroad and port) facilities, economic activity in the town has been at a new low. Two developments in shipping account for the rather bleak picture today. Even before the earthquake, the construction of a railcar-loading dock facility at Whittier, coupled with the introduction of sea-land vans and containerized shipments direct from the West Coast to Anchorage, had reduced Seward's importance.[44] An even more important development occurred during the post-

Table 8-7	ESTIMATED FEDERAL EXPENDITURES TO SEWARD ($THOUSAND)

Short-term Recuperation		
Emergency Rehabilitation		$2,708
Debris Clearance	2,500	
Health and Sanitation	208	
Long-term Recovery		
State and Local Facilities		10,370
Transportation	5,000	
Local	2,860	
State	2,140	
Public Buildings	870	
Local	250	
State	620	
Educational	1,200	
Public Utilities	1,800	
Urban Renewal Project	1,500	
Federal Facilities (Alaska Railroad)		13,000
TOTAL		$26,078

Data Sources: Office of Emergency Planning; Alaska Railroad; Department of Housing and Urban Development.

44. Increased use of air freight to various inland Alaskan destinations also reduced the tonnage transported by water. See Real Estate Research Corporation, *Land Utilization and Marketability Study, Seward Urban Renewal Project, Seward, Alaska*, Alaska State Housing Administration, Anchorage, 1964, p. 13.

disaster period when the port of Anchorage was needed to handle direct shipments from the West Coast. For the first time, freighters attempted to enter Cook Inlet during the winter by loading down the stern of the ships and going fast enough to break the ice. The experiment was such a spectacular success that, for all practical purposes, Anchorage is now considered an ice-free harbor. As a result, its port facilities have been greatly expanded and modernized from their prequake status. A 150-foot extension of the north end of the dock undertaken at a cost of $750,000 and a new $1.8 million petroleum tanker dock have been constructed. Anchorage would not have been built as rapidly, or perhaps at all, if it were not for the bold experiment with the ice that yielded positive results. Economic progress in shipping to southcentral Alaska thus occurred because of widespread technological progress in the industry (containerization) and specific postdisaster changes (breaking the ice at Anchorage).

The position of Seward today can best be summarized by some comparative figures. Table 8-8 indicates the change in shipping patterns from 1961 to 1966 for the three principal southcentral Alaskan ports serving the Anchorage area. As the years 1964 and 1965 represent the period of restoration of transportation facilities in Seward, these tonnages alone are not representative of a permanent structural change. Although work on the city dock and inner harbor facilities was essentially completed by June 1965, Seward could not receive large quantities of freight until 1966, since the Alaska Railroad had not been fully restored. During 1966, however, when facilities had been completed, the average number of boats arriving in Seward per week decreased from a prequake average of between two and three to less than one. As shown in Table 8-8, Seward's percentage of the total tonnage shipped to the three ports (Anchorage, Seward, Whittier) clearly has also fallen accordingly. During the prequake year of 1963 Seward received 55 per cent of the tonnage while in 1966 it only received 4 per cent. The increased use of automated facilities for unloading cargo also contributed to the reduction in the number of employed

Table 8-8	FREIGHT TONNAGE[a] SHIPPED TO INDIVIDUAL PORTS IN SOUTH-CENTRAL ALASKA AND PERCENTAGE OF TOTAL (1961–1966)

	1961	*1962*	*1963*	*1964*	*1965*	*1966*
Anchorage	268 (26%)	352 (31%)	382 (34%)	749 (60%)	1080 (83%)	907 (86%)
Seward	631 (62%)	670 (58%)	622 (55%)	186 (15%)	37 (3%)	44 (4%)
Whittier	119 (12%)	132 (11%)	121 (11%)	303 (25%)	177 (14%)	109 (10%)

Data Source: Corps of Engineers.
[a] In thousands of short tons.

longshoremen to 38, compared to the 160 full-time employees and the 60 part-time workers needed before the quake.[45]

The anticipated Universal Seafood plant never did materialize, but the town restored the damaged Halibut Producer's Co-op, which has a staff of six and offers 30 jobs but only on a 4-month seasonal basis.[46] The establishment of a Coast Guard station in the area during 1965 and an Air Force recreation camp in 1966 also brought approximately 70 military personnel to Seward. But the situation for the civilian residents in the town is not bright, as shown by the comparative figures in Table 8-9. Despite complete remodernization and urban renewal developments in the town, the Alaska Department of Labor estimates that 440 people migrated from the city of Seward between March 1964 and July 1966. Over 17 per cent of the remaining work force was unemployed during 1966. These adverse developments prompted the city manager to request additional funds from the Economic Development Administration (EDA) in the spring of 1966 to build new facilities as a means of reducing the unemployment rate. In November 1966, EDA approved a public works grant for $378,000 and a twenty-year loan for $162,000 at $4\frac{1}{8}$ per cent to dredge the harbor further, repair dock facilities, and build a warehouse. Construction on these projects began in February 1967 and was completed one year later.[47]

A long look backward, using the total expenditures detailed in Table 8-7, indicates that each of the 1340 residents remaining in the town two years after

$Table\ 8\text{-}9$	ACTUAL PRE- AND POSTQUAKE ECONOMIC STATUS OF CIVILIAN POPULATION IN SEWARD (BASED ON ANNUAL AVERAGES)

	Prequake (1963)	Postquake (1964)	Postquake (1966)
Population	1770	1640	1340
Total Work Force	1000	770	740
Total Employment	900	660	610
(Total Unemployment)	(100)	(110)	(130)
Unemployment Rate	9.9%	14.3%	17.5%

Data Source: Alaska Department of Labor (Employment Security Division).

45. These figures were given to us in personal communications with Fred Waltz, city manager of Seward, April 1966.

46. Real Estate Research Corporation, *op. cit.*, p. 3.

47. The funds for these projects were authorized under the Public Works and Economic Development Act of 1965 (PL 89-136) to aid areas of high unemployment. Normally 70 per cent of the project is financed by a grant from EDA with the community contributing the remaining portion. Because of Seward's desperate plight, EDA funded the entire project by supplementing its normal grant with a special twenty-year loan.

the quake could have been given a lump-sum payment of more than $22,000 to move elsewhere, thus permitting the town to die in peace rather than having to request more Federal funds. Ironically enough, Seward was scheduled to be named an All-American City in early April 1964, when the quake postponed the festivities; two years later, however, when rebuilding had been completed, the town received this long-awaited award.

CONCLUSIONS

The empirical evidence in this chapter indicates that a community may benefit economically from a disaster through a rapid inflow of capital for rebuilding purposes and the adoption of technological innovations to meet crisis situations. Occasionally the physical effects of the occurrence may directly benefit the region. A case in point is the tornado that ripped through the city of Topeka in June 1966. According to Mayor Charles W. Wright, Jr., the swath cut by the storm carved out a path almost identical to the one proposed by the city for a new superhighway and thus prematurely razed buildings that were scheduled for demolition. Unfortunately, Federal funds were not available for the city of Topeka to purchase the land on the proposed site of the highway; consequently, most of the damaged structures have now been rebuilt and may have to be torn down again at a future date.[48]

Fishing after hurricane Carla was better than at any time since the early 1940s because the surging water cleaned the coral reefs of mud and silt, redistributed the food producing areas, and thereby increased the number of fish available.[49]

But these unexpected side-benefits are the exception rather than the rule. What seems more typical are the comments appearing six months to a year after a disaster, expressing surprise at the speed with which the community has recovered and the prosperity that now reigns. An example of this reaction is found in the following clipping that appeared in the December 17, 1964, issue of the *Indianapolis News*.

---

48. Personal letter from Mayor Charles W. Wright, April 24, 1968.
49. Harry E. Moore et al., . . . *And the*

Winds Blew, The Hogg Foundation for Mental Health, University of Texas, Austin, 1964, p. 113.

Prosperity Follows Alaska Quake Ruin (Anchorage—AP)

With its first post-quake Christmas approaching, the city's merchants have taken a close look at yuletide spending and find the current business picture as bright as the twinkle in Santa's eyes.

The consensus is that business this Christmas season promises to be perhaps the best ever—despite the big shake of March 27.

Employment is up and the Salvation Army's Christmas kettles are ringing out a tune of quarters and dimes far louder than in past years.

Vance Phillips, co-proprietor of two large department stores, said:

"This will be our biggest year by quite a bit. Every year so far has been the best and 1964 is no exception. There are just more people around this year and they are not holding back in shopping."

Mayor Elmer Rasmuson, who also is president of the National Bank of Alaska, commented "probably the season will be one of the best we have ever seen in Anchorage."

This view is shared by William Renfro, executive vice-president of the Matanuska Valley Bank.

"All the people we talk to, customers of the bank, particularly in the retail trade, seem to be enjoying an excellent business this season," Renfro said. "The reason they give is earthquake reconstruction work—much of the work has gone on later than usual and there are just more payrolls."

Yvonne Krotke, manager of the State Employment Service Office in Anchorage, said quake reconstruction work has resulted in lower unemployment and a higher than normal level of winter employment.

This concluding optimistic note about the recovery process leads us to the next part of the book, where we examine more specifically the role of the Federal government in postdisaster operations.

Part IV

THE ROLE OF THE FEDERAL GOVERNMENT IN NATURAL DISASTER

<table>
<tr><td>

Chapter Nine

</td><td>

The Small

</td></tr>
</table>

Business Administration

Disaster Relief Program

THE SMALL Business Administration has operated a disaster-loan program since 1953. The major features of that program are its wide coverage, extreme flexibility, and quick response. Individuals, business concerns including corporations, partnerships, and cooperatives, churches, charitable organizations, and other nonprofit organizations qualify for disaster loans once their area has been designated a disaster area.[1] This broad coverage applies in all types of natural disasters, with the congressional authority for disaster loans stated in such a way as to allow the Administration considerable discretion with regard to qualification of applicants, loan size, maturity, and other loan characteristics.

The first section of this chapter outlines some salient features of the SBA disaster-loan program. The next section presents some relevant statistics on the size of loans granted since the disaster-loan operation became a part of the Small Business Act. Then comes a more detailed analysis of SBA disaster

---

1. See *Federal Disaster Relief Manual*, rev. ed., Committee on Government Operations, U.S. Senate, U.S. Government Printing Office, 1963, p. 92. See also *Small Business Act*, committee print, Select Committee on Small Business, U.S. Senate, 89th Congress, First Session, August 30, 1965, and "Disaster Loans," Small Business Administration; Office of Disaster Loans, ND 560-1, September 1967, Chaps. 5–8.

home loans in the Alaska earthquake. This last section demonstrates in a concrete way the versatility exercised by the SBA in making disaster loans. It is a case study illustrating how SBA loan analysts actually determine the loan size and maturities. For the purpose of inferring how these loan characteristics are determined, the SBA action in the Alaska earthquake is probably typical of their thinking in other disasters, at least in those that have occurred since the earthquake. The last section briefly discusses one major aspect of lending policy in hurricane Betsy and sets the stage for our analysis of equity in disaster relief in Chapter 10.

*T*HE SBA DISASTER-LOAN PROGRAM

The SBA makes three types of natural-disaster loans. Displaced business loans, those made to businesses to meet hardships caused by displacement due to urban renewal or highway construction, are excluded from our definition. (1) Physical-disaster loans are made when property damage has occurred because of natural disaster; these are by far the most important disaster loans made by the SBA and account for 98 per cent of all SBA disaster loans and 96 per cent of the value of all loans. (2) Economic-injury loans are allowed to businesses that suffer loss of revenue because of postdisaster conditions such as blocked roads and washed-out bridges. The purpose of an economic-injury loan is to supply working capital for businesses cut off from their normal trade. (3) Product-disaster loans can be made to businesses that have suffered economic injury due to an inability to process or market a product for human consumption because it has become contaminated or toxic through natural or undetermined causes. The SBA has made very few of this type of loan.

Physical-disaster loans have been interpreted broadly. Primarily, they are granted for repair or reconstruction of buildings, but items such as furniture and personal belongings are frequently included. However, no disaster loan will be issued for the purpose of building protective devices such as retaining walls, fences, and seawalls unless these were previously in place and were destroyed by the disaster.[2] In view of the otherwise liberal policy of the SBA,

---

2. "Disaster Loans," p. 32.

this latter restriction seems irrational, since funds loaned for protective purposes could reduce probable future losses and thus lessen the likelihood that the SBA would be needed a second time.

On occasion the SBA provides funds to relocate a business outside of a flood-disaster-prone area. In that case, no future *flood-disaster* assistance is to be given for any physical loss to property located on the site from which the disaster victim was relocated as long as the area remains disaster prone.[3]

Practically anyone suffering uninsured damage in a disaster area is qualified for a loan if there is a reasonable indication that he will be able to repay it. In cases where the SBA thinks the applicant cannot "afford" the loan, he is referred to the Red Cross for assistance. According to an SBA national directive,[4] it is not necessary that disaster-loan applicants show inability to obtain funds from some other source. However, the agency does not like to make a disaster loan if there is sufficient evidence that the individual can obtain other funds on reasonable terms without causing hardship to himself. There are no hard and fast rules in the procedure. In actual practice, the SBA does not investigate a person's financial position beyond determining his ability to repay the loan.[5] Therefore, few are turned down on the grounds that they have other resources; in fact, some are given loans even when their ability to repay appears questionable. There is no legal restriction on the amount that the SBA can loan to any person.[6] The agency normally follows a rule of thumb that the size of the loan should not exceed the amount of the loss. Thus, the loan is not intended to provide expansion of facilities or modernization beyond that normally expected with the passage of time. But this rule is very flexible, and, as will be shown later, the SBA can and has loaned amounts far exceeding that of the physical loss.

The law is more explicit with regard to maturity and interest rate. Today the maximum term is thirty years with the possibility of extension or suspension of payment of principle and interest for five years if the Administration determines that the extension is necessary to avoid severe financial hardship. Before the Alaska earthquake, the legal maturity maximum was twenty

---

3. *Ibid.*, pp. 36–37. The SBA national directive is specific on this point, but we were not able to determine whether the policy has ever been strictly enforced.

4. *Ibid.*, p. 31.

5. Ability to repay is not defined in the national directive. As we shall indicate later, ability to repay is probably related to the ratio of monthly income to monthly mortgage obligations.

6. *Small Business Act*, p. 10.

years.[7] The interest rate is not to exceed 3 per cent per year except for displaced-business disaster loans, for which it may be higher. For these loans, the interest rate is not to exceed the average interest paid on all U.S. government obligations plus .25 per cent. Virtually all disaster loans granted by the SBA since 1953 have been at 3 per cent per year.

*T*HE SIZE OF SBA DISASTER LOANS

The average citizen is likely to be familiar with the role of the Small Business Administration in the very large disasters that gain headlines in the newspapers. Those are the disasters we referred to in Chapters 1 and 2. In each of those disasters, damage assessment was about $100 million and above, and the SBA loaned more than $2 million in each case. However, in the majority of all disasters the SBA has loaned relatively small amounts. This fact is shown in Table 9-1.

The table reveals several important features of the SBA disaster-loan policy. In one half of the disasters, the SBA has loaned less than $50,000 per disaster. Not indicated in the table is another interesting fact. In all but one of

| *Table 9-1* | DISTRIBUTION OF SBA DISASTER LOANS BY CLASS OF DISASTER[a] |

Total Value of SBA Disaster Loans	No. Disasters	Ave. No. Home Loans Per Disaster	Home Loans Ave. Value	Av. No. Business Loans Per Disaster	Business Loans Ave. Value
Under $50,000	161	3.0	$2,965	1.7	$6,021
$50,000–100,000	45	8.1	3,530	5.7	7,509
$100,000–1,000,000	87	25.7	4,265	14.4	10,869
$1,000,000–10,000,000	21	186.4	5,867	144.0	13,240
$10,000,000 and over	6	1,046.8	5,435	797.0	30,946

Data Source: Small Business Administration, "Disaster Loans Approved and Applications Pending."
[a] Includes all disasters for which the SBA made any loans through the Alaska earthquake in 1964.

7. See in Chap. 2, "Recent Federal Legislation: Effect of Alaska Earthquake."

the minor disasters, the total number of loans made was less than twenty-five. As a matter of record there are forty-four disasters for which the SBA made only one loan. These statistics demonstrate that no disaster is too small for the SBA and also provide circumstantial evidence as to the partly political nature of the disaster-loan program. The Administrator's decision to declare a disaster area is based upon field reports by the regional offices that include statements about the extent of the damage, extent of insurance coverage, and probable number of applications.[8] As an internal SBA rule of thumb, no area is declared a disaster area if it is thought that less than twenty-five home loans will be made; but the figures in Table 9-1 show clearly that this rule has been broken on many occasions.[9]

To further demonstrate the flexibility of SBA policy we have taken a closer look at the distribution of loans in the five major disasters that occurred in 1964 and 1965. These data are presented in Table 9-2, and cumulative distributions for home and business loans are shown in Figures 9-1 and 9-2.

There is no statutory limit on the size of loans. For the five disasters listed in Table 9-2 the average home loan size varied from $2690 in the Mississippi floods to $21,381 in the Alaska earthquake. This large variation can be explained by three factors: (1) different physical characteristics of the disasters; earthquakes and tornadoes tend to be totally destructive whereas most floods and hurricanes are not; (2) average price of real property much higher in Alaska than along the Mississippi; (3) SBA provided additional funds for debt retirement in the Alaska earthquake.[10] In general, different disasters generate different requirements and the SBA responds to individual requirements.

In the cumulative distributions, hurricane Betsy and the Mississippi floods exhibit the same kind of pattern for home loans. In both of those disasters, about 70 per cent of all home loans were for amounts less than $2500. In hurricane Betsy, each borrower had the privilege of writing off up to $1800 of his loan. Thus, if we considered only the actual loan (exclusive of this write-off privilege), the cumulative distribution for hurricane Betsy would be even further to the left. An intermediate pattern is given for the Palm Sunday tornadoes and the

---

8. "Disaster Loans," p. 13.

9. It is curious that the average size of loan is related to the size of the disaster. In large disasters the SBA loans large total amounts of money, and the average loan is also relatively large. This might indicate that disasters that cover a large area tend to be intensely violent too and/or that the SBA is more lenient in granting loans in the large disasters than in the small ones.

10. See the following section of this chapter.

Table 9-2 — DISTRIBUTION OF SBA DISASTER LOANS IN FIVE LARGE DISASTERS SINCE 1964 BY PER CENT

Loan Class	HOME LOANS					BUSINESS LOANS				
	Alaska Earthquake	Northwest Floods	Palm Sunday Tornadoes	Mississippi Floods	Hurricane Betsy	Alaska Earthquake	Northwest Floods	Palm Sunday Tornadoes	Mississippi Floods	Hurricane Betsy
$500 and under	.5	.7	2.0	5.3	1.4	.2	—	—	.7	1.1
$501–1000	5.1	8.7	9.5	25.5	5.3	1.0	2.4	4.6	4.2	4.6
$1,001–2,500	7.7	17.9	19.3	36.4	63.3	4.0	6.8	12.6	14.7	29.0
$2,501–5,000	14.5	25.1	20.0	19.9	14.6	5.5	11.3	20.7	16.8	13.6
$5,001–10,000	16.3	24.9	20.7	11.6	11.6	10.0	22.9	14.9	23.1	17.0
$10,001–25,000	22.0	20.8	24.7	1.3	3.4	21.7	29.0	28.7	23.1	17.9
$25,001–50,000	25.7	1.9	2.0	—	.1	17.0	14.0	12.6	8.4	11.0
$50,001–100,000	7.2	—	1.4	—	—	21.8	7.8	4.6	5.6	3.9
$100,001–150,000	.7	—	—	—	—	5.7	2.0	1.1	1.4	.8
$150,001–250,000	.2	—	.3	—	—	7.8	1.7	—	2.1	.7
Over $250,000	.1	—	—	—	—	5.3	2.0	—	—	.5
No. of loans	809	414	295	302	26,192	823	293	382	143	1,791
Average size of loan ($)	21,381	6,860	8,304	2,690	3,451	92,867	49,013	16,702	19,658	17,242
Standard Deviation ($)	23,964	6,227	16,814	2,306	3,122	247,293	245,748	21,126	34,452	50,159

Data Source: The data in this table were derived from computer printouts furnished by the Small Business Administration. Note that the total value of loans implied by the average loan size and the number of loans differs from the figures shown in Table 2-4, which were taken from a different source. The cause of the discrepancy is unknown. Therefore, this table requires an assumption that the true percentage distributions are not affected by those discrepancies in the totals.

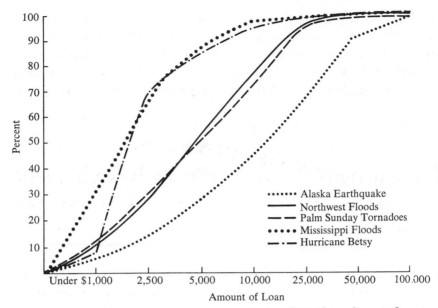

FIGURE 9-1.   *Cumulative distributions of value of SBA home loans in five major disasters.*

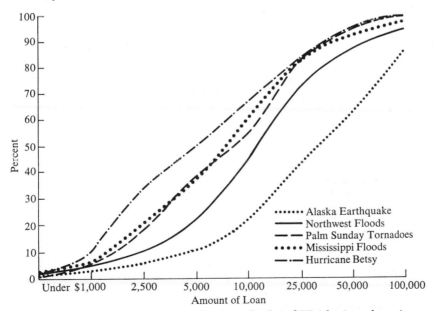

FIGURE 9-2.   *Cumulative distributions of value of SBA business loans in five major disasters.*

Northwest floods. In those disasters only 30 per cent of all home loans were under $2500. The Alaska earthquake is in a class of its own with only about 10 per cent of all home loans less than $2500 and almost 10 per cent in excess of $50,000. The pattern for business loans is more variable than for home loans, but again the size of loans in Alaska was much higher than in the other areas.

CHARACTERISTICS OF THE SBA DISASTER HOME LOANS IN THE ALASKA EARTHQUAKE OF 1964

The discussion that follows is based on a carefully analyzed sample of fifty home loans made by the Small Business Administration following the Alaska earthquake.[11] The data were taken at random from loan folders on file in the SBA Washington office. Some of the sample characteristics are presented in Table 9-3.

The analysis of this sample was undertaken to describe the SBA's policy by reference to what was actually done rather than to some vague statements

Table 9-3	CHARACTERISTICS OF SAMPLE HOME LOANS MADE BY THE SMALL BUSINESS ADMINISTRATION IN THE ALASKA EARTHQUAKE[a]

Number in Sample	50
Average Amount Requested (Dollars)	24,308
Average Amount Approved (Dollars)	23,160
Standard Deviation of Approvals (Dollars)	16,031
Average Maturity Requested (Years)	21.2
Average Maturity Granted (Years)	19.0

[a] Only loans in excess of $2,500 are included because of an ambiguity in classifying loans below that amount.

11. A similar analysis of business loans was undertaken but will not be reported because of our rejection of the hypothesis that the sample was drawn from the complete population. For example, SBA figures show that the average business loan approved was $92,000 with a standard deviation of $247,000 (see Table 9-2), but for our sample the average was only $49,000 and the standard deviation was $56,000. Evidently, many of the folders for the large business loans were missing from the SBA Washington files that we analyzed.

about their overall disaster-loan program. The reader should remember that the present policy of the SBA differs somewhat from what it was at the time of the Alaska earthquake and that therefore some of the policies implied below are not necessarily consistent with statements made in the first section of this chapter. He should also recall the discussion in Chapter 2 that indicated how the Alaska earthquake led to changes in SBA policy.

▷ DEBT-RETIREMENT LOANS

The distinctive feature about the Alaskan disaster-loan program was a provision allowing an earthquake victim to borrow in order to retire a previous debt. Undertaken for the first time in the Alaskan disaster, the granting of this kind of loan demonstrates more clearly than any other activity the broad discretionary powers of the Administrator in giving disaster relief.[12] When first granted in 1964, debt-retirement loans had no permanent status, that is, they were not approved explicitly by any law or internal SBA directive. Debt-repayment loans were not granted again until the Fairbanks, Alaska, flood in August 1967. In the following month, however, they were incorporated as an explicit feature of SBA policy as stated in National Directive 560-1.[13]

The new policy allows for debt-repayment loans on a case-by-case basis in hardship situations. Where payments on the previous debt plus the new SBA debt cannot be met by the disaster victim, the holder of the old lien will be asked to reset payments on the balance of the loan by using the original maturity. If total payments are still so high to cause undue hardship, the SBA can repay the old, relatively high-cost loan or have it reduced. Thus, the SBA can loan low-cost money to a disaster victim in order that he may retire a previous debt.

Since this new procedure generalizes a policy first used in the Alaska earthquake of 1964, it is useful to understand how debt retirement actually worked in that disaster. Suppose the earthquake completely destroyed a $20,000 home that had recently been purchased, so that the outstanding debt was equal to the purchase price. In this situation the owner would need a new

---

12. A debt retirement loan is subject to much criticism on the ground that it basically is inequitable. See Chap. 10 of this book.

13. Small Business Administration, Standard Change No. 10/National Directive 560-1, September 15, 1967, p. 30.

home and would be obligated to pay off the outstanding debt as well. The SBA would have loaned him $40,000 with which he could purchase a new home and pay off the original debt. Normally the double-sized debt would require monthly payments in excess of those previously committed; nevertheless, it would provide considerable relief. In many cases, as we shall note later, the term of the loan was extended to ease the burden further. If the commercial mortgage rate were 6 per cent and a twenty-year mortgage is assumed on the previous loan, the predisaster monthly payment would be $143, whereas the postdisaster payment on the double-sized loan at 3 per cent and a thirty-year maturity would be $168. However, this is an extreme case, one in which the owner had acquired no equity in the home.

The following is an actual case. Homeowner *A* suffered damage of about $10,000, but he took out a $33,000 loan from the SBA. $23,000 went to retire an old mortgage, divided about two to one between first and second mortgages. Monthly payments after the SBA loan were about $20 less than before it. This loan is typical because it illustrates that the SBA loan policy often has the effect of reducing monthly payments. Considering all cases in the sample where some substantial debt existed before the earthquake, the SBA debt-retirement provision in the Alaska earthquake resulted in a lowering of the monthly payment in about three of every four cases. For those persons who used the debt-retirement privilege, the average loan was approximately $30,000, and just slightly above half (52 per cent) was used to pay off old mortgages.

How frequently was the debt-retirement privilege used? Considering all home loans above $2500, 60 per cent received debt-repayment loans,[14] and in only one case out of fifty sampled did the SBA refuse this kind of a loan to someone who had requested it.[15] Most of those who did not receive a debt loan had no outstanding debt, whereas others did not request one because their previous mortgages were forgiven under the special forgiveness clause. Thus, the SBA was extremely lenient in granting debt-retirement loans.

The decision to grant debt-retirement loans in the case of the Alaska earthquake is easy to defend administratively. In Alaska, unlike most disaster areas, destruction was frequently total, and since most economic growth had been of recent origin, many homeowners were burdened with significant mortgage debts. To pay off an old loan at relatively high interest rates in addition to a new low-cost loan would have been impossible for many families. Therefore,

---

14. See Table 9-4.

15. The loan folder does not indicate why the loan was refused.

it would have been an empty gesture to have offered a straight replacement loan without debt retirement. The only recourse for many families would have been to declare bankruptcy and possibly leave Alaska.

By granting debt-repayment loans, the Federal government not only helped families whose property had been destroyed. In a very real sense, financial institutions, although in competition with the SBA, were beneficiaries of the Federal loan program. Bankruptcies would have resulted in considerable losses for local banks and savings and loan associations and for many out-of-state institutions, such as the Bowery Savings Bank in New York, that owned many Alaskan mortgages. Although it is unlikely that any single holder of Alaskan mortgages outside the state would have suffered huge losses, they probably would have been set back enough to make them skeptical of the value of Alaskan mortgages in the future. In an indirect way, this would have jeopardized the credit of Alaskans and caused an increase in their conventional mortgage rates, thus curtailing the growth of the 49th state. The Alaskan politicians who fought for more disaster funds were certainly aware of the potential effects of the earthquake on the credit position of their state.

▷ LOANS REQUESTED VS. LOANS APPROVED

Eighty-five per cent of the loans requested were approved by the SBA. This percentage is approximately the same as the average for all disasters. Of the persons who received loans, 90 per cent received the full value of their requests and only 6 per cent received less than the amount they asked for. The other 4 per cent actually received more than their original request because the loan analyst felt that those applicants had asked for too little, given their circumstances. Table 9-3 shows that for all home loans above $2500 the average approval was for $23,160, or 95 per cent of the average request. For all home loans, including those below $2500, the average request was $20,471 and the average approval was $19,513. Relatively few asked for very small loans, but they were usually approved even though some were of a dubious nature. For example, in the case of one person who requested a $1000 loan for repairs, the analyst made this comment, "Earthquake damage is questionable— home is run down and is in need of maintenance." Loan analysts evidently tended to consider the full amount requested valid if they approved the loan at all.

▷ POLICY REGARDING LENGTH OF LOAN

The SBA was also generous with regard to maturities. Where a substantial amount of damage was done, borrowers sought twenty- and thirty-year maturities. At the time of the Good Friday earthquake the Small Business Administration was restricted to a maximum maturity of twenty years. In April this restriction was eased in favor of longer-term loans, but even then instructions were passed to the field to use thirty-year amortizations only "as required, not as standard practice." Sixty-six per cent of the loans granted provided for maturities requested by the applicants. In 28 per cent of the cases, the SBA approved loans with shorter maturities than those requested, but this figure, as we shall observe, is misleading. In the remaining cases, more liberal maturities were granted.

"Only as required" is, of course, a very vague direction. How was the thirty-year maturity actually used? About one third of the cases in our sample requested thirty-year maturities. Slightly less than half who requested the longer maturities were granted them, and about half were cut back to twenty years. However, this statistic is misleading, for a closer scrutiny of the loan folders revealed that although some were turned down on a thirty-year loan (the agreement was written on a twenty-year loan in most instances), in many cases the monthly payment schedule was based on thirty-year amortization schedules. This, of course, greatly reduces the monthly payment for twenty years, at which time the balance of the loan, presumably, would have to be re-financed. Such a loan is more favorable to the borrower than one amortized out at twenty years. Most twenty-year requests were approved. The average maturity approved was 18.9 years, whereas the average request was 21.2 years. It is fairly apparent that the SBA was also generous with respect to the loan term.

▷ SIZE OF MONTHLY PAYMENT

If any single factor can be cited as having the major impact on SBA loan attitude in Alaska, it would be the size of the monthly payment. The amount of the monthly payment is determined by the amount of the loan, the term of the loan, and the rate of interest, given as 3 per cent. Even though the SBA followed a liberal loan policy, it cannot be stated that the Administration acted with total disregard to the safety of the loans it made. It is apparent from a study of the loan files that the SBA tried to arrange the various characteristics of the loan in such a way that the monthly payment would not be larger than that which the borrower had been making. Thus, we see little relationship between the size of loans granted and the monthly income of the borrower or the net worth of the borrower. The loan analyst tended to view the amount of the applicant's previous monthly payment as the amount he could be expected to bear. Considering the many loans which had to be processed in a relatively short period of time, this policy seems reasonable. In effect, the SBA loan analyst assumed that previous lenders had made a more complete analysis of the borrower's ability to pay, based on his present wealth broadly interpreted. Implicit in this attitude by the loan analyst is the feeling that the previous financial lender had already weighed all the risks and had found the applicant to be worthy of a loan requiring the scheduled monthly outlay.

To demonstrate how this policy worked in practice, we cite an extreme case. Mr. X requested a loan for $33,000 for a thirty-year term. $30,500 was needed to retire an outstanding debt. Mr. X was granted the full loan but the maturity was reduced to twenty years, just about equalizing the old and new monthly payment. On the other hand, Mr. Y requested a loan for $9000 for ten years. After an exchange of letters, the loan size was increased by $4900 to allow Mr. Y to pay off his old mortgage, and the term was extended to twenty years to reduce the monthly payment.

However, this logic can be carried to excess, and, indeed, it frequently was. It can also lead to inequities, as we shall point out in the next chapter. Mr. Z requested a loan for $31,900, of which $17,200 was for debt retirement. This person had a relatively high monthly income, but also his nonmortgage monthly obligations were high. It was argued that he needed a loan to make the necessary repairs on his home and that he needed an additional amount in order to retire his previous high-cost loan since he had already overextended his financial position. Of course, by this logic any extravagant person could always argue that he needed some assistance in reducing his monthly payments (either by reducing his mortgage rate from 6 per cent to 3 per cent or by lengthening the term) in order to be able to meet them!

▷ FINANCIAL CHARACTERISTICS OF BORROWERS

We have pointed out a few instances in which there appeared little justification for a home loan. That is probably the consequence of any massive aid program and in particular when the agency is under severe pressure to grant many loans in a relatively short period of time. In spite of one's judgment that many un-justified loans were made, it would be difficult to support a claim that the SBA did not maintain due regard for the taxpayer's money. Certainly the income and net-worth levels of Alaskan borrowers seem sufficiently high to raise little question about their credit worthiness.

Average family income in our sample was $14,424 or about two thirds of the average loan size. Considering that conventional mortgage lenders are usually willing to make loans two to three times the size of one's income, SBA home loans in Alaska were relatively conservative. The conservative nature of these loans is brought out even more clearly by comparing the ratios of monthly mortgage payments to monthly incomes before and after the earthquake. This comparison is given in Figure 9-3. The line marked prequake gives the cumu-lative distribution in percentage of the ratio of the amount of monthly mortgage payment to monthly income before the earthquake for the home loans in our sample. For example, for 63 per cent of the home loans, the family monthly income exceeded the monthly mortgage payment by more than six times. These

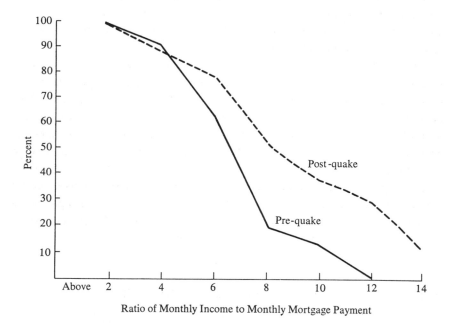

FIGURE 9-3. *Ratio of monthly income to monthly mortgage payments of Alaskan homeowners before and after 1964 earthquake.*

prequake loans had been made by private lenders. After the earthquake, when the SBA refinanced many of these loans at lower interest rates and longer terms, the ratios increased markedly. That is the meaning of the dashed line being outside the solid line in almost all places. Since a higher ratio usually indicated a safer loan, we must conclude that the SBA Alaskan home loans appear relatively safe despite the haste with which they were made.

No one in our sample reported an income below $6000 per year and about one fourth of the borrowers had incomes in excess of $18,000 per year. Average reported net worth was approximately $36,000, with considerably more variance than was the case with income. Some families reported no net worth. On the whole, however, this was not a poor group. Furthermore, monthly payments on other debts were not excessive and the average monthly payment on SBA loans appeared to be well within the abilities of the borrowers taken as a group. In only a few cases does it appear that the SBA granted a loan for which the borrower was overcommitted.

▷ SOME USES OF SBA LOANS

We previously stated that a large portion of the total loan value was for the purpose of retiring old mortgage debt. Replacement, repairs, land purchase, and personal property were the other uses of SBA funds. Table 9-4 gives a breakdown of our sample showing the various ways the recipients of SBA loans utilized the funds.

Debt repayment was by far the most significant use of disaster borrowing. The SBA previously had not loaned money for this purpose. Extrapolating from our sample, the SBA loaned almost $7 million to Alaskan homeowners

Table 9-4	USES OF SBA DISASTER LOANS (HOMES) IN THE ALASKA EARTHQUAKE

Use	Per Cent of Total Loans Providing Funds for Special Use[a]	Per Cent of Total Value
New Property	24	25.6
Repairs	74	28.4
Personal Property	20	1.8
Land	16	3.5
Debt Retirement	60	39.6
Other	6	1.2

Data Source: Random sample taken from SBA loan files.
[a] Since most loans provided funds for two or three uses the figures in this column total more than 100 per cent.

for debt retirement, and that is more than they loaned to homeowners for all purposes in any previous disaster with the exception of hurricane Carla. Whether or not the granting of debt-repayment loans is an advisable government disaster policy will be discussed in the next chapter.

Borrowed funds used for land, personal property, and other purposes accounted for only 6.5 per cent of the total. In quite a few cases large fissures in the earth rendered some land unusable for home sites but the homes were not totally destroyed. When possible, these homes were moved to other locations requiring some new land purchases. Repairs, excavation and construction of new basements, and moving expenses almost always constituted costs much in excess of the land costs. A typical example is the case of a $45,000 loan divided in the following way: $22,500 for repair and moving expenses, $6100 for land and $16,000 for debt repayment. In other cases, repairs and relocation costs were slight compared with amounts borrowed to retire old mortgages.

Most of the funds granted to replace personal property were used for the purchase of furniture. Some went to replace clothing, jewelry, and even tools. The justification for some of these loans is difficult to understand. In one case $6800 was approved for the replacement of household furnishing that were supposedly destroyed or damaged. How the furnishings were damaged without any damage to the home—at least, no home damage was claimed—is not at all clear. One suspects that this particular loan amounted only to a cheap long-term consumer loan. Judging from the man's statement about his other debts and monthly income, the borrower was on the brink of financial disaster before the earthquake. In another instance, the Small Business Administration loaned a person $12,000 to pay for some construction materials he had purchased to build a lake cottage that was not affected by the earthquake. Once again it is hard to understand the justification of such a loan.

▷ LOANS IN HIGH-RISK AREAS

Shortly after the earthquake, a geological survey of Alaska was made, and certain areas were designated *high-risk areas*. At least 20 per cent of the loans made by the SBA were related to properties located in these areas, and some of these loans were for large sums of money.[16] This is not surprising, of course,

---

16. We say "at least 20 per cent" because it is not always possible to determine from the loan folder whether a property was in a high-risk area. One fifth of our sample was definitely located in such areas.

since major damage occurred in the high-cost Turnagain residential section of Anchorage. What is surprising, however, is that the SBA loaned money to repair those homes and pay off old mortgages without requiring the loan recipients to take out earthquake insurance. Provision #5 on the SBA Authorization Form 304 clearly states that the borrower must provide insurance, "including comprehensive coverage . . . in amounts and for such risks as are satisfactory to Small Business Administration." Evidently this provision was either not enforced or the SBA did not consider the risk of future earthquakes high. The latter assumption clearly is absurd. Failure to force borrowers to purchase earthquake insurance on homes mortgaged to the SBA is, in our opinion, a gross mistake. For a $30,000 wood frame house, the additional charge would not have exceeded $42 per year. That would not have placed a great burden on the borrower and would have protected the SBA against potential loss in future earthquakes.

SBA LOANS IN HURRICANE BETSY

In the preceding sections we have stressed the apparent freedom with which the Small Business Administration operates its disaster-loan program. Although lack of specific regulation does allow the Administration to respond quickly and flexibly to almost any situation, it also encourages ad hoc congressional manipulation of its disaster operations. It has become evident since the Alaska earthquake that the SBA disaster-loan program has been infused with a degree of pork-barrel philosophy. Congressmen vote special legislation for some disaster area because there is always the possibility that their areas might be next. Frequently, actions are taken that cannot be justified as a matter of economics or equity.

The best example of the way that the Small Business Administration has been misused is the case of hurricane Betsy in late 1965. Congress passed the Southeast Hurricane Disaster Relief Act of 1965, which allowed a borrower to write off up to $1800 of his SBA disaster loan. As a result of hurricane Betsy, the Small Business Administration loaned over $120 million, mostly in small loans, with about $40 million subject to the write-off provision.[17] If the loans for this

---

17. "National Flood Insurance Act of 1967," *Report of the Committee on Banking and Currency, U.S. House of Representatives*, October 16, 1967, p. 8.

disaster are paid off on the average of ten years, given the assumptions that will be elaborated in Chapter 11 (2-per cent loss in the interest rate and a 3-per cent default rate) an extra loss of $10 million, not discounted, will be incurred. Thus, the total financial cost to the Federal government of hurricane Betsy will be approximately $50 million. This is by far the largest loss the Federal government has realized in any disaster. In fact, it could have made loans of approximately $700 million for the same loss without the write-off provision. Looked at in another way, it appears that the Federal loss in hurricane Betsy was as large as it had been in all previous disasters combined. There is nothing wrong with this per se, but we feel that the rehabilitative results were not achieved in the most economical manner.

The Federal gift in the case of hurricane Betsy can be equated with the debt-retirement privilege in the Alaska earthquake. The average forgiveness grant per borrower was $1430. As will be explained in the next chapter, an SBA twenty-year disaster loan of $6250 is worth approximately $1430 to the borrower, if the borrower's discount rate and the market rate are both 6 per cent. Therefore, instead of giving each borrower $1430 the Federal government could have increased his loan by $6250 and he would have been just as well off. This additional loan could have been called anything, even *debt retirement*. Debt-retirement loans are potentially inequitable and so are any other devices that achieve similar results. The following chapter is given to an explanation of this rather complex matter.

Chapter Ten | Equity in

Disaster Relief

IN CHAPTER 2 we briefly traced the recent legislative history of Federal disaster aid programs and noted that low-cost loans to private citizens rather than grants have been the preferred method of assistance. On those occasions when grants have been made, euphemistic expressions have been substituted for the term. In the Alaska earthquake, for example, the Federal National Mortgage Association accepted the "forgiveness" of some disaster victims holding FHA mortgages for a payment of $1000; and in the Southeast Hurricane Disaster Relief Act of 1965, the Small Business Administration was authorized to "cancel" up to $1800 of an individual's obligation to repay an SBA loan.

Grants have never been popular in any domestic aid program. Farmers have preferred to "sell" their crops to the Commodity Credit Corporation rather than receive direct subsidy payments. In the early stage of their development, airlines were subsidized for carrying the mail. Domestic mining interests have been furthered by sales to the strategic stockpile. Disaster victims have been subsidized through low-cost loans. From an analytical point of view a low-cost loan is equivalent to a grant. However, a grant program makes it clear that someone else has to pay the bill, thus facilitating an understanding of the welfare implications of aid.

The purpose of this chapter is to explore some of the welfare effects of the present Federal loan program, to draw attention to the loan-grant equivalence, and finally to suggest some criteria for avoiding perverse welfare effects of disaster relief to the private sector. Throughout the discussion attention will be

203

centered on disaster loans of the Small Business Administration since that agency is the principal source of relief to individuals suffering losses from a disaster.

Loans, grants, and relative welfare

The disaster-loan program of the Small Business Administration makes sense only if viewed through humanitarian lenses. A study of the record with a banker's eye could be unsettling. As one reviews the SBA disaster program, he must constantly remember that the Federal government is not primarily a profit-seeking organization and that, if it were, it never would have become involved with disaster relief. Evidently, the agents who are charged with receiving and analyzing applications feel that the principle of sound finances can be stretched when there exists a social need. The following remarks, taken from a loan specialist's comments in an actual case, are, we believe, illustrative of the approach that the organization follows in deciding on the merits of a particular request.

> Mr. X's financial condition is described as "heavy," yet his "only" liability consists of a mortgage debt around $14,000. He "has a large family to support" and it would "put the applicant in a bind" if he were required simultaneously to meet payments on an SBA loan of $6000—necessary to replace part of his business—and the [high-cost] payments on the current mortgage. Therefore, the SBA ought to loan him $20,000 (at 3 per cent) since "approval of the full amount would definitely take a strain off the family budget."

A commercial lender no doubt would have considered the large family irrelevant and the heavy financial conditions distressing. The SBA, on the other hand, seemed to consider these problems as more convincing evidence for approving a larger loan. In this particular case the recommended amount was authorized.

We share the belief that persons put under considerable financial stress due to natural calamity ought to have somewhere to turn for relief. We believe also that low-cost financial assistance should be provided and that profit seeking is an inappropriate goal for the Federal government if it is the relief agency so involved. However, it is by no means clear that the present role of the Federal government in the private sector is ideal, good, or efficient.[1]

Basically there are three approaches to disaster relief.

1. Straight grants by the government or some other agency to the victims of natural disaster.

2. A governmental disaster-loan program similar to the present apparatus administered by the Small Business Administration.

3. A disaster insurance program.

In this chapter our concern will be with the first two approaches, reserving discussion on insurance for the concluding chapter of the book. An individual's loss may be fully redeemed by a grant or only partially reimbursed. Except where noted, the discussion in this section is based on full grants. Later on we consider the more realistic case of partial grants.

No disaster relief program, regardless of how it is managed, can be operated without cost to someone. It should be obvious that the cost to the government of out-and-out grants for full reconstruction will be greater than low-cost loans for restoration of damaged facilities. This does not necessarily mean that a loan program is more efficient than a grant program. In the former, the recipient shares more of the cost of the disaster than he does in the latter and so unquestionably he is better off under a system of grants. But someone has to pay the bill. In this case the Federal government collects from all the people through its powers of taxation and dispenses to a subset of people as their disaster patron.

The disaster program in any one instance provides substantial relief to relatively few people while reducing the income of many very slightly. However, no one is better off in an absolute sense. If A's home has been destroyed by a tornado, he is still slightly worse off than before the catastrophe even when his home is restored through outright government grants. He is a net loser by the amount of his increased taxes. So are all of the others from whom taxes have to be collected. There is no reason why relative welfare positions must be altered.

---

1. Each of these words has a vastly different connotation. A statement that something is ideal or good implies value judgments, which may differ among persons. If we accept the conventional economic meaning of the word *efficient*, an efficient form of disaster relief can be described as one in which the aggregate welfare of the recipients is maximized to the limits of a given relief fund.

A low-cost-loan program practically assures a change in relative welfare positions. Under a government loan program, A has recourse to relatively low interest money and this reduces his loss somewhat. But to the extent that the government makes loans below its borrowing rate (including transactions cost) taxes have to be higher by the amount of the gross government subsidy; of course, they would be even higher if full compensatory grants were made. Under the loan program those who have suffered property damage lose absolutely as do the rest of the population, but at any positive interest rate the disaster victims lose relatively as well. If the loan is limited to the amount of the loss, the victim's absolute loss will always be greater than that for the average taxpayer, who pays only a fraction of the government's loss of interest on a disaster loan. We also assume no tax write-off.

If natural disasters struck in a perfectly random manner, so that each person had exactly the same probability of being injured (and further if the marginal tax rate were constant), then it would not matter which of the two programs were in effect. Probabilistically speaking, A would infrequently gain and frequently lose, but the weighted sum of gains and losses would cancel out.

The total economic cost of any disaster to the nation is the replacement cost of the property destroyed. This is true regardless of whether or not there were a relief program. If there were no government aid program at all, the loss in welfare would be the sum of the welfare losses of the injured people, which in general will be equal to the cost of reconstruction. In welfare terms, though, it is not possible to state whether one method is more efficient than the other without knowing something about each person's welfare function.

Evidently, those responsible for running our government have ruled that the disaster victim ought not have to bear the full cost of his loss. Up to very recent times, our society has preferred to operate a low-interest-loan program rather than a system of grants. As we shall demonstrate later, it is possible to devise a grant system whose welfare effects are equivalent to those of the present loan system. The grant system explicitly indicates to the public that some are being taxed to the relative benefit of others. Since the issue of payment would be less confused than under a loan program, people in all parts of the country might be induced to register their own welfare feelings through voting and/or letters to congressmen. The major advantage of a loan program is that the individual pays most of the cost of rehabilitation. Persons who live in disaster-prone areas would thus pay a relatively high cost for living in them if the loan amount were not allowed to exceed the loss and the loan interest rate were positive.[2] And those persons, we think, should be responsible for most of the risks they had willingly assumed in advance. To structure this analysis, we shall construct a generalized welfare function for any individual.

THE WELFARE FUNCTION

A systematic discussion of welfare presupposes an orderly relation between welfare and the variables upon which it depends. In the following discussion we shall assume that welfare is a function of four variables. Exact specification of the function is unnecessary for our purpose. The variables are (a) the future income stream, (b) the rate of interest, (c) past acquired nonincome assets, and (d) a payments schedule on contracted debt. In functional form we assume

$$U_0 = f(Y_0, Y_1, \ldots Y_T; r; A_0; P_0, P_1, \ldots P_T) \tag{1}$$

The Ys represent the income stream starting at the present (Y_0) and continuing for all future time periods, i.e., $t = 1, 2, \ldots T$; r is the rate of interest at which the income stream is discounted to obtain its present value. A_0 is the value of assets at the present time. It has a special interpretation in the function. It is the subjective value of all assets not intended to earn money income which are held by an individual. Those assets usually have a market value and could be converted into income-bearing assets, but they are not converted because their subjective value exceeds their market value. Most durable goods are nonincome assets of which an owner-occupied home is the best example. Rental property is not included since the return from that kind of asset would be included in income. The series of Ps in the function stand for the pay-out schedule on liabilities contracted in the past. This series also must be discounted by some r to show the present cost of the payments pattern. If one's time discount factor

---

2. When the disaster-loan rate is below the market rate, the borrower captures the difference between the two rates; and if the size of the loan is greater than the loss, it is conceivable that the borrower's profit could exceed the loss. This point is discussed in more detail below under "Loans in Excess of Loss."

is equal to the market rate of interest, the present cost of all future payments will equal the bookkeeping conception of current liabilities.

Alternatively, the welfare function could be expressed as

$$U_0 = f(Y_0', Y_1', \ldots Y_T'; r; A_0) \tag{2}$$

where $Y_1' = Y_i - P_i$. Y' is defined as unobligated income, and for some purposes it will be convenient to use this equivalent expression of the welfare function.

Several implications of this welfare function are worth noting. If it is assumed that one's time discount factor is equal to the market rate of interest, an individual will purchase a home to live in rather than rent a home only if his subjective valuation of the home is greater than its market value. Of course, the act of purchase reveals this preference. On the other hand, if an individual purchases a house to rent it, he does so because the marginal rate of return on the home is greater than the market rate of interest. The Y's in equation 2 increase. It would be possible to treat A_0 in the welfare function as a part of the income stream, but the imputed income should be based on the subjective valuation of the asset rather than on its market value; and that is equivalent to stating that the marginal rate of return in satisfaction is greater than the market rate of interest.

From looking at equation 2, it is evident that an individual who loses assets in a disaster must suffer a loss of welfare unless an equivalent value is returned to him as a gift. A loan at a negative interest rate could restore his predisaster condition, but an interest-free loan in the amount of the loss, if it were not continuously renewable, would still leave him worse off after the disaster. In the latter situation A_0 would be unchanged but the Ys would be reduced since repayment of the loan becomes an additional obligation against income.

Other ways for restoring a disaster victim's welfare are theoretically possible. For example, an increase in A_0 in equation 1 along with an increase in the Ps could achieve that result. An individual might desire a larger or better home but had not been able to contract for one before the disaster because of his own income limitations or other credit restrictions. If he were able to take out a low-cost loan after the disaster, say from the SBA, to build the better home, conceivably he could be better off. While that outcome is not likely, it could be achieved if the individual had a very high time discount factor, which would mean that he lived essentially for the present and is not bothered much by a large debt.

THE DISASTER RELIEF PROGRAM EVALUATED BY WELFARE CRITERIA

▷ SOME PERVERSE EFFECTS: AN EXAMPLE

We have heard frequently that the Good Friday earthquake was "the best thing that ever happened to Alaska." With reference to the welfare function described above, Alaskans could be better off if the increased liabilities of those affected by the earthquake were more than compensated by an increase in income and/ or nonincome assets. To demonstrate how it is possible to achieve an absolute welfare gain within some of the existing disaster programs we offer the following example. We shall assume that all assets are valued at market prices, or that subjective value is equal to market value. Suppose someone had just purchased a $20,000 FHA-insured home and had signed a twenty-year mortgage at 6 per cent for the entire amount. Then some disaster completely destroys the home. Immediately his asset position would be reduced by the full amount and his liabilities as defined would be unchanged. Undoubtedly, he would be worse off. Suppose also that he were allowed to write off his mortgage for a $1000 for-giveness payment. At that point, his liabilities would be reduced from $20,000 to $1000. He still would be worse off since the value of his assets would have been reduced by more than his liabilities. However, assume further that he were able to borrow $20,000 from the SBA at 3 per cent in order to purchase a home identical to the one he lost. At this point, his asset value would have been restored, but since the periodic payment stream at 3 per cent is considerably less than at 6 per cent his liabilities in the sense defined would have been reduced from their predisaster level. If the individual's time discount factor were 6 per cent, the difference in the present costs of a $20,000 loan taken at 6 per cent and one taken at 3 per cent would be $4581 and that difference, called an *interest rate differential windfall*,[3] is the amount by which the individual's liabilities would have been reduced as a result of the SBA loan. Taking account of the $1000 forgiveness payment, the individual's liabilities would be $3581 lower

---

3. This concept and its computation are discussed in considerable detail later in this chapter under, "Low-Interest-Rate Loans as Windfall Gains." Calculations in these examples assume annual payments and compounding.

after the disaster than before it. This situation, where the individual obviously is better off after a disaster, we shall call Case *A*.

CASE A

Time and Event	Assets	Liabilities	Net Assets
Before Disaster	20,000	20,000	0
Immediately after Disaster	0	20,000	−20,000
After Mortgage Forgiveness	0	1,000	−1,000
After SBA 3-per cent Loan	20,000	16,419	3,581

We now consider two other cases. Suppose that someone owned an identical $20,000 home but had completely paid the mortgage. The bookkeeping entries for Case *B*, using the same government policy, would be recorded as follows:

CASE B

Time and Events	Assets	Liabilities	Net Assets
Before Disaster	20,000	0	20,000
Immediately after Disaster	0	0	0
After Mortgage Forgiveness	0	0	0
After SBA 3-per cent Loan	20,000	15,419	4,581

Anyone in this situation clearly is worse off after a disaster. Net assets have been reduced by $15,419 because the individual had no outstanding mortgage balance before the disaster and thus could not benefit from the government's forgiveness program.

Case *C* describes a situation in which the homeowner had taken out insurance. As the owner's original equity position is exactly restored, it is intermediate between cases *A* and *B*.[4]

CASE C

Time and Event	Assets	Liabilities	Net Assets
Before Disaster	20,000	0	20,000
Immediately after Disaster	0	0	0
After Mortgage Forgiveness	0	0	0
After Insurance Payments	20,000	0	20,000

A comparison of the three cases reveals some startling conclusions. The system of disaster relief that has been used in some past disasters tends to dis-

---

4. In case C it does not matter whether the loan had been paid off before the disaster. Also, insurance is not so good as a free gift because the insured person has had to make periodic payments in order to have his assets restored.

criminate in favor of persons who live on credit and against those who have made provision for the future by insuring and saving. It is particularly discriminatory against saving. If it were made a permanent part of any relief program, such a system would tend to undermine personal qualities on which most citizens place high value. In a sense, therefore, that kind of system operates in a perverse way.

The element in the system that contributes most of its perversity is the mortgage forgiveness. That constitutes an outright grant. A loan at an interest rate lower than the market rate is also equivalent to a grant. But there is a major difference: Everyone has access to the loan whereas the mortgage forgiveness is available only to persons who do not completely own their homes. From an equity point of view, grants ought to be as universally available as loans.

Selective grants such as mortgage forgiveness are not the only source of discrimination. Low-cost loans in amounts greater than the loss if extended to some and not to others are discriminatory too. We shall theoretically justify this assertion later in this chapter; for the moment we simply cite an example of how this discriminatory policy may have worked in the past. Following the Alaska earthquake the SBA approved funds for debt repayment, thus offering the possibility of extending the size of the loan to well beyond the loss. In the welfare function the effect of this policy is to increase A or Y'. Due to the low interest charge on these loans, there is a chance that a person's welfare might actually improve as a result of the disaster.

▷ SOME PERVERSE EFFECTS: THEORETICAL ANALYSIS

Any form of relief that alters relative welfare positions between individuals we consider inequitable. Those systems also tend to promote perverse incentives. However, for the moment our objective simply is to point out that a person's welfare can be enhanced after a disaster only if his income- or nonincome-bearing assets increase or if the discounted value of his future payments stream decreases. The immediate effect of a disaster is to reduce income or assets, and wealth must decline if something of value has been destroyed. Income or assets could increase by a gift or a low-cost loan in excess of the loss. Yet the latter possibility would seem to be precluded if the SBA followed its stated goal of only "restoring the victim's property to its predisaster condition."

There is evidence that the SBA has not always restricted its loans to this goal. In some cases, it is probably true that some people have been better off after a disaster than before it; and in all cases, it is true that people who suffered property damage were better off with SBA loans than they would have been without them even if, in an absolute sense, they were worse off after the disaster. Even though someone has to pay for disaster aid, the overall welfare effects probably are favorable; at least we would consider them favorable if the political decision to give aid is endorsed by most citizens.[5] Disaster relief, therefore, might bring aggregate gains rather than losses in welfare, yet it would be wrong to assume that everyone benefits. Some people undoubtedly are injured by disaster relief, and we now turn to consider how injury might be minimized in the interest of equity.

Let us consider individual welfare in the disaster area and forget about the slight loss in welfare in the rest of the country. It has been demonstrated that an injured person X could be better off after a disaster than before it. In another part of the disaster area, Z may have suffered no property damage. Although it is impossible to make any meaningful interpersonal comparisons of subjective utility (i.e., we cannot say that X is better or worse off than Z), in the situation postulated X has definitely improved his position relative to Z. It is even possible for X to move ahead of Z because of the event.

Other results are possible under the present program. Suppose that A and B suffer equal damage and each obtains a loan that will just exactly restore his property to its predisaster state. Suppose, however, that A has a lower monthly income and is able to convince the loan agency to extend his loan to a thirty-year maturity while B obtains a standard twenty-year maturity. Again, as we

---

5. Aid supplied by organizations such as the Red Cross results in an unmitigated improvement in aggregate welfare, to the extent that a person is willing to donate to relief agencies. There is an actual gain on the part of the people who pay for the disaster. Presumably, a contribution of one dollar to charitable organizations brings more satisfaction to the donor at the margin than any other usage.

This line of inquiry suggests a conceptual test to determine whether Federal involvement in a natural disaster improves national welfare. Suppose that the Federal government withdrew from all disaster relief and some private, non-profit organization took over the responsibility, raising its funds through donations. If this organization could borrow at 6 per cent and loan at 3 per cent, it would need to raise enough money to pay the difference plus operating expenses plus losses due to default. On a disaster loan of $125 million (approximately the amount loaned by SBA in hurricane Betsy), the annual interest loss would be $3,750,000, which would continue for the average maturity of the loan, say twenty years. Discounted to the present at 6 per cent, this loss over twenty years amounts to $32.7 million. Assume no default loss and operating expenses. If the charitable organization could voluntarily raise that amount, we could then say that the people who helped finance the rebuilding of New Orleans did so without loss of welfare.

shall demonstrate in a moment, *A* improves his position relative to *B*'s and may even move ahead.

A disaster-loan program is perverse if (1) it makes someone better off in an absolute sense after the disaster than he was before it, and/or (2) if there exists the possibility that relative welfare positions will be altered as a result of the loan policy. We see no reason for using a disaster-loan program to further normal welfare goals, particularly if the program discriminates against others, i.e., if it is perverse. Alteration in relative welfare positions, if desirable, should be achieved with other measures which are fully open to public scrutiny.

The elimination of these possible perverse effects within the operation of the existing SBA program will improve this form of relief in terms of a welfare efficiency criterion. Specifically, if the Administration would follow its own stated rule to restore the victim's property to its original condition, perverse effect No. 1 would be impossible; for it is evident that a person cannot be better off after a loss than he was previously if only the amount of the loss is restored.

Low Interest Rate Loans as Windfall Gains

The elimination of perversity No. 2 requires more than a summary explanation. First, the reader should have some quantitative idea of the economic value a disaster victim receives from the SBA liberal loan policy. The amount gained from borrowing at 3 per cent when the opportunity cost is a higher rate, say 6 per cent, we shall call a *rate differential windfall.*

When an individual borrows from the SBA at a lower rate than that prevailing in the loan market, he receives a privilege worth a calculable sum of money. If the maturity of the available commercial loan and the SBA loan is the same, the monthly payment to the SBA will be lower than the payment required by a commercial lender. For example, a twenty-year amortized loan of $30,000 at 6 per cent requires a monthly payment of $214.93, whereas the typical payment under a comparable SBA loan of the same maturity at 3 per cent is $166.38. The difference of $48.55 per month can be considered a gift from the government continuing for twenty years. The monthly difference can be treated as a net income flow. The present value of this flow depends upon the opportunities for investment open to the borrower. Let us assume that a home investment returns 6 per cent a year net. Under that assumption, the present value of a monthly income stream of $48.55 for twenty years is $6777. This sum is the rate differential windfall.

Table 10-1 shows the rate differential windfalls corresponding to various loan amounts and maturities. The table assumes that the best investment alternative, the opportunity cost, is 6 per cent. Suppose the amount of the loan is $20,000 and the maturity is twenty-five years. In that case the rate differential windfall is $5318. Of course, if the opportunity cost is higher than 6 per cent the rate differential windfalls will be smaller than those shown in the table; they will be larger than the figures in the table if the opportunity cost is smaller than 6 per cent.

Long-term Maturity Loans as Windfall Gains

The total windfall for a low-interest loan of a given size can be increased even further by extending the maturity. The prospect of a longer-term loan per se is somewhat distasteful but that distaste is more than offset by the favorable effects of a reduction in the size of the monthly payments. The additional benefit that accrues to a borrower as a result of a maturity extension we shall call a *maturity differential windfall*. Like the rate differential windfall, the maturity differential windfall is worth a calculable sum.

Using the shorter of two loans as a reference point, maturity differential windfalls are easily calculated from Table 10-1. For example, if a standard $10,000 loan with a twenty-year maturity is extended to twenty-five years, it is worth $369 ($2659 − $2290) to the borrower. Specifically, let us consider two individuals both receiving a $30,000 loan, but *A*'s loan carries a twenty-year maturity and *B*'s is for thirty years. A comparison of the two long-run payment schedules is given in Table 10-2.

| *Table 10-1* | RATE DIFFERENTIAL WINDFALL GAINS RESULTING FROM A 3% LOAN IF MARKET RATE IS 6% AND THE BEST INVESTMENT OPPORTUNITY IS 6% (DOLLARS)[a] |

MATURITY	AMOUNT OF LOAN					
Years	5,000	10,000	15,000	20,000	25,000	30,000
5	380	760	1,140	1,520	1,900	2,280
10	686	1,372	2,058	2,743	3,429	4,115
15	932	1,864	2,797	3,729	4,661	5,593
20	1,145	2,290	3,436	4,581	5,726	6,871
25	1,329	2,659	3,988	5,318	6,647	7,976
30	1,489	2,977	4,466	5,955	7,443	8,932
35	1,626	3,253	4,879	6,505	8,132	9,758
40	1,745	3,491	5,236	6,981	8,727	10,472

[a] Values have been calculated from compound interest and annuity tables on the basis of annual payments schedules. They have been rounded to the nearest dollar.

Because B's loan has a longer maturity, his monthly payments are $39.88 less than A's. Discounted at 6 per cent the present value of the income stream for the first twenty years of the loan is $5574. For the last ten years of his loan, however, B continues the monthly payments of $126.50 whereas A has no further obligation. Thus, from months 241 to 360, B has a negative advantage that has a present value of $3438. On balance, B is better off by $2136.[6]

Variation in the lengths of loans is a way of giving preferential treatment. It is an effective and legal method for achieving the same result that could be obtained by lowering the rate of interest. We illustrate this point by referring back to Table 10-1. Assume the twenty-year, 3-per cent loan as a standard one with annual payments being made. If X is allowed to borrow $30,000 at 3 per cent, he would receive a rate differential windfall of $6871 *and* a maturity differential windfall of $2061. His total windfall would be $8932. Y, who gets the standard loan, would receive no maturity differential windfall and his total windfall would be the rate differential windfall on a twenty-year loan, $6871. If the loan agency had discretion over the interest rate and for some reason decided that X was to receive a total windfall of $8932, it could have achieved this objective by granting him a twenty-year loan at 2 per cent. Or more precisely, if the opportunity cost of money is 6 per cent, as we have been assuming, on the basis of present value alone an individual would be indifferent between a thirty-year maturity at 3 per cent and a twenty-year maturity at 2 per cent.

Loan analysts who recommend longer maturities for some and shorter maturities for others are discriminating as surely as if they recommended different interest rates. We do not necessarily feel that discrimination is improper or irrational so long as the public clearly understands and sanctions the

Table 10-2	MONTHLY PAYMENT SCHEDULES FOR A $30,000 LOAN FOR 20- AND 30-YEAR MATURITIES CALCULATED AT 3%

Months	A's Monthly Payments	B's Monthly Payments	B's Advantage	Present Value of B's Advantage[a]
0–240	$166.38	$126.50	$39.88	$5574
241–360	Nothing	126.50	−126.50	−3438
				2136

[a] Assumes a discount rate of 6%.

6. Based upon annual payments schedules, the maturity differential windfall would be $2061, as seen in Table 10-1.

practice. But in our opinion the public understands little about the mathematics of finance; that it would countenance varying maturities but object to varying interest rates gives credence to that opinion. We simply believe that the Federal loan policy should be consistent with respect to this problem.

In the context of our earlier discussions on welfare, it is clear that if one person is granted a maturity differential windfall while another is denied it, the welfare of the first person is improved relative to that of the second, if all other features of the loan are the same. Perhaps his welfare should be advanced with the Federal loan, but if so, we would prefer that the loan policy be explicit on this matter. No doubt, lowering the interest charge to 2 per cent in the case of some borrowers while maintaining 3 per cent for others would make the intended result explicit.

The Small Business Administration is too circumscribed by regulations and tradition to effect a satisfactory remedy to this problem. On the one hand, it is charged with making low-cost 3-per cent loans to disaster victims and, on the other, it is criticized by its opponents for not heeding certain principles of sound finance. The truth of the matter is that its job is one of aid and not of sound finance. This does not mean, however, that it can be oblivious to its default rate. As it is charged with the task of granting relief, so it is charged with the duty of protecting the public's money. The SBA does not enter a loan negotiation with an attitude of indifference as to whether the borrower repays or defaults. Indeed, it attempts to tailor the loan to fit the borrower's ability to repay. This is why it grants maturities longer than the standard twenty-year term, and why legislation now allows the SBA to loan money up to thirty years.

Varying the Interest Rate and Maturities to Eliminate Perversity

The method of protecting the public's money by adjusting the loan maturity clashes with what we consider to be the public's notion of equity. It certainly is in opposition to one of the welfare principles we have discussed, i.e., that a disaster should not be a cause for advancing some above others. Yet the conflict of interest is not inevitable.

A harmony of interest can be achieved with a slight alteration of existing policy. A twenty-year, 3-per cent loan can be considered the standard loan so that the maximum amount of relief a disaster victim could receive would be the rate differential windfall on a twenty-year loan. If the loss were $10,000, the windfall would amount to $2290, or 23 per cent of the loss, and if the loss were $20,000, the windfall would be $4581 and so on. If the SBA thought that the monthly payments on a twenty-year loan would be too high in relation to the individual's ability to pay, thereby jeopardizing the loan or making it more risky from the government point of view, then the SBA should be authorized to increase both the maturity and interest charge in such a way that the maturity differential windfall would be just exactly taxed away. The trade-off between interest charge and maturity would achieve the following results:

1. It would eliminate the maturity differential windfall that potentially is a source of discrimination in violation of some principle of equity.
2. It would compensate the government for granting a more risky loan and thus more adequately protect the public's money.
3. It would still allow for a reduction in the size of monthly payments, making the terms of the loan more agreeable to the borrower.
4. If the individual were willing to sacrifice some interest for a longer maturity, he would, in fact, be better off by revealing a preference for these alternate terms.

Table 10-3 shows the rates that would have to be charged in order to eliminate the maturity differential windfall. It assumes a variety of standard loans, i.e., one could consider the standard to be ten, fifteen, or twenty years and, indeed, there is no reason why it should be the same in all disasters.

Let us take a hypothetical loan case to describe how this policy would work in practice. In a disaster where the standard loan is taken as 3 per cent and twenty years, X requests a loan of $20,000 for twenty-five years. If granted for twenty-five years, the interest rate charge would be 3.5 per cent. For the loan requested, the monthly payment would be approximately $100 whereas for the standard twenty-year loan the monthly payment would be approximately $112. In either case, the present value of the opportunity to borrow from the SBA would be the same. Under the current system of 3 per cent rates, the monthly payment on a twenty-five year loan would be about $95.

Table 10-3	RATES OF INTEREST WHICH ELIMINATE MATURITY DIFFERENTIAL WINDFALLS FOR A LOAN OF CONSTANT AMOUNT[a]

Assumed Length of Standard Loan (Years)	*Maturity of Loan (Years)*						
	10	*15*	*20*	*25*	*30*	*35*	*40*
10	3	$3\frac{7}{8}$	$4\frac{5}{16}$	$4\frac{9}{16}$	$4\frac{3}{4}$	$4\frac{7}{8}$	$4\frac{15}{16}$
15		3	$3\frac{5}{8}$	4	$4\frac{1}{4}$	$4\frac{3}{8}$	$4\frac{1}{2}$
20			3	$3\frac{1}{2}$	$3\frac{3}{4}$	4	$4\frac{1}{8}$

[a] Assumes a 6% market rate of interest.

Each applicant would respond differently to the schedule of interest rates and maturities, and the exact combination could be worked out by the borrower and the representative of the Federal loan agency. The borrower would benefit although not nearly to the extent he benefits under the current system if his maturity is extended, and so would the taxpayer. Most of the arbitrariness that exists in the present system would be eliminated, and the scope of the government in altering relative welfare positions of individuals would be reduced.

▷ LOANS IN EXCESS OF LOSS

To restore a victim's property to its predisaster condition is the stated purpose of the SBA disaster-loan program. Nothing in this statement of purpose can be construed to imply that loans in excess of the *physical* loss should be excluded.[7] Yet it seems evident that the statement would preclude granting a debt-repayment loan that would make the victim better off after the disaster than he was before it. Certainly, we see no reason why a person should be able to look upon a disaster as a fortunate occurrence.

To indicate the extent to which improper use of debt-repayment loans can be taken, we cite an extreme case from the Alaskan experience. The earthquake caused $23,000 damage to the property of Mr. X. He applied for a business-disaster participation loan from the SBA for $249,000 of which the SBA's share was 90 per cent, i.e., $224,100, a local bank furnishing the rest. This loan was taken for the purpose of refinancing an old debt. If the local bank rate was 8 per cent, the prevailing rate on business loans, the combined loan was financed at an average rate of approximately 3.5 per cent. Interest payments on the old debt averaged about 6.25 per cent (most at 8 per cent but a rather large loan granted earlier by SBA at 4 per cent).[8] The annual difference in interest payments before and after the quake amounted to $5400. This annual difference considered over a period of, say, twenty years has a discounted value in excess of $50,000 figured at any reasonable rate.[9] Thus, a natural disaster increased Mr. X's wealth by at least $50,000.

---

7. In Chapter 9 we referred to loans in excess of loss as debt-retirement loans as that was the main purpose for which the additional amount was granted in the Alaska earthquake.

8. This earlier loan was made under the normal SBA loan program, not under the disaster relief program.

9. The present value is $63,000 figured at a personal discount rate of 6 per cent and $54,000 figured at 8 per cent.

The case of Mr. X is not typical, but there is a significant number of instances in which people emerge from a disaster better off than they were when they encountered it. In terms of our welfare criteria, this is a perverse outcome. Not only does it bring about a different ordering of welfare positions, but it also makes a mockery of what most Americans consider to be virtues—thrift and providing for the future with insurance. Thus, the person who borrows to the limit is the one most likely to benefit from a disaster if cheap debt-repayment loans are available. If loans in excess of loss were prohibited, no one could possibly be better off after a disaster than before it, and the reordering of individual welfare positions would be unlikely.

We do not necessarily think that debt-retirement loans should be discontinued in the future if the Federal government is to be involved in disaster relief. They can serve a useful function. In most cases, it would seem that the size of a debt-repayment loan ought not to exceed the loan for replacement, since under normal conditions it is not possible that the debt on a property completely destroyed would exceed the loss. Although this may seem to be a reasonable limit to debt-repayment loans, it has no specific economic basis. In some Alaskan cases, in fact, the debt-retirement loan did exceed the replacement or repair loan, and we think that kind of practice, should be eliminated.

Suppose that the disaster lending agency operated on the belief that monthly payments after the disaster should not exceed those before the disaster. If amortization schedules and a basic twenty-year loan are considered, post-disaster payments will be considerably higher than predisaster payments if the loan is not allowed to exceed the property loss. Assuming a commercial predisaster mortgage rate of 6 per cent and a relief rate of 3 per cent, the relief lending agency would have to grant a debt-retirement loan about 3.5 times the repair or replacement loss in order to equalize the pre- and postdisaster monthly payments.

To clarify this point, suppose that someone owed $17,500 on a 6-per cent twenty-year mortgage. His annual payment would be $1526. Suppose that a natural disaster caused $5000 damage. In order to equalize the pre- and post-disaster payment, the victim would have to be granted a loan of $22,500 at 3 per cent out of which he could finance the repairs and retire the old 6-per cent loan. The $17,500 used to retire the old loan is 3.5 times the disaster damage.

We do not suggest that such liberal loans ought to be made. Our present concern is to point out how large a loan must be in order to restore the victim's absolute predisaster welfare position. By our definition any loan in excess of the loss can have perverse effects; and there is no logical stopping point beyond a loan size that is equal to the loss.

A policy of restricting Federal loans to replacement or repair follows from the general proposition that relative welfare positions ought not be disturbed as a result of Federal disaster relief. The capricious character of natural disasters assures that the ordering of individual welfare will be upset, for some will suffer property damage whereas others will be unharmed. Of course, those who are injured always lose their relative position immediately after the catastrophe; the purpose of disaster relief is to minimize the loss in accord with certain social constraints. Society approves low-cost loans but probably would not condone complete indemnity. Thus, acceptable disaster relief cannot prevent some backsliding of the injured relative to the uninjured.

Debt-repayment loans favor some of the injured relatively to others. A family that loses its debt-free home is going to be worse off with respect to income flow even at a zero loan rate if continuous refinancing is not available, but another family that is allowed to retire a large debt relative to its loss can actually improve its position. A policy that approves a debt-repayment loan not in excess of the amount of loss will insure that no one will actually improve his position, given the present Federal loan rate. However, the family with a prior mortgage debt will advance relatively to one that had no previous debt.

We see no way of preventing this result short of eliminating debt-repayment loans. If it can be argued on other grounds that debt-repayment loans serve a useful social need, then they should not be discontinued. We simply conclude that there is no economic argument favoring them. And precisely for that reason we prefer a Federally supported insurance program over direct Federal aid.

▷ DIRECT GRANTS AS A SUBSTITUTE FOR LOANS

Direct grants can achieve the same welfare goals as loans and ought to be much easier to administer. It would be possible to calculate the windfall benefit from any loan and make a direct grant in that amount. The Federal agency would not have to bother with collection problems, default, or legal problems in case of default. It would also make explicit the effect of Federal aid. In effect it would be cheaper.

But we favor a direct-grant program over subsidized loans for another reason. It would allow the victim to spend the aid funds any way he saw fit. If his own welfare is advanced by allocating relief funds to other activities, then there is every economic reason to allow him to do so. In this case total welfare might not be advanced only if the taxpayers' welfare functions depended upon the manner in which disaster victims spent their aid, that is, if individual welfare functions are not independent of each other. If taxpayers disapproved of any use of the relief funds other than for reconstruction, then total welfare might be decreased.

Conclusions

We have proposed, as a welfare criterion, that Federal disaster relief should be administered in such a way as to leave the predisaster ordering of individual welfare positions unchanged. Consistent with this criterion we have suggested the following rules of action:

1. The maximum amount of a disaster loan would be that which just exactly restores the victim's property to its predisaster state.
2. Interest charges on loans with maturities in excess of the standard maturity should be raised by an amount that would tax away the maturity differential windfall.
3. Debt-retirement loans ought not to be granted except in exceptional cases, and they should never exceed the amount that makes the victim better off after the disaster than he was before it.
4. In no case should full indemnity—such as mortgage forgiveness—be granted to disaster victims.

Chapter Eleven | The Cost of

Federal Relief

PREVIOUS CHAPTERS have documented the extent to which the Federal government has become involved in recovery activity following natural disasters. Its various agencies and departments provide technical assistance, equipment, materials, and many essential services to stricken areas. Although these types of relief are the sources of significant community benefits, their economic costs to the government, i.e., their marginal costs, are relatively low. In most cases the distribution facilities already exist.

By far the most costly type of assistance given natural disaster victims is financial. A grant under PL 875 to restore public facilities is a complete loss from the point of view of the Treasury of the United States. More fundamentally, it is a clear transfer payment from one group of people to another and eventually must be paid for in full out of taxes. Another kind of transfer payment is the loss in Federal revenues due to the tax write-off provisions that are applicable to disaster victims who have suffered real property losses. A third kind of transfer results from low interest rate loans from the SBA as has been demonstrated in the previous chapter.

Because of our ultimate interest in developing a system of disaster insurance, the purpose of this chapter is to estimate the financial costs to the Federal government of its disaster relief programs. The savings to the Federal government that would result from eliminating the current forms of relief to the private sector could be used as a partial subsidy in a disaster insurance program. For this reason we shall consider only those Federal costs related to the potentially insurable properties in the private sector. Local governments usually self-insure public facilities, and these are not likely to be affected by any private insurance scheme. Therefore in the following discussion expenditures under PL 875 will not be included as a Federal cost.

$\mathcal{F}$EDERAL LOSSES DUE TO TAX RELIEF

For tax purposes, disaster losses are treated as casualty losses and are afforded special treatment under the Federal tax laws. Damages to grounds, dwellings, automobiles, boats, furniture, and other uninsured property used for personal or business purposes come under this category. When an individual loses a home or furniture in a natural disaster, the amount of the loss, less $100, can be used as an offset against normal taxable income to establish a new basis for computing income taxes.[1] Losses to business such as rental properties can be treated as a current business loss, and inventory losses are reflected as a current operating expense in the cost of goods sold. If the accrual method is used in calculating farm income, damage to crops and livestock are deductible as inventory losses.

In general, the loss claimed cannot exceed the cost of the property. Thus, if a home that cost $15,000 is completely destroyed in a hurricane, the maximum loss claim is $15,000 even if the prehurricane fair market value might have been greater than that amount. In the case of businesses, the depreciated cost is relevant. All of the loss must be claimed in the year of the disaster; however, if the loss exceeds taxable income it may serve as the basis for a tax refund for the previous three years. And if the preceding three years are not sufficient to absorb the loss, it may be carried forward for five years.

In order to determine the amount of tax relief a disaster victim can receive, it is necessary to know his income as well as the deductible loss. If the disaster loss is small compared to income, the marginal tax rate is relevant for computing the amount of relief. If the disaster loss is large compared to income, the

---

1. The reader interested in the particulars of how casualty losses are treated under the Federal income tax law is referred to "Disasters, Casualties, and Thefts," Internal Revenue Service, U.S. Treasury Department, Document no. 5174 (10-66).

average tax rate is more relevant. As an example, suppose X has a taxable income after deductions of $12,000 and has suffered a disaster loss of $10,000. If he is married and files a joint return, his tax would be $290 after deducting the disaster loss and $2260 before deduction. Tax relief in this case would be $1970, or approximately 20 per cent of the loss. Had the loss been only $4000, the victim could have claimed 22 per cent of the loss, since that is the marginal tax rate for the income bracket $8000–$12,000.

The appropriate individual tax rate for disasters probably varies considerably. Data on the incomes of families affected by disasters is not available; therefore, it is not possible to state precisely the appropriate rates. The SBA data presented in Chapter 9 gave us some idea of the distribution of disaster losses, and we judge that, on the average, disaster losses are slightly less than the average annual income of property-owning people. However, without specific information, it is best to use a range of assumptions about the tax rates that apply to disaster write-offs. For the calculations that follow, we shall assume a lower limit of 15 per cent and an upper limit of 25 per cent. This broad range will allow for some property losses to corporations, which have a higher write-off rate than the average individual.

The total tax loss to the Federal government can be estimated by multiplying the tax rate by the total private noninsured losses. The percentage of total disaster losses sustained by private property (tax deductible) is uncertain. In the specific disasters that we have studied in Chapter 2, damage to private property as a percentage of total damage has varied within a wide range, from

Table 11-1	ESTIMATED LOSS OF FEDERAL TAX REVENUE DUE TO NATURAL DISASTERS, 1953–1965 ($MILLION)

Year	Low Estimate[a]	High Estimate[b]	Midpoint Estimate
1953	19	56	38
1954	48	141	95
1955	69	204	137
1956	8	23	16
1957	32	94	63
1958	14	41	28
1959	11	32	22
1960	26	78	52
1961	34	102	68
1962	18	54	36
1963	12	36	24
1964	84	250	167
1965	129	381	255

[a] Computed as 5.4 per cent of damage estimates in Table 1-8.
[b] Computed as 16 per cent of damage estimates in Table 1-8.

25 per cent for the Alaska earthquake to 93 per cent for hurricane Carla.[2] Averaged out over several large and many small disasters for any given year, we think that private property losses would be between 60 and 80 per cent of total losses for any year. Insurance frequently covers a large percentage of those losses in the cases of hurricanes and tornadoes and practically none in the case of floods and earthquakes.[3] On the basis of sketchy information, we shall assume that 20 to 40 per cent of private disaster losses are insured today and are therefore not tax deductible.

Thus, in our calculations, we shall make the following assumptions:

1. Sixty to eighty per cent of total disaster losses pertain to private property.
2. Sixty to eighty per cent of private property damage is not insured.
3. The tax rate applicable on casualty (disaster) write-off is between 15 and 25 per cent.

Loss of Federal tax revenues as a percentage of total disaster loss is obtained by multiplying the preceding ratios. Since each of the three factors has a high and low value, it is possible to obtain six combinations. However, we are interested only in deriving the minimum and maximum combinations to compare with the average, or midpoint, estimate. On the basis of these assumptions, loss in Federal revenue would vary between 5.4 and 16 per cent of the total estimated disaster losses; an average estimate of 10 to 11 per cent, we think, would be the proper order of magnitude. Our estimates on Federal revenues lost due to tax write-offs from natural disasters are given in Table 11-1.

FEDERAL COST OF LOW-INTEREST-RATE LOANS

The Federal cost of low-interest-rate loans can be broken into three components:

1. The difference between the Federal borrowing rate and the disaster-loan rate.
2. The default rate on disaster loans.
3. Administrative and legal costs.

---

2. These percentages are inferred from Table 2-5.

3. This is seen clearly in Table 2-4.

The annual Federal loss due to low interest loans can be calculated as the difference between the borrowing and lending rates multiplied by the value of outstanding loans. Thus, when the Federal government borrows at 5 per cent and lends at 3 per cent it loses 2 per cent of the loan value for the first year and 2 per cent of the unpaid balance during all remaining years if the borrowing rate remains unchanged. If the value of new loans issued in any year exceeds the repayment of past loans, the annual Federal loss will rise. Table 11-2 indicates that since fiscal year 1964, new loans issued by the SBA have far exceeded repayment of old loans. In fact, the inventory of outstanding loans has just about doubled in each of the last three fiscal years shown in the table.

The Federal loss on disaster loans must also take account of loss due to default and administrative expenses. At present the Small Business Administration estimates the default rate on disaster loans to be approximately 3 per cent. No data exist on the cost of administering the disaster-loan program, and we shall exclude this third component of the Federal loss from our calculations.

Assuming the given interest rates, the financial cost to the Federal government of operating a disaster-loan program in fiscal year 1966 was $12.8 million: $6.4 million was due to the difference between the borrowing and lending rates (i.e., .02 × $320 million) and the remaining $6.4 million was due to the eventual default loss, not discounted, on the value of loans disbursed in fiscal year 1966 (i.e., .03 × $213 million).

| *Table 11-2* | SBA DISASTER LOANS OUTSTANDING AT END OF FISCAL YEARS ($MILLION) |

Fiscal Year	Cumulative Disbursements	Cumulative Repayments	Loans Outstanding
1954			.3
1955	5.3	.4	4.9
1956	36.0	2.2	33.8
1957	48.2	7.6	40.6
1958	65.9	15.2	50.7
1959	74.2	25.1	49.1
1960	78.5	35.1	43.4
1961	92.2	44.4	47.8
1962	127.1	56.1	71.0
1963	150.2	69.9	80.3
1964	173.9	84.1	89.8
1965	256.6	100.3	156.3
1966	469.3	148.5	320.8

Data Source: Small Business Administration.

$\mathcal{F}$ORECAST OF FUTURE FEDERAL COST IN PRESENT DISASTER PROGRAMS

In 1964 and 1965 the Small Business Administration approved loans amounting to approximately 7 per cent of total disaster losses. Unless Congress initiates a new approach to disaster relief, it is not likely that the SBA will be involved to any lesser degree in the future. In Chapter 1 we estimated that disaster losses will amount to $750 million per year on the average over the next decade. On the basis of that estimate of loss and no change in disaster policy, SBA loans over the next ten years will be at least $50 million per year on the average. If the default rate remains at 3 per cent, the financial loss to the Federal government from this source alone will be at least $1.5 million per year.

Loans outstanding at any given time depend upon the rate of previous loan approvals and the rapidity with which borrowers pay them back. Most SBA loans are repaid well in advance of their maturity dates. From a study of four large disasters, we have found that disaster loans were repaid in about one half the time allowed.[4] These loans were repaid on the average within four to five years. With the recent trend to longer maturities we believe that loan repayments in the future will be made over a longer period of time than in the past. Our guess is that average loan maturities in the future will not be less than twelve years and that loans will not be paid off in less than six years. Using the assumption that SBA loans per year will total at least $50 million, we estimate the balance outstanding over the next decade will level off at some figure in excess of $300 million. Finally, assuming an interest-rate loss of 2 per cent to the Federal government on disaster loans, the Federal cost due to the interest-rate component will be in excess of $6 million annually.

---

4. This figure was obtained from a sample of financial records maintained by the Small Business Administration.

Relevant data are given in the following table.

Disaster	Number in Sample	Average Maturity (months)	Average Repayment (months)	Repayment/ Maturity
Hurricane Diane (1955)	41	108	49	.45
Northwest Floods (1955)	41	109	65	.60
Michigan and Wisconsin Tornadoes (1956)	25	135	59	.43
Hurricane Donna (1960)	38	63	43	.67

Adding the two components, we forecast that the minimum financial loss to the SBA will be around $8 million per year over the next ten years. Table 11-3 gives an estimate of the total Federal cost to the private sector, due to the two major sources that we have discussed.

Table 11-3	FORECAST OF ANNUAL FEDERAL COST OF PRESENT DISASTER PROGRAMS OVER THE NEXT DECADE ($MILLION)[a]

	High Estimate	*Low Estimate*	*Midpoint Estimate*
Cost Due to Tax Write-off[b]	126	41	84
Cost Due to Low-interest Loans[c]	8	8	8
TOTAL	134	49	92

[a] Assumes annual disaster damage of $750 million.
[b] See section of this chapter entitled "Federal Losses due to Tax Relief."
[c] See section of this chapter entitled "Federal Cost of Low-Interest-Rate Loans."

<table>
<tr><td>$Chapter\ Twelve$</td><td>The Need</td></tr>
</table>

for Comprehensive

Disaster Insurance

CRITICISMS OF CURRENT DISASTER RELIEF PROGRAM

THE INTRODUCTORY chapter of this book indicated that losses from natural disasters over time have risen proportionately with the increase in national wealth despite improved technology, better building-code regulations, and large sums of money spent by the Corps of Engineers on damage-prevention projects. However, beginning with the Alaska earthquake, the Federal government has aggravated the problem even further by increasing the scope of its assistance through special legislation. Several *specific* criticisms can be leveled against the equity of the current system of disaster relief:

A. The amount of aid forthcoming to victims of a disaster depends upon Federal classification of the area as well as any special congressional legislation. Regions not designated as disaster areas by the President or some executive office such as the SBA will be forced to rely on conventional financing for rebuilding if they do not have insurance coverage. In contrast, individuals in a Federal disaster area will receive low-interest SBA loans and possibly outright grants from Washington.

B. The Federal policy frequently rewards the gambler at the expense of the prudent or cautious individual. Special disaster policies, such as mortgage forgiveness in Alaska and a $1800 forgiveness clause on SBA loan repayments following hurricane Betsy, tend to encourage economic actions that an individual would most likely consider unsound under normal circumstances. For example, Anchorage residents are now anxious to obtain long-term mortgages with small down payments on their homes so as to be in a position to take advantage of the government's generosity if another disaster hits. It does not make any sense for them to tie up their capital in real estate, since debt was rewarded at the expense of saving following the earthquake.

C. The most disturbing aspect of Federal relief is that it does nothing to discourage individuals from moving into disaster-prone regions (e.g., flood plains), thus perpetuating the need for more loans and grants in the future. In fact, Federal aid to some individuals or businesses that rebuild in the same location may cause them to be better off after the disaster than they were before. Examples of this form of relief were discussed in Chapter 10 in the section on equity following a disaster.

By modifying the SBA loan policy in the directions outlined in Chapter 10, it is possible to cope with only some of the problems of disaster relief; individuals moving into disaster-prone regions will still be essentially guaranteed subsidized aid after future catastrophes. Some form of disaster insurance based on risk provides a means of protecting individuals before the unexpected happens, thus obviating the need for large-scale Federal relief. At the same time, unwise development of disaster-prone areas should be curtailed. This chapter will develop a comprehensive insurance system that should be equitable, marketable, and economically meaningful. To provide some perspective on the problem, let us first look at current insurance-industry policies with regard to various disasters.

CURRENT DISASTER INSURANCE POLICIES

▷ FIRE

Since the word *disaster* commonly refers to an event affecting a large group of people, fires are not normally classified under this heading unless a number of homes or businesses are damaged. Because blazes are generally localized, insurance companies are able to sell policies at premiums that are small enough to attract a large number of insurers but large enough to pay for the losses of a few. Furthermore, an individual wants to carry fire insurance on his house in order to avoid the heavy liability that a fire would bring to him if he were not insured. Therefore, practically every homeowner in the country pays the small premium for fire insurance although he will probably never actually collect on the policy.

▷ EXTENDED COVERAGE ENDORSEMENT

Today it is standard practice for a financial institution to require that a home-owner carry extended coverage (EC) along with fire insurance as a condition for a mortgage on a house. Extended-coverage protection, never issued as a separate policy but always in conjunction with fire insurance, is uniform throughout the country, covering damage from "windstorms, hail, explosion, riot, riot attending a strike, civil commotion, aircraft, vehicles, smoke." It was not always that way. Prior to 1937 any peril other than fire was covered by a special rider (e.g., windstorm damage), so there was no uniform required procedure when a homeowner obtained a mortgage. During that year, the insurance industry included EC as an endorsement to the fire clause. The policy was initially popular only in the Midwest, where tornadoes had always posed a threat. In the 1940s, however, after a series of storms and hurricanes caused severe wind damage in other regions, EC protection became more widespread and eventually was required by banks before they would issue a mortgage. The development of a comprehensive homeowners' policy in the mid-1950s represents the most widespread type of coverage available today. Contents and furnishings as well as property are protected against the specified man-made or natural catastrophes.

Let us look more closely at the available coverage against tornado and hurricane damage provided by the present EC endorsement.

Tornadoes

Insurance companies have been willing to include losses from this type of disaster as part of the EC endorsement because wind damage is normally limited to a relatively small area. Although no part of the country is immune to tornadoes and other windstorms,[1] their frequency and damage is greatest

---

1. During 1957, for example, the only three states not hit by tornadoes were Maryland, Nevada, and Rhode Island.

in the central portion. By eliminating seacoast and other hurricane-prone areas from consideration, we can demonstrate how EC rates reflect differences in tornado-damage potential for various parts of the United States. Windstorm-prone areas are also subject to hail damage, and these two components comprise most of the losses under EC for inland areas. Table 12-1 presents 1965 EC figures for a wood frame home (for each of the six regions delineated by us in Chapter 1.) These averages were obtained by weighting each state rate by its relative percentage of the regional population.[2] As would be expected, homeowners in the central portion of the country must pay the highest rates for protection against wind damage from tornadoes.

Hurricanes

[EXPERIENCES IN TEXAS]

Hurricanes occupy a very ambiguous position with regard to insurance protection, since damage from wind is covered but water damage is not.[3] Some

Table 12-1	REGIONAL COMPARISONS OF ANNUAL EC RATES FOR 1965, WOOD FRAME HOMES[a] ($50 WIND AND HAIL DEDUCTIBLE, EXCEPT AS NOTED IN APPENDIX A, TABLE 12-4)

Region	EC Rate
Northeast	.123
Southeast	.133
Ohio Valley	.106
North Central	.174
South Central	.313
Western	.064

Data Source: State insurance records.
[a] Seacoast and beach areas with special rates not included in regional calculations.

2. Differences in rates between states in one region do exist, but they are generally much smaller than interregional differentials, as shown by the individual state figures presented in Table 12-4, Appendix A, for wood frame homes and brick joisted mercantile buildings.

3. The standard EC endorsement today does, however, cover water damage to a building if the walls or roof were first breached by the direct action of wind or hail. Marked consequences can result from such a distinction as evidenced by

the problems following hurricane Carla, which hit the Texas Coast in 1962. Several days after the disaster, Governor Price Daniel of Texas "warned insurance companies against using the 'fine print' in their policies to escape or reduce payment of hurricane and windstorm losses resulting from hurricane Carla." Other comments by Red Cross President General Alfred Gruenther and other public officials made the insurance industry appear as a villain by their not paying for total hurricane damage. One official was quoted as saying publicly that, "If the

perspective on insurance problems caused by hurricanes in the United States can be gained through a brief summary of changes in coverage within Texas from 1900 to the present.[4] At the time of the great hurricane and tidal wave that struck Galveston in 1900, killing 6000 and destroying an estimated $30 million in property, a typical insurance policy excluded loss caused by flood, or any kind of waves. Following a coastal hurricane in 1915, courts ruled that existing policies covered only damage "caused by water or rain entering the building through openings in the roof or walls made by the direct action of the winds." However, a severe hurricane in 1943 prompted the State Board of Insurance to rewrite the EC clause so that it included protection from windblown water. Coverage of damage from tidal and surface water was still excluded. Losses from windblown water, particularly in the Galveston and Houston area, were so severe over the next few years, however, that the board withdrew its "windblown" provisions in 1949 and reverted to the earlier, more restrictive coverage, which still applies today.

After hurricane Carla in 1962 time-consuming surveys, and court suits were necessary to settle the wind-water controversy. Adjustors were forced to make the most minute distinctions to allocate the proportion of the claim they should pay. An example taken from Moore's book illustrates this point:[5]

> Stereophonic sound equipment in a home was destroyed by being battered and flooded. The adjustor surveyed the situation and determined that a window probably broken by wind had allowed water to enter and ruin the cabinet. But the cabinet would have protected the electronic equipment, it was argued, from water blown through the broken window; hence, flooding must have caused this portion of the damage. Settlement was made on the basis of an estimate by a cabinet maker for repair and refinishing of the cabinet, with the owner taking the remainder of the loss. If the homeowner had been able to demonstrate that all of the water

---

insurance companies get away without paying for water damage, they will be getting away with murder." According to a spokesman from the insurance industry, "There probably is no storm at any time in which the insurance companies were subjected to more abuse, more misunderstanding, more grief and more downright hostility than they suffered through Carla." Harry E. Moore et al., . . . *And the Winds Blew*, The Hogg

Foundation for Mental Health, University of Texas, Austin, 1964, pp. 184–187.

4. This material was compiled by the Texas State Board of Insurance following hurricane Carla and is presented in Moore et al., *op. cit.* pp. 190–193. The Texas State Board has prescribed the language of insurance policies and fixed maximum prevailing rates since 1913.

5. Moore et al., *op. cit.*, p. 188.

entering came through the wind-broken window, he would have been entitled to coverage on his total loss.

The wind-water conflict may also produce settlements that offend a person's sense of justice, as demonstrated by the following comparison taken from Moore's book.[6] One contractor built his home with the best available materials so that it withstood the Carla winds but later was flooded and almost wholly destroyed. His damage claim was disallowed. Nearby, another house built of cheap materials had its shingle roof disintegrated by the wind early in the storm. The claim for total loss was allowed.

The result of the Carla experience was a compromise between the insurance industry and claimants, with homeowners recouping approximately $65 million of the $170 million damage suffered by them.[7] The severe losses to the insurance industry prompted the Texas State Board of Insurance to permit a rate increase of 27 per cent in counties along the Gulf Coast and adjoining counties inland.

Comparative Rates for Geographical Areas

Table 12-2 contrasts the normal EC rates in 1965 with seacoast and beach rates for wood frame houses. The higher rates shown for dwellings near the water reflect the wind-loss potential from hurricanes. States north of Virginia have received mostly water damage from these storms, so inland rates prevail for the entire state. The West Coast area has not been subject to hurricanes, so only one EC rate is computed for each state in this section of the country. Differences between normal and special EC rates are largest in Southern states bordering on the Eastern Seaboard, where there is a low probability of inland damage from tornadoes and a much higher probability of wind losses from hurricanes. Texas, on the other hand, frequently has tornadoes and windstorms inland and hurricane winds along the coast; thus, rate differentials within the state are not appreciable except for the territories of Galveston Island and North Northwest Inland, where special charges were put into effect following hurricane Carla.

▷ EARTHQUAKE INSURANCE COVERAGE

Insurance companies have been placed in an awkward position when trying to develop a meaningful series of earthquake rates based on risk. Relatively few

---

6. Moore et al., *op cit.*, p. 188.

7. *Ibid.*, p. 178. Total insurance payments to the private sector (homes and businesses) from hurricane Carla totaled $100 million, as shown in Table 2-4.

shocks have occurred in populated areas of the world, so the industry has had to rely primarily on geologists' and seismologists' theoretical reports.[8] Yet earthquake policies are available throughout the country. Except for nine Western states where damage potential is relatively severe, there is one standard manual used to determine these rates. Regions are divided into four zones on the basis of risk, with premiums varying with type of construction. Rates for the Western states are calculated by the Pacific Fire Rating Bureau on the basis of three different hazard zones and eight types of construction ranging from

Table 12-2	COMPARISON OF BEACH, SEACOAST, AND NORMAL (INLAND) ANNUAL EC RATES FOR 1965 FOR STATES AFFECTED BY HURRICANES, PER $100 OF INSURANCE ($50 WIND AND HAIL DEDUCTIBLE, EXCEPT AS NOTED)

STATE	WOOD FRAME HOMES		
	Normal Rate	*Seacoast Rate*	*Beach Rate*
Alabama	.11	.18	.27
Florida	.12		
Seacoast Zone 3		.18[a]	.18[a]
Seacoast Zone 2		.27[a]	.27[a]
Seacoast Zone 1		.40[a]	.40[a]
City of Key West		.40[b]	.40[b]
Monroe County (except city of Key West)		.60[b]	.60[b]
Georgia	.11	.20	.30
Louisiana	.16	.27	.27
Mississippi	.158	.178	.178
North Carolina	.10	.36[a]	.72[a]
South Carolina	.16	.34[a]	.60[a]
Texas	.31	.39	.39
Galveston Island		.44[c]	.44[c]
North Northwest Inland		.64	.64
Virginia	.054	.10	.10

Data Source: State insurance records.
[a] $100 wind and hail deductible.
[b] $200 wind and hail deductible.
[c] $250 wind and hail deductible.

8. The Coast and Geodetic Survey (CGS) has recently made efforts to develop a methodology for systematically collecting earthquake damage statistics. This research was stimulated by a provision in the Southeast Hurricane Disaster Relief Act of 1965 (PL 89-339) following hurricane Betsy, which authorized a three-year study to determine the feasibility of earthquake insurance. In a report prepared by Frank E. McClure in April 1967, for the CGS entitled "Studies in Gathering Earthquake Damage Statistics," a detailed study was made of the damage and losses by class of construction from data available following the Bakersfield, California, earthquakes during the summer of 1952.

wood frame structures, the most stable, to buildings with clay, tile, unreinforced hollow concrete block, or unreinforced adobe walls, the most vulnerable.[9] Table 12-3 compares the weighted average annual rate in 1965 on wood frame houses for each region of the country.[10] An 80-per cent coinsurance clause is stipulated for all policies except in the state of Washington, where no such requirement exists.[11] The averages presented are based on a 5-per cent deductible for policies written in the nine Western states[12] and full coverage for the rest of the United States; a 2-per cent deductible in these latter states would reduce the rates by 25 per cent. Thus the true differential between the Western region and the rest of the United States is even greater than Table 12-3 indicates.

In many of the non-Western states it is possible for homeowners to purchase an Earthquake Damage Assumption Endorsement with the amount of protection being the same as the fire and EC provision. This endorsement contains the 2-per cent deductible, and thus the rates for dwellings would be 25 per cent lower than the full coverage rates shown in Appendix A. In the Western

Table 12-3	REGIONAL COMPARISONS OF ANNUAL EARTHQUAKE RATES FOR 1965 FOR WOOD FRAME HOMES,[a] PER $100 OF INSURANCE (80% COINSURANCE REQUIRED EXCEPT IN WASHINGTON)

Region	Earthquake Rate
Northeast	.038
Southeast	.032
Ohio Valley	.028
North Central	.034
South Central	.024
Western	.125

Data Source: State insurance records.
[a] Full coverage in states not using separate manuals, 5% deduction otherwise (see Appendix A, Tables 12-5 and 12-6 for classification).

9. This earthquake insurance classification scheme was developed by the Pacific Fire Rating Bureau. For a detailed description of the types of structures falling under each class, see Pacific Fire Rating Bureau, *Earthquake Rules and Rates*, August 1, 1957, pp. 23B–23D.

10. As in the EC calculations presented in Table 12-1, the rate for each state is weighted by its relative population with respect to the region. Data for each of the individual states are assembled in Tables 12-5 and 12-6, Appendix A.

11. A coinsurance clause requires the individual to keep his property insured to a stipulated percentage of its full value (in this case 80%) before the company will cover him for the entire amount of any loss suffered. If the person does not take out the required percentage of insurance, then he is only partially reimbursed for any loss incurred, according to the policy conditions.

12. In general, it is possible to purchase full coverage in these states at somewhat higher rates, but few people actually do.

states, the overwhelming majority of property owners chooses this Earthquake Damage Assumption Endorsement, which is attached to the fire and EC clause, although it is still possible for them to purchase a separate earthquake policy. The endorsement can be used in Western states with any type of property, not just dwellings as in the rest of the country. Only the endorsement rates are presented in Appendix A.

Residents in earthquake-prone areas have not been encouraged to take out policies, since many insurance companies are concerned about the possibility of suffering severe losses if a large number of buildings in one area is destroyed or damaged by shocks or tremors. Coverage is viewed as a special service to customers holding other policies with the company rather than as a profit-making operation. Consequently, agents have not promoted earthquake insurance, nor have property owners expressed a great interest in coverage.[13] As a result, less than 5 per cent of the property in California insured against fire is also protected against the earthquake peril.[14] In Alaska, the percentage figures are even smaller. Between 1960 and 1966, the total earthquake premiums written by all companies doing business in the state were never higher than 1.2 per cent of the amount written for fire.[15] One cannot attribute this lack of coverage in Alaska to unusually expensive policies, since most homes are of wood frame construction, for which the rate is lowest. A sample list of rates for residental construction in Alaska is presented in Table 12-7, Appendix B; the stated premium for wood frame houses is only $1.10/$1000. According to Anchorage insurance firms, a large voluntary demand for coverage on the part of residents did not occur following the Good Friday disaster, since most homeowners felt that another serious earthquake would not take place in their lifetime.

▷ FLOOD AND WATER DAMAGE COVERAGE

It is practically impossible for property owners to protect themselves against floods or water damage from other storms, even if they are willing to pay a high

---

13. See P. J. Kelly "Disaster Insurance", *Best's Fire and Casualty News* (July, 1965), pp. 20–36.

14. P. G. Buffington, "Earthquake Insurance in the United States—A Reap-

praisal," *Bulletin of the Seismological Society of America*, vol. 51, no. 2, April 1961, p. 326.

15. Based on data from Alaska Insurance Reports, 1960–1966.

premium. Insurance is only available on personal property such as jewelry or furs (covered by a floater policy, which insures against damage to the object regardless of change of location) or motor vehicles (covered by comprehensive insurance) or boats, shipping equipment, and cargo in transit (covered by marine insurance).[16] In a few isolated cases, flood insurance has been purchased by a commercial enterprise. For example, the J. P. Horne Department Store in Pittsburgh arranged a package deal with several companies following the severe floods of 1936. Initially the store was actually required to install flood gates and other protective devices on a test basis each year as a condition for insurance. These restrictions have recently been relaxed due to the high cost of testing, so that only a dry-run check is made of the equipment in storage. If flood warnings are issued these devices can easily be installed. Reservoirs have also been constructed upstream by the Corps of Engineers during the past few years; the annual insurance premiums have since been lowered as a result of the reduced flood risk.

During the past fifteen years the insurance industry has been studying the feasibility of some form of coverage against water damage. Following the disastrous floods which affected the North Central states in 1951 and 1952, the factory mutual insurance companies sent questionnaires to 25,000 of their fire insurance policy holders in the country. Of those who responded, only 10 per cent were interested in any form of flood protection, and then only if the rates were low. Since the premiums charged on high-risk property would necessarily have to be large, most corporations preferred to remain uninsured and deduct their flood losses from Federal income taxes.[17] Homeowners would undoubtedly be more willing to purchase policies even at high rates since their tax write-offs would normally be less than that of a corporation and a large part of their equity would be tied up in their own dwelling units.

Two reports by the American Insurance Association[18] have amassed detailed data on losses from recent floods as well as outlining alternative methods for calculating the actuarial rates to be charged in hazard-prone areas. Both studies concluded that flood insurance did not provide an attractive com-

---

16. Tunnels and bridges are the only nonmoveable objects for which it is possible, under an all-risk policy, to buy insurance against water damage.

17. "Federal Disaster Insurance," *Report of the Committee on Banking and Commerce, U.S. Senate*, Staff Study, January 1956, p. 241.

18. *Studies of Floods and Flood Damage* (1952–1955) and *Studies of Floods and Flood Damage* (1962 report). The American Insurance Association is a voluntary nonprofit organization of 168 stock companies writing all lines of insurance through independent agents and brokers.

mercial venture for profit-making purposes. Up until recent months, the attitude of insurance firms toward providing this type of coverage could be summarized by a quotation appearing in the staff report for the Senate Banking and Currency Committee in 1956:

> Because of the virtual certainty of the loss and its catastrophic nature and the impossibility of making this line of insurance self-supporting due to refusal of the public to purchase such insurance at the rates which would have to be charged to pay annual losses, companies generally could not prudently engage in this field of underwriting.[19]

▷ CONCLUSIONS

Several conclusions can be reached about the rationale behind the insurance industry's coverage, or lack of coverage, against various natural disasters.

1. Companies encourage individuals to take out insurance policies if there is a small risk of large-scale damage to any area, e.g., fire insurance.

2. Insurance firms willingly provide coverage against a natural disaster that potentially affects any part of the country, e.g., tornadoes. The relatively low premiums of many are used to pay for the high damage of a few.

3. Insurance companies are concerned with their public image and, therefore, are willing to provide earthquake insurance to customers if they request it.

4. Until this year companies have been opposed to flood insurance because of the relative certainty of the event in particular regions and the assumption that only individuals in those hazard-prone areas would be interested in a policy, thereby necessitating unusually high rates.

$\mathcal{F}$RAMEWORK FOR COMPREHENSIVE DISASTER INSURANCE SYSTEM

If experience has proven that a natural disaster can strike any area of the country, insurance companies will include protection against these losses under

---

19. "Federal Disaster Insurance," *op. cit.*, p. 238.

the standardized extended coverage endorsement. Catastrophes that are considered to be regional will either be covered by a separate policy (e.g., earthquakes)[20] or not insured at all (e.g., floods and water damage from hurricanes). This section will consider the basic framework for developing a system of insurance that not only satisfies economic criteria but also takes into account feasibility and marketability considerations.

▷ NATURE OF PREMIUMS

It is much easier to talk theoretically about a basis for insurance premiums than actually to calculate the rates. Suppose, for example, that a man wants to insure his $30,000 house against fire damage. If the insurance company determines that the expected annual loss on a home of this type of construction and value is $30, then the loss portion of the rate per $1000 will be $1. Utilizing this concept of premiums based on degree of risk for developing a system of comprehensive disaster insurance, the implications of an insurance program should be clear. Individuals in disaster-prone regions would pay the price for living there; fees would be highest in areas most likely to receive severe damage from natural disasters.[21] This actuarially sound principle for determining rates differs from the government's recent attitudes toward disasters in the United States. Once a stricken community or region has been classified as a disaster area, unusually large amounts of Federal grants and loans are now made for rehabilitation.

▷ SPREADING THE RISK

Insurance companies are only interested in marketing policies for which diversification of risks is assured. If the entire portfolio of a particular insurance firm covers individuals in the same general location against the same disaster, then it is either feast or famine for the company. Two actual cases will illustrate

---

20. Although seismologists claim that no area of the country is immune from earthquakes, only the western part of the country has suffered any appreciable damage during the last 100 years. Insurance companies, therefore, look at shocks as a regional rather than a national problem.

21. Even today the requirements on home mortgages reflect the risk of living in a particular area and the absence of

some forms of insurance coverage (e.g., against water damage from hurricanes). Thus, if a person wishes to buy a home on the Middle Atlantic Coast, he characteristically makes a down payment that reflects the proportional value of the building to the total value of the property. If, for example, a cottage is worth $10,000 and the land $12,000, the $10,000 down payment protects the bank from disaster damages to the dwelling.

this point. In 1897 the first trial at establishing flood insurance in the United States was made by a newly established stock company in Cairo, Illinois, with branch offices in St. Louis and New Orleans. The firm had no trouble attracting customers, since there had been enormous property damage during the previous two years from the overflowing of the Mississippi and Missouri Rivers. Coverage was granted against losses to houses, contents, and livestock. During 1898 there was a surplus because of relatively small water damage in the area, but the following year there was such tremendous flooding that the premiums of the previous year and the stock capital were not sufficient to pay for all the insurable losses. Another flood later in the year brought further losses, which completely wiped out the home office of the company.[22]

During the late 1920s about thirty American fire insurance companies issued flood insurance and were congratulated by the American insurance magazines on having placed this coverage on a sound basis. Following the extraordinary floods during 1927 and 1928 in nearly all parts of the United States, one of these magazines wrote, "Losses piled up to a staggering total which was aggravated by the fact that this insurance was largely commonly treated in localities most exposed to flood hazard. . . . By the end of 1928 every responsible company had discontinued this insurance."[23] From that time until recently, flood insurance has never been considered a realistic profit-making operation.

One way to achieve diversification is through reinsurance between firms in the industry. If a particular company feels that too large a percentage of its portfolio is nonindependent, transferring some policies to several other insurance firms will spread the risks. This is called *reinsurance*. The greater the amount of reinsurance that takes place, the larger the overall underwriting expenses due to the transactions costs of making these switches. As a practical matter it may be difficult for small regional firms in the industry to charge competitive rates and still diversify enough to protect themselves against an unusually large loss from a natural disaster.

▷ GOVERNMENT REINSURANCE PROVISION

The preceding discussion indicates that there is an added price to pay for protection against extreme events because of a large variance in losses over time.

22. Alfred Manes, *Insurance: Facts and Problems*, Harper and Publishers, New York, 1938, p. 160.

23. *Ibid.*, pp. 161–62.

When an insurance firm starts issuing policies it either has to amass enough capital to be used as a reserve fund for handling unusually large pay-outs or it must reinsure with other companies. Either of these actions will be costly. By building up reserves, the firm will suffer an opportunity loss reflected in the difference between their own rate of return and the return on the nonrisky investments in which their reserve capital will be held. Reinsurance is also expensive since transferring policies to other companies involves an additional underwriting expense. Thus, the insurance rate would have to include one of these added costs. The experience of the stock company in Cairo, Illinois, previously cited is a good example of the dire consequences resulting when flood insurance is issued without adequate protection either in the form of reserves or reinsurance.

Government reinsurance is a relatively inexpensive way of protecting firms against an extreme loss in the near future. They are saved the trouble of going through the costly underwriting and transfer procedures of finding other members of the industry who are willing to purchase a share of their risk. By paying a certain percentage of each disaster policy to some designated Federal agency, companies would be protected against any unusual losses from natural disasters. In other words, the government would come to the rescue much in the same way as the Federal Deposit Insurance Corporation has promised to do in case a bank has a run on its deposits. Companies with large reserves might prefer to reinsure themselves rather than pay a percentage to the Federal government for such protection against unusual losses. Their reasoning would be the same as that of large corporations who self-insure against losses today: The high costs of outside protection justify taking the risk with one's own capital.

SUGGESTED DISASTER INSURANCE PROPOSALS

The above framework suggests several possible forms of coverage that we will now analyze from the point of view of both economic and marketability criteria.

▷ COMPULSORY INSURANCE

The simplest device from the administrative point of view would be for the Federal government to require all homeowners to take out a comprehensive disaster insurance policy offering protection against all natural hazards. Premiums on each residence would thus be a type of property tax reflecting the risk of living in a certain area. This method has the undesirable characteristic of forcing individuals who own their homes outright to purchase insurance even though they may prefer to gamble by not obtaining coverage. The suggested scheme does not begin to cóme to grips with the actual problems involved in marketing the policies. For one thing, a person now living in a hazard-prone area might not be able to afford the relatively high premiums that would be charged him. Furthermore, he might be unwilling to relocafe his home in an area where the rates would be lower because this move would be both economically and sociologically too costly. By *sociologically* costly we refer to the re-adjustment problems one is bound to encounter when pulling up stakes and resettling in a new environment. The repercussions of the compulsory insurance requirement would thus be so severe as to make it highly unlikely that this system would even get off the ground.

▷ LONG-TERM INSURANCE

Another possibility is to market long-term comprehensive disaster insurance (e.g., fifty-year policies) based on risk in a manner similar to the way life insurance is issued today. This idea stems from the concept of property life insurance that was developed and put into practice in Germany during the 1920s. In essence, property is given a personal character by assuming that objects have a limited lifetime just as human beings do. In the event of complete destruction of property, a capital sum would be granted for replacement purposes; funds would also be provided for repair when events occur that have a deteriorating effect on the property.[24] The rationale for developing such a plan for disaster insurance[25] is that companies must be guaranteed premiums for a long time span if rates are to be based on expected losses. Of course, if some form of government reinsurance were instituted to protect companies from unusually large losses, there is no reason why rates under an annual policy would have to be unusually high.

Proponents of long-term policies contend that companies could effectively

---

24. For a more detailed description of property life insurance see Manes, *op. cit.*, pp. 168–175.

25. A proposal of this type for flood

insurance is detailed in a series of four articles by John S. McGuiness, "Is Flood Insurance Feasible?" *Insurance Management Review*, April 24–June 5, 1965.

discourage homeowners from canceling their insurance after a short period of time for a stated cash value by requiring a large enough initial investment so as to give the customer a vested interest.[26] In essence, a long-term insurance policy makes the optimistic assumption that property is efficiently located today on the basis of cost/benefit criteria and that it should remain there in the future. Unfortunately, too many structures have been built in certain areas as a result of insufficient information on the part of homeowners and a generous policy of Federal and local disaster relief. Long-term insurance would do nothing to discourage the resident from repairing or rebuilding his damaged property in the same area following a disaster. In contrast, a short-term insurance policy with differential rates would help achieve the long-run objective of relocating this property on safer ground.

▷ SEPARATE COVERAGE

Another possibility would be to issue separate insurance against natural disasters losses not included under the present EC endorsement. In other words, a separate policy would be available for damage due to water and another one for protection against earthquake losses. This is the approach advocated by the Southeast Hurricane Disaster Act of 1965, which authorized separate studies of the feasibility of flood and earthquake protection. A private-Federal flood insurance bill has recently been passed by Congress as a result of a HUD flood study. For more details on Federal legislation with regards to disaster insurance see Appendix C. Advocates of separate coverage claim it is desirable to have individual bookkeeping accounts for each type of damage (i.e., water, wind, and earthquake). A look at the record clearly reveals that natural disasters frequently involve two or more of the elements. Hurricanes are the prime example, since wind and water are both culprits; earthquakes frequently trigger huge tidal waves as well as fires. If all disasters were incorporated into one package, the large adjusting expense incurred today when the actual cause of damage is determined would be obviated, and overall rates could be lowered accordingly.[27] Furthermore the variance in losses would also be reduced, because more disasters would be included in one package.

---

26. McGuiness, *op. cit.*, June 5, 1965, p. 32.

27. A detailed description of the problems facing the insurance industry following hurricane Carla is found in Moore et al., *op. cit.*, Chap. 9, "Insurance: Resource for Rehabilitation," pp. 177–193. For a brief discussion of these problems see pp. 232–234 of this chapter.

A SUGGESTED COMPREHENSIVE DISASTER INSURANCE SCHEME

In this section a proposal will be presented for including protection against floods, hurricanes, earthquakes, and other limited disasters under the EC endorsement that normally accompanies fire insurance. The suggested system takes into account not only economic criteria but also marketability and political factors, and therefore seems superior to the alternative schemes already presented.

▷ DEVELOPMENT OF THE SYSTEM

Nature of Premiums

Rates on the current value of property already built in disaster-prone areas will be determined actuarially, but the stated premium will be partially subsidized by the Federal government. Only in this way would residents want to purchase policies from the private companies who would be marketing the insurance.

A good theoretical economic case can be made for providing some form of subsidy. Today the value of property partially reflects the benevolent attitude of the Federal government toward disaster victims. If suddenly this generous assistance were discontinued and insurance based on risk substituted in its place, the resale price of the house would drop by an amount directly related to the reduction in benefits from the free or low-interest relief that the individual formerly had available to him if he suffered damage. (Specifically, the decrease in value would be determined by the probability of various amounts of damage multiplied by the expected windfall gains through grants and/or long-term, low-interest loans.) One solution would be to grant a lump-sum payment to every property owner as compensation for this reduction in value. The justification for such a payment would be that the change in government attitude could not have been foreseen when the house was originally built. From a political point of view, outright grants have never been very popular. They also are not likely to achieve the desired effect of encouraging individuals to purchase insurance. If a lump-sum payment were given, insurance rates on existing property would naturally be based on the full actuarial premium. The individual would then have the option to purchase a policy at these high rates or to take his chances. If there were another disaster and he did not have insurance, he would undoubtedly demand aid from Washington. The political facts of life indicate that if enough people put pressure on their congressmen, they will get low-cost relief. It seems preferable to transform the lump-sum payments into a subsidy on insurance rates, thereby encouraging people to purchase coverage.

The subsidizied rate can take one of two forms: It can be granted for a fixed period of time (e.g., ten years) after which the full actuarial premium will be charged, or it can be provided year after year, but only on the portion of property that still has not received any damage from a disaster after the insurance system was put into effect. In either case, the subsidy could be determined so that it would be equivalent to the lump-sum payment that the Government could have offered to the homeowner.[28]

A fixed-time-period subsidy has the administrative advantage of simplicity. For the first T years, every homeowner would have his insurance premium partially paid for; at the end of this period he would be on his own. Under the alternative system, some homeowners might continue to receive a subsidy for $T + n$ years or more because they had not received any destruction, whereas others whose homes had been washed away during the first year of the program would start paying the full rate almost immediately.

Ironically, it is the simplicity of the first system that should make it extremely difficult to implement from the political point of view. To translate an old French proverb quite freely, "Nothing endures longer than the temporary." In this case, suppose an insurance subsidy was provided for a ten-year

---

28. Let L represent the lump-sum payment which the government would make as compensation for the decline in the value of a given home due to a change in its disaster relief policy. To find the annual amount of the subsidy (A) on this home, based on a fixed time period (T) which would be equivalent to L on a present value basis, we simply compute

$$L = A \int_0^T e^{-it}\, dt = \frac{A}{i}(1 - e^{-it})$$

$$A = \frac{iL}{1 - e^{-it}}.$$

If the subsidy were based on the value of property not yet destroyed by a disaster, then the conversion process becomes more complicated. Let us make the simplifying assumptions that the value of a fully repaired home remains constant over time and that damage occurs at the rate e^{-Dt}. To determine the initial value A' such that the total expected subsidy is equivalent to L on a present value basis we compute

$$L = A' \int_0^\infty e^{-Dt} e^{-it}\, dt = \frac{A'}{(D + i)}$$

$$A' = (D + i)L.$$

period. Just before this grant expired, homeowners would undoubtedly put pressure on their congressmen to extend the subsidized rate for another short period. Some would use the argument that their insurance rate should not be increased since they have not even received any damage during this time period. It would be hard for politicians not to sympathize with this complaint.

A system of insurance in which the value of the premium is determined by the amount of damage actually incurred has a greater chance of succeeding politically than its counterpart. People who receive damage *should* expect to pay more the next year, not only because they have collected from the government but also because the recent disaster provides statistical fuel for a rate increase. Congress will have much less of an incentive to maintain low rates after providing these victims with insurance compensation. For these reasons we subscribe to an insurance premium for which the subsidy on each piece of property will be revised over time in accordance with damage actually incurred.

The subsidy could be partially or even totally financed by additional funds that the Federal government would receive or save over its present disaster relief operations in the private sector. For example, individuals would be prohibited from writing off property losses for tax purposes since they would now be protected by insurance. Federal agencies such as the SBA would save money by not having to make forgiveness grants or low-interest loans to homeowners and businesses suffering losses.

If a subsidy were given to new property or additions to existing facilities, then this proposed system would actually be encouraging further developments in hazard-prone areas. Therefore the full rate would be charged on any increase in value to present property or on developments occurring after the insurance system was initiated. In this way, individuals would have explicit information as to the expected cost of new construction and should take positive action only if the calculated benefits make the action appear to be worthwhile. In the long run, as old property decays or is destroyed, we will achieve our objective of having everyone fully bear the risk, as well as it can be determined, of living in a certain area.

Spreading the Risk

The government should require this comprehensive disaster coverage on all VA and FHA homes, which comprise about 20 per cent of the housing market. In order to induce banks and financial institutions to force homeowners and businesses to buy this policy before issuing a mortgage, the Federal agencies would have to modify their current role in postdisaster recovery. For example, the SBA would have to make it very clear that in the future its relief program would be limited solely to relocation expenses if a family wishes to move from a disaster-prone area to safer ground. A step in this direction was taken by the SBA when they provided funds to relocate a home or business outside of a flood-prone area. No future flood disaster assistance is to be given for any physical loss to property constructed on the site from which the disaster victim was relocated, as long as the area remains disaster-prone.[29] Explicit policies restricting federal aid to hazard-prone areas would compel banks to require this proposed comprehensive insurance just to protect their own investments from disaster losses and possible declarations of bankruptcy on the part of the mortgagor. There is a legal advantage to developing a comprehensive form of extended coverage rather than having separate policies for flood and earthquake insurance. Homeowners who have already arranged for a mortgage with a bank cannot be required to buy a separate policy covering other disasters. On the other hand, if protection against other catastrophes were included as part of the new EC clause, then they would be required by the bank to purchase this insurance, since the old coverage would not be available.

Government Reinsurance

One of the reasons why the insurance industry has refused to market flood policies and shied away from earthquake coverage is the possibility of suffering unusually large losses from a severe disaster. A program of government reinsurance whereby companies would pay a small charge for protection from any unusual losses would permit rates to be calculated on the basis of expected annual losses over a number of years plus the small reinsurance charge. Private companies would still market policies, just as they do for other forms of coverage, but would now know that following a series of severe catastrophes they would still be assured of financial stability.

▷ OPERATION OF THE SYSTEM

An advantage of the proposed system of dual premiums (i.e., subsidizing the value of existing property and charging a full rate on new developments) is that

---

29. Small Business Administration, "Disaster Loans," National Directive 560-1, July 12, 1966, pp. 36–37. The SBA national directive is specific on this point, but we were not able to determine whether the policy has ever been strictly enforced.

individuals suffering damage from a disaster will be encouraged to move to a safer location unless the benefit/cost ratio dictates that they ought to stay. The time to induce action on the part of residents is when they have the flexibility to relocate their property, such as immediately after having suffered damage from a disaster. To achieve this desired effect, the insurance system must be supplemented by meaningful Federal and local agency programs.

To illustrate this point, let us consider the operation of the proposed system in the case of a family living on the flood plain whose $25,000 dwelling receives $15,000 worth of damage. Their comprehensive insurance policy will reimburse them for their damages.[30] However, the insurance premium on the portion of their house destroyed (i.e., $15,000) would no longer be subsidized if the family chose to rebuild in the same location. This factor alone should lead the home-owner to think about moving to a safer and less costly area unless there were some special benefits of living near a river bank. If the family were not able to relocate elsewhere, the SBA could play a helpful role by offering long-term low-interest loans to cover the difference between the insurance payment and the cost of rebuilding and relocating a home in a low-risk region. Local agencies and developers could also play a role by taking steps toward developing new areas in safer regions and providing information on ways to protect one's home from future damage. Sociologically, there may be some roadblocks to mobility on the part of residents, but through these economic incentives and the flexibility generated by disaster damage, some positive changes might be forthcoming.

The preceding discussion refers to the short-run problems of relocating residents in hazard-prone areas who may not have been aware of the problems when they originally settled. The main advantage of the dual premiums from the long-run point of view is that it presents the true cost of building new property in disaster-prone areas but does not explicitly prohibit settlement in those areas. Thus, if individuals are willing to pay the price of living in a particular region they would, and should, be permitted to do so. The incentive structure of a system of insurance with premiums based on risk would have the effect, however, of discouraging unwise investments and gradually inducing present occupants to move to safer areas. In the long-run, the same effect as flood-plain regulations can be achieved in a less costly way through insurance.

---

30. For simplicity we are assuming no deductibles on their policy. The same line of reasoning holds if deductibles are in effect.

A comprehensive system of disaster insurance would also form the basis for coordinating the activities of various Federal agencies and groups involved in preventing losses from future catastrophes. For example, one way to protect property from severe water damage is through the relatively inexpensive method of flood proofing.[31] Currently most residents who could benefit from this preventive action are not aware that it even exists. An insurance system would explicitly call attention to this alternative by indicating the reduced rates that would be charged if a home was floodproofed to various degrees. The owner could then determine whether the cost of the investment was justified by the resulting benefits in the form of lower insurance charges.[32]

The feasibility of flood-control projects for an area could also be determined in the same manner. It would be in the interest of a community to use its taxes to erect dams or levees when the benefits to residents, in the form of reduced insurance rates on property reflecting the lower risk of potential damage from floods or hurricanes, exceeded the discounted cost of the project.

▷ CRITICAL EVALUATION

Noncompulsory Nature

If the proposed system were not made compulsory by the Federal government, the most serious potential problem would relate to individuals who received substantial damage but had no insurance. From a purely economic point of view, the answer as to what would happen to them is clear: they would, and should, suffer the consequences. In effect, this attitude exists today when a dwelling is damaged by fire and the homeowner is not covered by insurance; he must pay all the losses himself. For this reason, all home buyers are required by the commercial banks to protect themselves with fire insurance before they are allowed to take out a mortgage. There is no reason why the same attitude could not prevail regarding natural disasters. If practically every house in a

---

31. For a detailed discussion of the principles and methods of flood proofing see the monograph by John Sheaffer, *Introduction to Flood Proofing*, Center for Urban Studies, University of Chicago, 1967.

32. Some preliminary research on this problem has been done by R. Lewis in conjunction with H. Kunreuther and J. Sheaffer. Actual data from various flood plain areas have been used to determine the reduced insurance premiums that result from various amounts of flood proofing. The results are detailed in an unpublished paper, "Flood Proofing and Flood Insurance: An Empirical Analysis," University of Chicago, May 1968.

community had insurance coverage and an earthquake caused widespread damage, then it would *not* be necessary to classify the region as a Federal disaster area except for the purpose of restoring public facilities. The isolated homeowner without insurance surely would not receive the same generous treatment as he does today. If everyone had been fully aware of the opportunity to protect himself from unexpected losses at reasonable rates, this person would simply be considered a gambler who lost.

If a subsidized premium were offered to current occupants of disaster-prone areas, the vast majority of property owners would then be able to afford the premiums. Banks and commercial institutions could then feel free to require the new form of extended coverage as a condition for continuing the present mortgage. In effect, this would mean that for the vast majority of property owners the new insurance would be compulsory on the value of their outstanding mortgages. Of course, there still would be the extremely poor individuals living near a river bank in shacks or shanties who could not afford insurance even at the most modest rates. Even now, when no flood insurance is available, these individuals are refused a low-interest loan from the SBA following a disaster because the agency feels they do not have the ability to repay the money. They must thus rely on contributions from the community or the American Red Cross to rebuild their homes, frequently in the same spot. There is no reason why this benevolent policy toward poverty-stricken individuals should change; disaster contributions are expected to be used for purposes such as these. The victim is happier and so are the people who donate the funds. In fact, it is highly likely that most of the other residents in town would prefer to pay the cost of building shacks along the river banks rather than having these "outsiders" invade their community. Charitable contributions thus have a definite purpose in postdisaster operations. We are objecting solely to the Federal government's paternalistic attitude toward the private sector through its forgiveness grants and low-interest loans.

Disaster Insurance Today or Tomorrow?

Some Federal agencies have voiced strong reservations about the possibility of developing a meaningful system of comprehensive disaster insurance in the near future.[33] They have felt that until very accurate information is available on probabilities and actual losses associated with certain types of disasters, an

---

33. See the report by President Johnson's Task Force on Federal Flood Control Policy, "A Unified National Program for Managing Flood Losses," Government Printing Office, Washington, D.C., 1966, pp. 38–39.

insurance program may do more harm than good. There is no denying that some unfavorable new construction would be undertaken if the suggested insurance costs were below the true but currently unknown rates. Certainly it would be nice to have extremely accurate figures with which to calculate rates, but since we presently do not have these data, the following question appears relevant: "Would total resource losses from disasters in future years be lower under a comprehensive insurance program based on approximate figures (to be improved over time) or by having no insurance program and continuing with the current system of relief until accurate rates could be calculated?"

Two points must be raised in this regard. Recent pilot studies by the Corps of Engineers, the Geological Survey, and the TVA have given us a much better feel for the magnitude and probabilities of flood losses over time so that there is a large amount of available data upon which to base rates for water damage.[34] Earthquake rates, albeit imperfect, are currently established for the entire country;[35] studies by the Coast and Geodetic Survey should lead to improvements in these figures within the near future.[36] However, even if these new data on water and earthquake damage had not been collected, one has only to look at the present form of disaster relief to recognize how ineffectual it has been in curtailing the growth of disaster-prone areas. In this sense, the present Federal policy has unwittingly been designed to encourage residents to locate in hazard-prone regions. It is hard to see how an insurance program, no matter how low the rates, could fail to improve this situation.

Another advantage of developing a system of comprehensive coverage today rather than tomorrow is that it will enable us to get better data on future losses than we could possibly have obtained solely from damage analysis by Federal agencies such as the Corps of Engineers and the Geological Survey. Insurance companies would be forced to keep records on payments to disaster victims and in this way would be able to up-date the initial imperfect rates and make them more accurate over time. It is not at all surprising to find that our

---

34. See Appendix C of the report to the President from the Secretary of the Department of Urban Development, *Insurance and Other Programs for Financial Assistance to Flood Victims*, Washington, D.C., August 8, 1966, which was required by the Southeast Hurricane Disaster Relief Act of 1965, PL 89-339, November 8, 1965.

35. It is quite likely that the insurance industry would demand an increase in earthquake rates over the current ones if they wanted to market policies on a large scale rather than perform a "good-will" service to customers as they are doing today.

36. See the report by Frank McClure, "Studies in Gathering Earthquake Damage Statistics," which was done for the Coast and Geodetic Survey in April 1967.

most complete damage statistics are on hail and windstorms (including torna-does) since these are the only natural phenomena entirely protected by extended coverage today.

Economic vs. Marketability Criteria: Setting Subsidized Rates

To preserve the differential nature of insurance premiums, the subsidy on the value of existing property in different areas must yield actual rates that still reflect relative risk. To take a simple example, suppose that locations A and B on the flood plain had respective actuarial rates of $5 per $100 value of insurance and $3 per $100 value of insurance. The difference between the two subsidies given to property owners in A and B would have to be less than $2, for the more risky property to be charged a higher absolute rate. It may be difficult to satisfy this criterion from the marketability angle if the people who can least afford insurance reside in the most dangerous areas. The Federal subsidy might then have to be disproportionately high for these residents to be in a position to purchase coverage. The government could follow one of two courses of action: It could let economic and equity considerations slide into the background by setting extremely low rates that these low-income people could afford, or it could follow our recommendation of preserving the relative risks associated with living in hazard-prone areas and entrusting the responsibility for aiding those persons not able to purchase insurance to the Red Cross and to private charity.

Conclusions

This chapter presents our answer to the principal question that has produced this book: "Should the high risk of a few individuals be spread equally among the entire population, as our present form of disaster relief tends to do, or should we institute some form of disaster insurance with rates reflecting the potential damage to an area?" We have shown in no uncertain terms that current federal disaster relief policy has been both inefficient and inequitable. It has been inefficient in that it has encouraged some property to be located in hazard-prone areas through an implicit guarantee of low-interest loans and grants if a disaster causes any damage. These structures would likely have been built elsewhere if such subsidized relief were not available. Federal policy has been inequitable in that disaster victims practicing so-called social virtues have been relatively worse off after the disaster than "imprudent" individuals suffering similar damage.

Comprehensive disaster insurance should lead to a much more efficient allocation of resources in the future and an elimination of the inequitable effects of the current system of federal aid to the private sector. By forcing homeowners and businessmen to bear the full risk of living in any area where previously they were subsidized after experiencing bad luck, we are suggesting a definite structural change in policy. Over the short run there are bound to be sociological and political costs; these have been explicitly considered in trying to develop an insurance system which still meets meaningful economic criteria.

Pervading this chapter is our strong feeling that economic analysis cannot be practiced in a vacuum if it is going to make some meaningful contributions to policy. It is relatively easy to present theoretically optimal solutions, but they are useless if they have no chance of getting past the paper stage. After having spent considerable time discussing possible implementation problems with members of the insurance industry and the Housing and Urban Development task force authorized by the President to investigate the feasibility of flood insurance, we are convinced that some form of subsidy on the value of property now located in hazard-prone areas is imperative. We have argued that this type of system can be given theoretical justification by using economic efficiency criteria. It is up to the reader to decide whether the proposed system of disaster insurance has a better chance of succeeding than the other alternatives outlined in this book. In this regard it should be pointed out that a variation of our proposal was incorporated in the National Flood Insurance Act of 1968.[37] The bill, in its original form, received endorsement by representatives of such diverse interest groups as the insurance industry, National Association of Homebuilders and elected officials in flood-prone areas. This support does not necessarily make the proposal a good one; in fact, some people would claim that it may be suspect just because it has received overwhelming approval. The principal feature of the Congressional bill, however, is that it forces *new residents* to pay the full actuarial rate on his property. Even if Congress continues to subsidize the premiums on existing structures ad infinitum (rather than decreasing the subsidy as the property receives damage), the system still will lead to an optimal allocation of resources in the long run. Homes and businesses constructed after the insurance system is inaugurated will pay

---

37. "National Flood Insurance Act of 1968." PL 448, 90th Congress, Second Session, 1968. For further discussion of this bill see Appendix C.

actuarially-determined premiums. Over time these structures will be the only ones remaining as the old property will have been destroyed or have decayed.

An insurance system would provide better information at lower cost than relying on other imperfect mechanisms such as information pamphlets currently being distributed by the Corps of Engineers. It is our hope that the flood insurance bill before Congress will be swiftly passed and eventually extended to cover other natural hazards, enabling the federal government to withdraw from its paternalistic role in relation to the private sector.

Appendix A

| Table 12-4 | STATE-BY-STATE COMPARISONS OF ANNUAL EC RATES FOR 1965 FOR BRICK JOISTED MERCANTILE BUILDINGS AND WOOD FRAME HOMES, PER $100 OF INSURANCE ($50 WIND AND HAIL DEDUCTIBLE EXCEPT AS NOTED)[a] |

Region	Brick Joisted Mercantile Building (with 80% coinsured damage)	Wood Frame Home
Northeast		
Connecticut	.09	.18
Delaware	.10	.10
District of Columbia	.068	.065
Maine	.07	.12
Maryland	.08	.08
Massachusetts	.10	.30
New Hampshire	.08	.18
New Jersey	.16	.16
New York	.06	.08
Pennsylvania	.10	.10
Rhode Island	.10	.30
Vermont	.06	.12
Virginia	.063	.054
Southeast		
Alabama	.07	.11
Florida	.13	.12
Georgia	.08	.11
Louisiana	.13	.16
Mississippi	.207F	.158
North Carolina		
Eastern	.16	.17
Western	.14	.10
South Carolina	.13	.16
Ohio Valley		
Indiana	.096F	.14
Kentucky	.084F	.10
Michigan	.096F	.10
Ohio	.096F	.10[b]
Tennessee	.096F	.11
West Virginia	.07	.08

(continued on p. 256)

GOVERNMENT: COMPREHENSIVE DISASTER INSURANCE

| Table 12-4 | STATE-BY-STATE COMPARISONS OF ANNUAL EC RATES FOR 1965 FOR BRICK JOISTED MERCANTILE BUILDINGS AND WOOD FRAME HOMES, PER $100 OF INSURANCE ($50 WIND AND HAIL DEDUCTIBLE EXCEPT AS NOTED)ᵃ |

Region	Brick Joisted Mercantile Building (with 80% coinsured damage)	Wood Frame Home
North Central		
Illinois		
Cook County	.066F	.07F
Balance of State	.125F	.16
Iowa	.132F	.18
Kansas	.283	.44
Minnesota	.11F	.11
Missouri	.19F	.20
Montana		
Division A (North and West of Continental Divide)	.12F	.14
Division B (Balance of Western Half)	.20F	.30
Division C (Eastern Half)	.25F	.40
Nebraska		
Eastern	.140	.20
Western	.262	.24
North Dakota	.19	.34
South Dakota		
East of Missouri River	.226F	.30
West of Missouri River	.247	.30ᶜ
Wisconsin	.09F	.11
Wyoming	.11	.18
South Central		
Arkansas	.192	.25
New Mexico		
Eastern	.130	.26
Western	.096	.14
Oklahoma	.276	.44
Texas	.193	.31
Western		
Alaska	.16F	.06
Arizona	.21F	.14
California	.05F	.04
Colorado		
Eastern	.158	.32
Western	.048	.08
Idaho	.05F	.05
Nevada	.20F	.16
Oregon	.125F	.125
Utah	.09F	.08
Washington	.05F	.06

Data Source: State insurance records.
ᵃ Seacoast and beach areas with special rates not included.
ᵇ $50 deductible for all perils.
ᶜ Areas west of Missouri River, except Rapid City pay a flat $20 premium in addition to premium developed from .30 rate. In Rapid City the flat premium is $40 and the mandatory wind and hail deductible is $100.
F = Full coverage.

| Table 12-5 | EARTHQUAKE ZONES AND ANNUAL RATES FOR 1965 FOR FRAME DWELLINGS AND BRICK JOISTED MERCANTILE BUILDINGS, PER $100 OF INSURANCE (FULL COVERAGE,[a] 80% COINSURANCE EXCEPT FOR WESTERN STATES USING SEPARATE TABLES) |

Region	Zone 1	Zone 2	Zone 3	Zone 4
Northeast				
Connecticut		X		
Delaware		X		
District of Columbia		X		
Maine	X			
Maryland		Balance	Western two counties	
Massachusetts	Eastern half	Balance		
New Hampshire	X			
New Jersey		X		
New York		X		
Pennsylvania		Extreme SE corner		Balance
Rhode Island	X			
Vermont		X		
Virginia[b]		X		
Southeast				
Alabama		Northern two fifths		Balance
Florida				X
Georgia		X		
Louisiana				X
Mississippi		Northern half		Balance
North Carolina		X		
South Carolina	X			
Ohio Valley				
Indiana	Extreme SW corner	Balance		
Kentucky	Western fifth	Balance	3 Counties south of Cincinnati	
Michigan			X	
Ohio			X	
Tennessee	Western quarter	Balance		
West Virginia			X	
North Central				
Illinois	Southern fifth	Balance		
Iowa				X
Kansas				X
Minnesota				X
Missouri[c]	Southeast sixth	Balance		
Nebraska				X
North Dakota				X
South Dakota				X
Wisconsin				X
Wyoming		X		

(continued on p. 258)

GOVERNMENT: COMPREHENSIVE DISASTER INSURANCE

| Table 12-5 | EARTHQUAKE ZONES AND ANNUAL RATES FOR 1965 FOR FRAME DWELLINGS AND BRICK JOISTED MERCANTILE BUILDINGS, PER $100 OF INSURANCE (FULL COVERAGE,ª 80% COINSURANCE EXCEPT FOR WESTERN STATES USING SEPARATE TABLES) |

Region	Zone 1	Zone 2	Zone 3	Zone 4
South Central				
Arkansas	Northeast fifth	Balance		
New Mexico		X		
Oklahoma				X
Texas				X
Western				
Colorado		X		
Frame Dwelling	.06	.04	.02	.02
Brick Joisted Mercantile	.13	.10	.07	.06

Data Source: State insurance records.
ª Reduce rates 25% for 2% value deductible.
ᵇ Rates are 10% below other Zone 2 rates.
ᶜ Frame-dwelling rates are .08 in Zone 1 and .05 in Zone 2.

| Table 12-6 | ANNUAL EARTHQUAKE RATES FOR 1965 FOR FRAME DWELLINGS AND BRICK JOISTED MERCANTILE BUILDINGS IN STATES USING SEPARATE MANUALS, PER $100 OF INSURANCE (5% DEDUCTIBLE FOR DWELLINGS AND 10% DEDUCTIBLE FOR MERCANTILE BUILDINGS. 80% COINSURANCE REQUIRED EXCEPT WHERE NOTED. EARTHQUAKE DAMAGE ASSUMPTION ENDORSEMENT ASSUMED) |

Region	Frame Dwelling	Brick Joisted Mercantile
North Central		
Montana	.143	.713
Western		
Alaska	.143	.713
Arizona		
Southern Border Counties	.114	.570
Balance of State	.084	.426
California		
Extreme Southeast Corner	.219	1.060
Sacramento and San Joaquin Valleys	.105	.532
Balance of State	.143	.713
Idaho	.142	1.060
Nevada		
Eastern One-Third	.105	.532
Balance of State	.128	.638
Oregon	.053	.190
Utah	.105	.532
Washington		
Eastern	.093ª	.238
Western	.147ª	.532

Data Source: State insurance records.
ª No coinsurance required.

Appendix B

| Table 12-7 | SAMPLE ANNUAL EARTHQUAKE INSURANCE RATES FOR RESIDENTIAL UNITS IN ALASKA[a] |

		RATE PER $1000 OF INSURANCE (DOLLARS)[b]			
		1–4 FAMILY RESIDENCE		5–20 FAMILY RESIDENCE	
Construction[c]	Mandatory[d] Deduction (Per Cent)	Building	Contents	Building	Contents
Frame Houses (3 stories or less in height)	5	1.10	1.10	1.10	1.10
Frame Houses (over 3 stories in height)	5	1.10	1.10	2.30	1.10
All or part brick, stone, or concrete (not concrete block)	10	5.30	4.20	5.00	4.20
All or part masonry-building veneer	15	17.50	1.10	16.60	1.10
All or part concrete block, tile, adobe, or metal	15	17.50	17.50	16.60	17.50

Data Source: Allstate Insurance Company, July 1964.
[a] Earthquake will only be insured as part of a fire policy. It may apply to one or more items of the fire policy, but it must be for the full amount of the item or items to which it applies.
[b] Building rates based on mandatory 80% coinsurance. For 90% coinsurance reduce above rates by 5%; for 100% coinsurance reduce above rates by 10%.
[c] If building is on filled ground, not firm natural ground, increase all earthquake rates 25%.
[d] Deductible per cent applies to actual cash value of the property insured, not to amount of insurance.

Appendix C

LEGISLATION ON DISASTER INSURANCE

The history of legislation on disaster insurance has closely followed the record of natural catastrophes affecting various parts of the United States. Following the disastrous Midwest floods of 1951, with total property and income loss estimated at $2 billion, President Truman sent a special message to Congress requesting a $400 million appropriation for a Federal flood-relief plan. He recommended that $50 million of this fund be set aside for financing a flood insurance program that would be administered by a Flood Disaster Administration, a small policy-making body of approximately thirty people chosen by the President. After extensive hearings both the Senate and House postponed any legislative action, and the bill was subsequently dropped from consideration.

During the next two years, interest in disaster insurance waned since there were no unusual catastrophes affecting the United States. However, following the 1955 hurricanes and floods, which caused even more extensive damage than in 1951, interest in legislation was renewed. Senator J. William Fulbright, Chairman of the Senate Committee on Banking and Currency, requested a study of the practicability of Federal disaster insurance with a view toward possible legislation in the next session of Congress. On the basis of a thorough report on Federal disaster insurance,[1] the Federal Flood Insurance Act of 1956[2] established three programs under the administration of the Housing and Home Finance Agency (HHFA) for aiding flood damage victims.

1. *Direct Insurance Program.* In order to permit marketability, fees charged to private individuals could be as low as 60 per cent of an estimated fair rate covering the expected loss from floods over a period of years. The difference between the actual fee and the estimated rate was to be covered by a Federal subsidy. Individuals were not required to take out insurance, but it was hoped that the relatively low rates would encourage most property owners to protect themselves.

2. *Reinsurance.* The HHFA Administrator could enter into reinsurance agreements with private insurance companies. Reinsurance fees were to be adequate to pay all claims for unusual losses over a reasonable period of years.

3. *Loan Contracts.* The HHFA was willing to guarantee any loans from financial institutions to private individuals covering flood loss. In case these funds were not made available on reasonable terms from private sources, the HHFA was obligated to make them directly. The amount of this loan could not exceed flood damage and was also subject to the limitations of $250,000 per person and $10,000 per dwelling unit.

This threefold plan was abolished in 1957, after being in existence for nine months, when Congress declined to appropriate funds for its operations.

Following hurricane Betsy, legislation was passed by Congress authorizing a nine-month study by the Department of Housing and Urban Development on the feasibility of some form of flood insurance and a three-year Coast and Geodetic study on developing more accurate earthquake insurance rates.[3] The

1. "Federal Disaster Insurance," *Report of the Committee on Banking and Currency, U.S. Senate*, Staff Study, January 1956.

2. PL 1016, 84th Congress, August 7, 1956 (70 Stat. 1078).

3. "Southeast Hurricane Disaster Act of 1965," Sec. 5.

HUD report, which was published in August 1966, concluded that some form of flood insurance was feasible, although rates in certain hazard-prone areas would be extremely high. Detailed data on potential damage from floods were presented for a number of pilot areas by the Corps of Engineers and the Geological Survey. These figures were detailed in a number of appendices accompanying the main report.

These positive conclusions from the HUD report as well as the new body of data led to Congressional action that culminated in the National Flood Insurance Act of 1968.[4] The law amends the Federal Flood Insurance Act of 1956 and provides for a national program of flood insurance. In essence, it subscribes to the system of dual premiums outlined in the comprehensive insurance scheme presented in this chapter. Although the actuarial and subsidized premiums would be estimated by the Federal government, private firms would still be marketing the policies. A system of government reinsurance is included so that companies will be protected from catastrophic losses in any one year. In order to integrate flood insurance with land-use management, the bill also provides that after June 30, 1970, no new flood insurance coverage (including renewals) would be provided in any area unless an appropriate public body had adopted permanent land use and control measures with effective enforcement provisions.

---

4. "National Flood Insurance Act of 1968," PL 448, 90th Congress, Second Session, 1968.

Index